Endangered

The Javan rhino story
The six-year journey to study and
protect one of Earth's rarest species

By

Dr Steve Wilson, PhD

Inspiring Publishers
P.O. Box 159, Calwell, ACT Australia 2905
Email: publishaspg@gmail.com
http://www.inspiringpublishers.com

A catalogue record for this
book is available from the
National Library of Australia

NATIONAL
LIBRARY
OF AUSTRALIA

National Library of Australia The Prepublication Data Service

Author: Dr Steve Wilson
Title: Endangered
Genre: Memoir, Wildlife, Conservation, Adventure, Scientific research

Paperback ISBN: 978-1-923449-36-7
ePub2 ISBN: 978-1-923449-37-4

*This book is dedicated to
my family and two special people*

*To my partner Tracy, Coen, Daly and Allira,
for your ongoing love and support through my journey,
thanks for all your help.*

*To the late Dr Widodo Sukohadi Ramono
04/04/1945 - 24/12/2020. For his lifelong contribution to
Asian rhino conservation, for friendship and support through my
PhD thesis journey, thanks for all the good times.
Never to be forgotten.*

*To the late Mohamad 'Aphuy' Syamsudin
25/10/1975 - 08/12/2021. For his unwavering support of my
PhD studies and active coordination of Ujung Kulon National
Park and rhino protection staff in support of my field work. I
couldn't have completed my doctorate without you're help, I will
always be grateful. RIP my friend, you were taken too soon.*

The above picture was drawn by my son, Daly Rainbow Wilson, a gifted artist, in 2020. The drawing depicts an adult pair of Javan Rhinos, showing the key differences between them, i.e., males are larger, heavier, and are horned. Females are less bulky and hornless. I had Daly's original drawing framed; It now sits in pride of place on a wall in our home, I smile every time I look at it!

About the Author

Dr Steve Wilson has a lifelong passion for wildlife and nature. Recently retired, Steve worked for nearly 18 years in the Australian zoo industry, including time working at North American facilities, followed by another 22+ years in the natural resource and catchment management space, both in Queensland and Victoria. Tertiary qualifications include a Bachelor of Applied Science (Parks, Recreation & Heritage), at Charles Sturt University, Albury, NSW, a Masters of Environmental Management majoring in natural resource management and a Doctor of Philosophy (PhD) awarded in 2021, for his thesis on the *'Factors shaping the conservation of the critically endangered Javan rhinoceros (Rhinoceros sondaicus)'*, both were completed through the University of Queensland's School of Biological Sciences, St Lucia, Brisbane. Steve enjoys natural history writing and has co-authored field guides on Western Queensland snakes, Lake Eyre Basin frogs and a book on Australian Goannas. An avid educator, Steve delivered regular nature-based radio programs on ABC Open in both Queensland and Victoria, has written over 50 articles and chapters on wildlife and nature for popular publications, natural history books and peer-reviewed science journals, including lead author for the species chapter on Javan rhino in the globally first released Springer book *'Rhinos of the World'*. Steve is also a member of the International Union of Conservation & Nature (IUCN) Species Survival Commission (SSC) 2021-2025, the SSC Asian Rhino Specialist Group 2021-2025 and the SSC Oceania 2021-2025 Group.

Acknowledgements

This book owes its existence to many people and respective organisations. To National Geographic for initial inspiration on the plight of Javan rhino. Hermawam, Head of Section Handeuleum Section 2 (rhino habitat), for in situ help and access to his staff when needed, many thanks. Special thanks and acknowledgment to the late Mohamad 'Aphuy' Syamsudin UKNP ranger, for field staff coordination and spatial mapping expertise, a great friend with good English! I miss you man! Haerudin, for bike transport (despite challenges with punctures/chickens) in poor road conditions during our community survey work. Usep, Tino and Hasan for going all out with community survey assistance and taking their bikes on some seriously bad roads to remote villages. Deddy (YABI), great assistance in working me through the complexities of Indonesian visas, research permits and KITAS, very much appreciated. Lukman, for picking me up at airports and getting me where I needed to go, many thanks. Dewo, hire car man extraordinaire, big thanks for getting me back and forth to Ujung Kulon, on good and bad roads, amazing driver with uncanny knowledge of Java's Road network. Asep and Irma, UKNP wildlife monitoring staff for providing usable rhino clips and mapping of wallow sites on the peninsula. Daryan, field coordinator UKNP rhino monitoring unit, for sharing his passion and knowledge of rhino behaviour, video clips and maps. Patat, UKNP ranger for survey help, many thanks. Samaya and Acep RPU team for survey help. Ujang UKNP ranger, great help coordinating surveys and in situ assistance. RPU staffers Sartol and Sarkhim, for help in the rain and wet conditions over the journey. UKNP ranger Apud, for assisting with visits to arenga plots and meeting with local wood carver. Agat, Head of Ujung Jaya Legon Pakis (traditional area) for in situ assistance. Entus and Ugang, UKNP rangers, for getting me out in a canoe on the Cigenter River. Special thanks and acknowledgment to the late Dr Widodo Sukohadi Ramono, Director of the Indonesian Rhino Foundation (YABI), for letters of support, organisational support, access to camera trap data, critical support in gaining approval for research visas and KITAS and great conversations on the conservation of rhino. Former Ujung Kulon NP Directors Haryono, Rahmat, Anggodo and current Director Andono from the Labuan office of Ujung Kulon National Park Authority, for letters of support, organisational support, access to camera trap data and maps, very much appreciated. Minggu, manager of the homestay and his family in Taman Jaya, always supportive, for comfy accommodation and tucker over the PhD journey. Hanif, Research and Education Officer/IRF Liaison to YABI, a great friend and help in coordinating on my PhD journey, special thanks. Ja Jaj RPU, for survey assistance. Yoga, Database Officer YABI, for mapping assistance.

Waladi, Manager RPU and JRSCA, many thanks for field support and organising, and for good operational conversations and insight. Ayani, Coordinator Habitat JRSCA, great in-situ support. Indra, GIS/Mapping guru, for always being eager to help, many thanks. Thanks to Mangaa 'Ma' a', driver at YABI, coffee and smokes in between the madness of Javan traffic and for getting me where I needed to go. My two Amila's, for Ujung Kulon NP permit approvals and research support. Doyok, local guide, and awesome jungle cook for help getting us around in the rain! Former Goulburn Broken Catchment Management Authority's CEO Chris Norman and Angus Emmott for my initial PhD application support and enthusiasm for my project. Dr Damian Michael at Australian National University for the letter of support and encouragement. Professor Hugh Possingham for letters of support and encouragement. Clare Campbell, Director

Wildlife Asia, for providing initial contacts in the rhino game, which got me started. Dr Marta Pascual, CEED and Ikerbasque Foundation, for social research support and providing relevant papers. Melisa Lewins for assistance regarding UQ Animal Ethics approvals. Peter Geddes for all things IT over a long period, thanks Pete. UQ's Gail Walter for consummate admin support over the PhD journey. Vanessa Campbell, special thanks for spatial mapping assistance and interest in my work. Karen Brisbane, for admin support and interest. Simon Casanelia, for spatial mapping expertise and always being interested. Darelle Backway and Andrea Muskee, computer troubleshooting wizzes, and for always being interested. Kaela McDuffie, big thanks for sorting out UQ Animal Ethics assistance. Georgina Hockings UQ Honours student, great conversations, and work on deciphering Javan rhino behaviour from videos. Rubén Venegas, Hernán Cáceres and Eduardo Gallo Cajiao PhD compatriots for UQ IT support and enthusiasm. Dr Simone Blomberg for statistical analysis advice over the PhD journey. Michael Tse, UQ Human Ethics Committee Coordinator, for practical advice and assistance. Kees Rookmaaker, Rhino Resource Centre, for assistance and guidance in sourcing information, particularly in the historical space, many thanks. Warmest thanks to the late Professor Colin Groves for his assistance in understanding museum specimens and cataloguing, and for good wishes. Tim Barlow and Rhiannon Sandford, editing prowess and honest feedback, you always made my papers read better; many thanks. Janice Mentiplay-Smith for providing her museum image of the last captive Javan rhino. Many thanks Jancie. Jo Deretic, acoustic analysis expertise and help in developing frequency sonograms and spectrograms of rhino vocalisations, and genuine enthusiasm for my work, special thanks Jo. My UQ Readers Associate Professor Diana Fisher and Professor Kerrie Wilson, many thanks for constructive feedback and support. Heather Christensen, for UQ assistance with travel issues, protocols and having great patience! Big thanks to GB CMA's Vicki Mackenzie for editorial and proofing assistance with my confirmation document. Special thanks to Nicole, David and Pam Fudge, for always being interested in what I was up to at any given time. David Williams, Eco Dev at Tatura, very grateful for discussions and guidance around data analysis and variables. To my great friend Inov Sectionov, International Rhino Foundation's Indonesian Programme Manager, based in Bogor with YABI, a very important cog in my PhD wheel, eternally grateful for all your help and support, I just couldn't have got there without your help! To my co-supervisors, Associate Professor Anne Goldizen and Dr Duan Biggs, many thanks for sharing your expertise and expanding my knowledge on all things academic. To Professor Salit Kark, my principal supervisor at the University of Queensland, wonderful support and guidance over my PhD journey; very fortunate to have you in my corner, much heartfelt thanks. Special thanks to my PhD Chair of Examiners at the University of Queensland, Associate Professor Diana Fischer, who attended the examination as adjudicator. Warmest regards to my two independent examiners, Associate Professor Dr Amal Bhattacharya from Raiganj University, India, and Dr Bibhab Kumar Talukdar, who heads up the IUCN Asian Rhino Specialist Group, and is the founder, CEO and Secretary General of Aaranyak, a leading wildlife non-government organisation based in Guwahati, India. Both gave up significant time to review my thesis and assessed and examined my thesis knowledge, which ultimately led to my doctoral approval. Heartfelt thanks. Additional thanks to Dr Bibhab Kumar Talukdar for writing the foreword for this book, and provision of the current and former Javan rhino distribution map, thank you and importantly, your continued contribution to Asian rhinos, is greatly appreciated. Many thanks to photographer Stephen Belcher for his amazing effort to take modern images of Javan rhino. Many thanks to Freelance Editor, Heidi Instone for making my manuscript read so much better, much appreciated. To Lodie, Wency and the broader ASPG & Inspiring Publishers team, wonderful to work with, many thanks. To my great mate Mike Hood and his extended family, for always being interested in my rhino adventures, many thanks. To my late godmother, Jenny Burrowes, for always trusting I would get there, and for showing interest in whatever I was doing at the time, a special thank you. To my family, parents Bill and Jude Pinder and favourite uncle Rob Whitehill for always being interested and supportive. My late brother Stewart, sisters Peta, Jenny and Cathy, for always showing support. To my talented kids, Coen for joining me on two field trips to Java and Sumatra, and help with editing, Daly for ongoing support and your amazing drawing of a male and female Javan rhino and Allira for supporting my PhD efforts and taking the journey with me, I couldn't have got there without you, extreme thanks, you guys were amazing. Special thanks and tribute to my late father, Leslie, for imparting the DNA and tools to find a way to expand on my love of nature, heartfelt thanks always. Most importantly, to Tracy, my partner for over 34 years, heartfelt thanks and love for always being there, I couldn't have got there without you, you deserve the most credit and thanks.

Preface

As I write this, I am 66 years old, and in my relatively short lifespan, humanity has lost significant habitat and wild places across the globe, with an estimated 35% remaining. The world's population is now over 8 billion people, noting there was around 2.7 billion when I arrived on the scene in 1959! Globally, just in my lifetime we have lost many significant species and subspecies such as the Western Black Rhino (*Diceros bicornis longipes*), Javan tiger (*Panthera tigris sondaica*), Bali tiger (*P. tigris balica*), the Baiji or Yangtze River Dolphin (*Lipotes vexillifer*), Lesser bilby (*Macrotis leucura*), Pinta Island Giant Tortoise (*Chelonoidis niger abingdonii*), Costa Rica Golden Toad (*Incilius periglenes*), the Javan rhino (Indochinese) subspecies (*Rhinoceros sondaicus annamiticus*), and the wild population of the Northern White Rhino (*Ceratotherium simum cottoni*) now functionally extinct with two ageing females remaining, and the Bornean Sumatran Rhino (*Dicerorhinus sumatrensis harrissoni*) once found across Borneo is now extremely rare, most likely functionally extinct, at present only two animals are known to remain.

As of December 2024, the IUCN Red List now includes 260,000 species, 44,300 of these are threatened with extinction, including, 41% of amphibians, 37% of sharks and rays, 44% of reef building corals, 34% of conifers, 26% of mammals, 28% selected crustaceans, 21% reptiles and 12% of birds. Humanity's hunger for more available land and natural resources continues unabated. Natural landscapes and their flora and fauna are under threat like never before, and far more resources are spent destroying nature than protecting it. I was motivated to make a useful and hopefully positive contribution to one of those at-risk species. The initial catalyst and inspiration for my interest in Javan rhino (*Rhinoceros s. sondaicus* or *'Badak jawa'*) occurred in 1967. As an eight-year-old with an insatiable fascination for nature, I learnt that a team of photographers were going into the jungles of Ujung Kulon, West Java, Indonesia, to photograph the Javan rhino in colour for the first time, which at the time were believed to number only 25 animals. I have clear memories of dreaming about this endeavour, the steamy jungle, lush tropical vegetation, how rare the rhinos were, would they find any, the risk of tiger attack, succumbing to dengue or malaria and battling the elements to secure these photos. Even as a young boy, I subconsciously began planning a way to visit Ujung Kulon, now a national park, and somehow study these amazing creatures. These enduring thoughts stayed with me through to November 2014, when I spent two weeks in Ujung Kulon and began formulating a plan to study these animals for my PhD. During this first visit to Ujung Kulon National Park, my expectations for what I would see and feel were high, and the experience did not disappoint. During November, the traditional monsoonal build-up was happening, the weather was erratic, bouts of heavy rain, sunshine, then corresponding periods of high humidity filled the air, and quickly I was drenched in sweat and ringing wet from rain and heavy droplets falling from the lush vegetation. Paddling a canoe along the rainforest-lined Cigenter River, a known Javan rhino haunt, was everything I dreamed of. I observed reticulated python (*Malayopython reticulatus* or *'Ular sanca batik'*) the world's longest snake, curled up in branches over water, noting the infamous green anaconda (*Eunectes murinus*) is slightly shorter but heavier by weight, the bright red, blue, and yellow flash of Javan stork-billed kingfisher (*Pelargopsis capensis javana* or *'Raja udang besar'*) Asia's largest, flying ahead of the canoe and troops of long-tailed macaques (*Macaca fascicularis* or *'Monyet'*) climbing down the mangrove branches to flash their eyebrows and protest as we paddled past. A Javan red giant flying squirrel (*Petaurista p. petaurista* or *'Bajing terbang'*) was jumping across branches high in the canopy, its shining red fur, which is quite striking in the sunlight, was eye-catching. A pair of the large and conspicuous oriental pied hornbill (*Anthracoceros albirostris* or *'Kangkareng'*) were calling to each other as they fed on *ficus* fruits high in the canopy. I really felt I was in the rhinos' last refuge. Rhino signs were everywhere, muddy slides and pathways where they had left the jungle to enter the water, horn rub marks on trees and flattened vegetation where they had clearly been feeding. On my first trip, the only thing that could have made the experience any better would have been to actually see a Javan rhino.

Over the six years and the many field and university trips that would follow, I was never able to get a complete rhino sighting in the field, usually it was a quick glimpse of a disappearing rhino backside charging off noisily after being disturbed at a wallow, or walking through wet, smelly, urine covered foliage, where a rhino was standing only seconds before. This is not unusual. In 2016, when I surveyed all 36 frontline staff, 78% of them had actually seen a Javan rhino in the field, and 22% had not, in spite of significant time, sometimes years of working in Ujung Kulon. This is okay, fortunately, I had access to the next best thing, camera trap footage, which would give me an undisturbed view and enabled me to learn about this amazing megaherbivore survivor. This book, in part, tells the natural history story of the Javan rhino through to present time, and the adjacent six-year PhD journey I undertook to find a way to study them and what I learnt. For example, I increased our knowledge of their social behaviour, uncovered secrets about their communication, their vocalisations, and wallowing behaviour, to name a few, and found practical ways to increase their habitat and food resources. It's a mixed bag of Javan rhino and local wildlife facts, my many local wildlife, community, rhino protection and national park staff adventures, what I actually discovered over my visits to Java and the people and places I interacted with and visited along the way.

I've tried to convey the information in an easy-to-read but not too sciency style, and aimed to keep the PhD information clear and interesting. References have been used sparingly across the book, relevant author references used are listed at the end of Parts I, II and III, with fully cited references in the bibliography at the end of the book, otherwise references have only been used as context and support components of the story. It's a memoir of my journey, the scientific research and the personal, hope you enjoy the ride, I did!

To assist the reader, and in defiance of academic convention, we have included species' latin, local and family names in brackets.

Dr Steve Wilson, PhD 2025

Foreword

I am very delighted to pen this foreword for a publication which is of immense importance and that is on a species which is critically endangered—the Javan rhino (*Rhinoceros sondaicus*), which is currently only found in one of the national parks in West Java, Indonesia. Currently, Ujung Kulon National Park in West Java, Indonesia, is the only abode of the critically endangered Javan Rhino which is also known as the Lesser one-horned rhino. The Asian Rhino Specialist Group, within the Species Survival Commission of the International Union for Conservation of Nature (IUCN) has been providing its technical inputs to all Asian rhino range countries in their efforts to secure the three species of Asian Rhinos—the Javan, Sumatran and the Indian greater one-horned rhino? While the Javan and Sumatran rhino is listed as critically endangered species, the Greater one-horned rhino is listed as vulnerable by the IUCN Red List of Threatened Species. Out of these three species of Asian rhinos, the greater one-horned rhino, found only in India and Nepal has made a remarkable comeback from the brink of extinction during early 20th century, from a population of fewer than 200 to current population of over 4000. This book, titled *Endangered, The Javan rhino story*, is authored by Dr Steve Wilson, with an aim to raise awareness, beyond the scientific community, as the author strongly feels, as conservation biologists, we all live and breathe the challenges rhinos and other wildlife and their habitats have been facing. It is a fact that the broader community at large is often unaware of the prodigious conservation effort in practice for many years and this book is an effort to share information on conservation efforts to secure the future of Javan rhino in Indonesia. I have been fortunate to visit Indonesia since 2008 in my capacity as Asia Coordinator of International Rhino Foundation and also as the chair of IUCN/ SSC; Asian Rhino Specialist Group and visited various parts of Ujung Kulon National Park with Rhino Protection Units of the Ujung Kulon National Park and Yayasan Badak Indonesia (YABI) and was fortunate to see two Javan rhinos in the National Park in wild habitat. Sightings of Javan rhino are very difficult in natural habitat due to its elusive behaviour. Javan rhino being a browser, often remains in the dense forest areas of the national park and on very few occasions it will move out to open areas like seashores or grazing areas. With natural succession taking place, it is essential to monitor the rhino population and changes in forest and waterbodies as part of the key habitat of Javan rhino. Steve did his rhino field work in Ujung Kulon National Park to unearth information needed to recommend future conservation needs and planning during his PhD studies. I am fortunate to be one of the two academic assessors of his PhD thesis and realised how important his research work was in that it contributes knowledge of the species and assists conservation and management to secure the future of critically endangered Javan rhino. The commitment shown by Steve during his six years of PhD work, to learn about Javan rhino in the wilderness, is indeed a valuable collation of knowledge on the species and its habitat, and what inspired me more is the final output of his research outcomes through *Endangered, The Javan rhino story*. I would recommend all the people associated with wildlife conservation not to miss reading this book, which has been written in a way the broader community can understand. Knowing about the critically endangered Javan rhino, whose global population is less than 60 itself, may trigger the needed spark among the minds of humans to collectively contribute to secure the future of Javan rhino in years to come to ensure that our next generations can see them in the wilderness alive! I strongly feel that one species on this world— namely, homo sapiens can create unlimited opportunities to save the species from the brink of possible extinction. We need to generate the strong will among humans to care for all living species on planet earth to reflect that humans are responsive towards the needs of planet earth's ability to support all life forms in harmony.

Bibhab Kumar Talukdar, PhD
Chair: IUCN/SSC; Asian Rhino Specialist Group
& Founder and Secretary General, Aaranyak
& Senior Advisor (Asian Rhinos), International Rhino Foundation

Contents

Part III:

PART I

Endangered—Introduction

There is significant evidence suggesting that the sixth mass extinction in the history of Earth is occurring. Unlike the distant past mass extinction events near the end of the Ordovician, Devonian, Permian, Triassic and Cretaceous periods, this current event is different in its causes, character and rates of extinction, largely resulting from anthropogenic or human-induced drivers. Globally, species are now going extinct ~100 times faster than background extinctions before humanity due to combined pressures and threats such as global climate changes, human population pressures, urbanisation, hunting and poaching, fragmentation of habitats, the introduction and spread of exotic species, a suite of pathogens and other factors, such as the unrelenting desire and need for more agricultural land. Despite 17% of the Earth's terrestrial areas and around 7.5% of the ocean's surface being declared as protected areas, significant gaps remain in the effective protection of biodiversity around the world, with existing protected areas varying in their resilience and ability to protect biodiversity and prevent extinction events.

The annual global trade and illegal trade of wildlife and wildlife products business alone is estimated to be worth between $10-23 billion USD. Global demand for productive land continues to be at odds with environmental protection requirements, often causing conservation disputes. As far back as 2009, the United Nations Food and Agricultural Organisation projected it will require at least a 70% increase in food production to feed a projected human population of 9.1 billion people by 2050. As of 2025, this projection is on track and may exceed the human population growth expectations and consequent food needs. Globally, despite ongoing attempts to meet the needs of both human population growth and nature conservation objectives, many challenges remain. For example, the overall conservation status of the world's mammal species continues to deteriorate, due to threats such as habitat decline and loss, and continued overexploitation.

In addition to reducing population numbers and abundances of various species, threats such as poaching and habitat loss, compounded by diverse and unique ecological traits of some species, have reduced the current ranges of many species from their historical extents. According to the International Union of Conservation of Nature (IUCN), 44 of the 74 largest terrestrial herbivores (>100 kg) are threatened with extinction (including 12 critically endangered or extinct in the wild), and 43 have declining populations. The majority of the large threatened terrestrial herbivores are found in developing countries, the exception being European bison or Wisent (*Bison bonasus*). The loss of large herbivores creates a trophic cascade, causing negative impacts across a broad spectrum of species, including apex carnivores, scavengers, small herbivores and small mammals, with consequent impacts on ecological system processes such as aspects of vegetation, hydrology, nutrient cycling and fire regimes.

The global growth in African palm (*Elaeis guineensis*) oil, which is now the most commercially traded vegetable-oil crop in the world, continues unabated. Because the oil palm's range is confined to the humid tropical zones, its expansion has come at the expense of biodiverse ecosystems, species diversity and carbon-rich tropical forests. The growing spectre of climate change looms large for ecosystems and their respective wildlife across the globe. Under the Brazilian Bolsonaro administration, destruction of the Amazon surged, doubling CO_2 emissions from wildfires between 2019 and 2020 and with deforestation reaching a 15-year high in 2021. The Amazon is steadily moving closer to the tipping point of becoming a carbon emitter and not a sequester. Central Africa's Congo Basin, the world's second-largest rainforest biome, now with the Amazon's decline, will become increasingly important for global climate stability and will need increased protection. Fortunately, through Brazil's recently elected President Luiz Inacio Lula da Silva's administration, reductions have begun, with the Brazilian Amazon deforestation rate falling by 22.3% in the year through July 2023. Our warming climate-induced thaw is driving rapid change across the Arctic Circle, opening the permafrost, exposing long-protected soil and releasing increasing amounts of methane, an unwanted greenhouse gas into earth's atmosphere. Antarctica is showing similar deterioration due to increased ice melt. This will reduce both poles' ability to reflect solar radiation, effectively warming our planet even further and impacting climate cycles. Again, humanity needs to be aware of this real emerging threat and take action to slow and stop it.

What are the drivers of terrestrial mammal decline?

A review of the Class Mammalia by Hoffman et al. (2011) recognised 5,487 extant species. Despite this incredible diversity, the overall conservation status of the world's mammal species continues to decline, with an estimated one-fifth of mammals threatened with extinction. Over 60% of the world's largest carnivores and largest mega-herbivores are threatened with extinction. Globally, it is estimated that at least 60% of primate species are threatened with extinction and 75% have deceasing populations. Mega-herbivore species, such as the Javan rhino (*Rhinoceros sondaicus*) and the Sumatran rhino (*Dicerorhinus sumatrensis*), now numbers under 60 and 50 respectively. Across Southeast Asia, humans have been hunting wildlife for at least 40,000 years. Hunting intensity has increased with rising human population densities and declining forested landscapes across the Asian region. For example, the first 90 years of British colonial rule across India instigated a system of rewards and bounties, driving an almost obsessive desire to hunt wildlife. For example, over 80,000 tigers (*Panthera tigris*) were hunted and killed during the period 1875 to 1925, averaging over 15 per week for 50 years. In recent times, the hunting of low-density populations of large mammalian fauna is likely to have a negative impact on population dynamics and long-term viability. Excessive overhunting for wild bushmeat across the developing world is becoming a critical factor in the decline of the largest terrestrial herbivores.

The global trend of increased wealth, especially in the Middle East, Russia and China, is expected to drive interest in many forms of hunting and increase demand for animal products such as rhino horn or tiger body parts. However, hunting, when managed properly, can generate substantial income that, at least in part, is directed towards conservation of target species and their habitats. For example, in Southern Africa, the development and shift of agricultural land to natural habitat for private game ranches has positively impacted the recovery of white (*Ceratotherium simum*) and black rhino (*Diceros bicornis*) numbers.

In the modern era, ongoing human population growth, consequent demand and rising GDP are related to significant growth in commercialised bushmeat hunting relative to subsistence hunting across many parts of the world. Rapid human population growth poses an ongoing threat to remaining wildlife populations. For example, in Asia, the preferred habitat of Javan rhino and Sumatran rhino is lowland rainforest, critical rhino habitat now being converted to oil palm and rubber plantations. Greater one-horned rhino (*Rhinoceros unicornis*) thrive in fertile floodplains, which are also prime human development sites for agriculture, logging and intensive cultivation. This rapid development has been supported by the expansion of agricultural land, corresponding rises in livestock numbers, causing increased isolation of protected and conservation areas and consequent decreasing wildlife populations. This situation is further exacerbated by threats such as logging, through creation of access roads, improved hunting equipment and ineffective or inadequate wildlife protection.

Global market demand increases for nonarboreal (e.g., rice, sugar cane and soybeans) and arboreal crops (e.g., natural rubber and oil palm), livestock (e.g., cattle) and tropical hardwood timber has driven broad-scale industry-supported deforestation across mainland Africa, Central and South America, Madagascar and Asia. The globalisation of financial markets and worldwide commodity boom has driven the ongoing demand for tropical timber and the expansion of industrial logging, driving deforestation and the economic imperative to expand road building in forested areas.

Habitat fragmentation exacerbates the effects of hunting by allowing hunters access to former remote areas and reduces the options for population growth of hunted species, should hunting ever be brought under control. Across Asia, large terrestrial mammal populations such as elephant and rhino are often exposed, because these habitats are under major pressure from conversion to agricultural activities and oil palm plantations. Allée effects have impacted many flora and fauna species. For example, individual reproduction and survival can be compromised in small populations through issues such as access to, or mate shortage (reproductive isolation), or lack of conspecific (same species) cooperation.

Often, the value humans attribute to the rarity of a species that can drive higher demand can, for example, increase poaching pressure and rapidly drive a species towards extinction, can be termed an anthropogenic allée effect. The anthropogenic allée effect often causes negative growth rates at low densities, driving populations to even lower densities, leading to an extinction spiral. In small, scattered, and isolated populations, it is only a matter of time before the average mortality rate exceeds the annual birth rate, and before the population goes extinct. The Sumatran rhino is a prime example of a species impacted by small populations and anthropogenic allée effect. Unusually, and unlike other rhino species, female Sumatran rhino ovulates only if induced by males (reflex ovulation). In fragmented or heavily hunted habitats, reproduction events fail to occur when the population becomes so low and isolated (reproductive isolation) that both sexes are unable to meet, contributing to impaired reproductive pathology such as tumours of the uterus and low or reduced sperm activity. Bottom line is, female Sumatrans need to be 'bare-hooved and pregnant,' otherwise they develop a rhino version of endometriosis, and the boys need to regularly 'mate and induce female ovulation'. I don't apologise for presenting the above information, it's real, and humanity needs to be aware, and importantly, work to turn things around. I've only been highlighting the risks to terrestrial mammals! Many species of marine mammals, birds, reptiles, amphibians, fish, invertebrates, plants and broader biodiversity and ecosystems face similar threats.

Evolution of the Rhinoceros Family

Early reconstructions of the evolutionary history and lineage of rhinoceros created a diversity of misconceptions and errors about rhinoceros systematics, phylogenies and nomenclature. These early phylogenies were founded on features now known to be significantly variable, i.e., molarisation of the premolars, which resulted in the division of early rhinoceros into too many species.

Today, four families are known, including the Amynodontidae, Hyracodontidae, Rhinocerotidae and the Paraceratheridae. All five living species possess the characteristic 'rhino horns' composed of keratinised hair, which decomposes at death and is not often preserved in the fossil record. Early forms of rhinoceros-like mammals belonging to the genus *Hyrachyus* are known from late Eocene (55.8–33.9 million years ago) deposits found in Asia, North America and Europe. These early forms resembled primitive horses and tapirs, none of which attained the larger size or horns that now characterise the modern species. Appearing in the late Eocene, and forerunners of the modern forms belong to the family Rhinocerotidae; these animals at the time were less prominent than two other families: the running rhinoceros (Hyracodontidae) and the aquatic rhinoceros (Amynodontidae). Ecologically and biologically successful due to their broad distribution and evolutionary persistence, rhinos have endured and thrived.

The aquatic Amynodontidae reached their greatest diversity in the late Eocene and early Oligocene (33.9–23.03 million years ago), especially in Asia. The third family of rhinoceros, the Rhinocerotidae, rose to prominence in the Oligocene period, after first appearing in the late Eocene in Eurasia. It was during this period that the trend towards larger, heavier bodied species and the key characteristics of modern Rhinocerotidae developed i.e., the appearance of boneless horns on the skull; broad feet with three toes and significant changes in dentition; premolars became more like molars, crowns of cheek teeth lengthened and the complexity of enamel patterns offered improved efficiency in handling a diet of coarse grasses for those species that were primarily grazers.

The recently treated fourth family, the giant rhinos (common name for the Paraceratheriinae), belonged to a remarkable lineage of the Rhinocerotoidea and lived across Eurasia in the Oligocene period. There are seven recognised genera (*Juxia, Urtinotherium, Paraceratherium, Dzungariotherium, Benaratherium, Aralotherium* and *Turpanotherium*). These animals grew to enormous sizes. For example, the giraffe-rhino (*Paraceratherium asiaticum*) is estimated to have weighed upwards of 34 tonnes and over 6 metres tall. Seriously, I would defy anyone not wanting to see this animal; it must have been an impressive sight. Today, our largest terrestrial mammal is the bull African elephant (*Loxodonta africanus*), which continues to grow until its 40+ years old and may reach 7+ tonnes and 4 metres in height, still impressive but tiny when compared to the giant rhino group. Many representatives of the family persisted successfully for millions of years. Recent North American fossil finds across the Badlands of the American West attest to their persistence. The Amynodontid genus (*Metamynodon*) is a prime example of a hippo-like rhino that ranged for 10 million years over much of North America. The massive and best-known species is *Metamynodon planifrons*, a form characterised by having massive teeth and large tusks that give it the appearance of a hippopotamus, some skeletons were over 3 metres in length. There is no doubt the success of rhinos was their ability to adapt and thrive on a nutrient-poor diet, and ability to exploit a diversity of habitats, which explains the broad distribution and their success as mega-herbivores.

Towards the end of the Miocene (23.03–5.32 million years ago), climatic changes are implicated in the demise of many rhino species. Across North America, almost the entire rhino fauna was eliminated, and in Eurasia, only two lineages survived; fortunately, one of these, the *dicerorhinines*, gave rise to a form similar to the Sumatran rhino of today. The well-known and famous woolly rhino (*Coelodonta antiquitatis*) was amongst this group, appearing in the *Pleistocene* (2.58 million–11,700 years ago) in China, moving west into Europe, and by the Upper Pleistocene, the woolly rhino was the most widely distributed rhino species ever recorded. Tragically, this ecologically successful species died out only recently in evolutionary timeframes, less than 12,000 years ago. The evolution of rhinos spans 50 million years, and the fossil evidence of greater than 60 genera and hundreds of species exists, forms that 'occupied nearly every ecological niche available to large mammalian herbivores'.

The common ancestor of extant species of rhino may date from 28 to 33 million years ago, with the next divergence within the group occurring only 1.0–1.5 million years later. Analyses of complete sequences of the mitochondrial 12S rRNA and cytochrome-*b* genes suggest that Asian and African rhinos diverged about 26 million years ago and that the Sumatran rhino forms a sister clade with the two species of *Rhinoceros*, the greater one-horned and Javan rhino.

The above synopsis of rhinoceros evolution has been drawn mostly from formative studies by Prothero, Guerin, and Manning 1989), and their work on the Evolution of Perissodactyls; and Shijie, Qigao and Tao (2022), and their work on the body mass of the giant rhinos (Paraceratheriinae, Mammalia) and its tendency in evolution.

Rhinoceros taxonomy and distribution

All rhinos belong to the mammalian order Perissodactyla (derived from the Greek words perissos, meaning odd in numbers and *daktulos*, meaning a finger or toe). The family Rhinocerotidae is included in the order Perissodactyla, together with the Tapiridae (tapirs) and Equidae (horses and asses). The Tapiridae are represented in one genus (*Tapirus*) with four species found in Central and South America and one in Southeast Asia, whereas Equidae is represented in one genus (*Equus*) with six species distributed throughout the world.

In 2013, an additional new species was added to the 17-living species of Perissodactyls, with the discovery and description of a new species of tapir, from southern Columbia and Brazil, the Kabomani tapir (*Tapirus kabomani*), one of the largest terrestrial mammals to be newly described, and the only new Perissodactyla in over 100 years. Local indigenous people undoubtedly maintained knowledge of the newly described species, suggesting a role for traditional ecological knowledge (TEK) in understanding the broader biodiversity of the region.

Modern perissodactyls are medium to mega-sized herbivores, ranging in size from the smallest equids (weighing 200 kg) to the largest rhinos (3,500 kg). Perissodactyls are united as a mammalian order by their limb and skeletal structure, and their body weight is borne by the large central digit. The Equidae (horses and asses) have a single functional toe on each foot (the third digit), while the Rhinocerotidae have three distinctive toes per foot. The Tapiridae, considered the closest to the ancestral perissodactyl form, possess four toes on the forefeet.

Perissodactyls move about on their hooves or digits, never on the sole with the heel touching the ground; the ulna and radius are reduced, which has simplified the wrist and ankle joints. The rhino families' characteristic and distinctive horns are present on the frontal bones of all living species of the Rhinocerotidae, are dermal in origin and retain no bony core as in the artiodactyls (e.g., antelopes, deer and bovids).

Living rhinoceros (African and Asian species), historical and current distribution, ecology

The Family Rhinocerotidae, a small group of mega-herbivorous mammals, have suffered significant reductions in distribution, range and numbers. The family Rhinocerotidae have three-toed hooves, a key characteristic of the odd-toed ungulate mammalian order Perissodactyla. The five living rhino species belong to the order Perissodactyla, suborder Ceratomorpha, family Rhinocerotidae and the two sub-families Rhinocerotinae, for *Dicerorhinus* and *Rhinoceros*; and Dicerotinae, for *Diceros,* and *Ceratotherium*. Living rhino species have 82 chromosomes, the exception being black rhino with 84, are amongst the highest for mammals, noting we humans have 46. Living rhino consist of four genera: *Dicerorhinus*, *Rhinoceros*, *Ceratotherium* and *Diceros*, of which only the latter two occur in Africa. The five extant species include the Black rhino (*Diceros bicornis*), white rhino (*Ceratotherium simum*), greater one-horned rhino (*Rhinoceros unicornis*), Sumatran rhino (*Dicerorhinus sumatrensis*) and the Javan or lesser one-horned rhino (*Rhinoceros sondaicus*).

All species are listed on the Convention on Trade of Endangered Species (CITES) Appendix 1, with three listed as critically endangered *D. bicornis, D. sumatrensis, R. sondaicus*, one as vulnerable *R. unicornis* and one as near threatened *C. simum* on the IUCN Red List (2024). There are currently two views regarding the number of black rhino subspecies. Groves & Grubb (2011) recognise eight subspecies, and Emslie and Brooks (1999) recognise four subspecies. For the purposes of this book, Emslie & Brooks (1999) descriptions have been used. Of the four black rhino subspecies, three extant subspecies remain: *D. b. bicornis, D. b. michaeli* and *D. b. minor. D. b. longipes* is now extinct. White rhino includes two subspecies, southern white rhino *C. s. simum* and northern white rhino *C. s. cottoni*. The northern white rhino (recently proposed as a separate species *C. cottoni*; Groves et al. 2010) became extinct in the wild in 2008. In 2009, four aged captive animals were transported to a Kenyan conservancy, the last hope for its survival (Leader-Williams 2013). As of 2025, only two animals, both non-reproductive females, remain; the last male died on March 19, 2018. With their large body mass and ability to thrive on a low-quality vegetation diet, rhinos have persisted over extended evolutionary periods, making them among the most biologically successful of the mammals. All five living rhino species are polygamous and polyandrous, with both males and females seeking multiple mates. Males are usually solitary, separating themselves spatially and temporally through olfactory communication using dung and urine to convey scent signals.

For the family Rhinocerotidae, the most stable and social bond amongst extant rhino species is between a female and calf. Intraspecific courtship and mating behaviour (e.g., male combat) are known to be aggressive and intense in all five species. For the family Rhinocerotidae, communication via vocal and olfactory signals (dung, urine, spray), pedal scent glands (cutaneous) are prominent as they have an acute sense of hearing and scent detection but relatively poor eyesight. Olfactory (scent/odour) signals can

11

also provide spatial information, for example, territory ownership and dominance or movements of a significant individual such as a dominant male. All five rhino species vocalise or call in various categories, including puffing, snorting, growling and the in-need-to-be-studied harmonic calls. Vocal and olfactory signals are the most important for communication amongst rhinos, however, their vocal communication has only been investigated to a very limited extent to date.

White rhino

Largest of the five species, the white rhino is characterised by its square lip which is an adaptation for grazing. Head-body: 340–420 cm; tail: 50–70 cm; shoulder height: 150–180 cm; weight: 2500 kg; but can range between 1800-3500 kg, with males larger and heavier than females. The head and body are massive, with a distinctive bump (nuchal hump) on top of its short neck, that helps support the head. The anterior horn is normally the larger of the two, and averages 90 cm but can grow up to 150 cm. Female horns are often larger and thinner, male horns are often shorter and bulkier. Gestation is 16 months; intercalf interval is 2–3 years in good habitat. Courtship is aggressive, with males actively chasing females and aiming to keep oestrus females within their breeding territories. May live up to 50 years. Males are sexually mature at 10–12 years, females at 6–7 years. Found in Southern Africa, including Southeast Angola, North-East Namibia, Botswana, Zimbabwe, South Mozambique, Swaziland and South Africa. The subspecies *C. s. cottoni* was historically present in South Chad, Central African Republic, South Sudan, North-East Democratic Republic of Congo and Uganda, is now extinct.

Black rhino

Third largest of the five species. Adult male and female black rhino are of similar size, with little dimorphism, although males tend to be heavier. Black rhinos have two horns; the anterior horn can reach 130 cm, the posterior horn is typically smaller, between

2–55 cm. Head-body: 300–380 cm; tail: 25–35 cm; shoulder height: 140–170 cm; weight: 900–1350 kg. The black rhino has a prehensile upper lip that aids in browsing foliage from shrubs. Compared to the white rhino, this species has a distinctive hollow-shaped back, and its ears are more rounded. Mostly solitary, males and females only come together for breeding. Courtship is violent, and mating can occur anytime of the year. Gestation is 15–16 months, intercalf interval is 2–4 years depending on habitat quality. May live up to 35 years in the wild. Black rhino tends to feed early morning and evening. During the heat of the day, they seek shade and rest, and use wallows if available. Black rhino is polytypic (two or more genetically different subspecies), and four subspecies are known. *D. b. bicornis* is found in Namibia, and West and Southeast Southern Africa. *D. b. longipes* was formerly found in Nigeria, Cameroon, Chad, Sudan and the Central African Republic, and was declared extinct in 2011. *D. b. michaeli* is found in Kenya, Rwanda and North Tanzania. Historically, it was also found in Sudan, Ethiopia and Uganda. *D. b. minor* is found in Central Tanzania, Zambia, Zimbabwe, Malawi, Botswana, Mozambique, North and Central-East South Africa.

Greater one-horned rhino

Second largest of the five species. Head-body: 335–346 cm; tail: 66 cm; shoulder height: 175–200 cm; weight: 1800–2700 kg. Adult males develop longer mandibular incisors (tusks) and have larger neck muscles than females. Incisors, more than horns, are used in combat. Horn length averages 25 cm in males, 24 cm in females, can range from 20–61 cm. This species has two distinctive skin folds that drape over the sides of the front and back legs. Mostly grazers, this species will browse when needed. Gestation is 16 months. Males form dominance hierarchies. Scent-marking occurs at dung heaps or middens, which serve as communication points and mark territorial boundaries. Males are sexually mature at 9 years, females at 4 years. May live up to 35 years in the wild. The long interbirth interval (3.8 years), means breeding opportunities are few, meaning heightened aggression occurs when females are in oestrus. Excellent swimmers, they can dive and feed underwater. Like most rhinos this species has a strong sense of smell and good hearing, but poor eyesight. This species is found only in India and Nepal.

Sumatran rhino

Smallest and rarest of the five species. Head-body: 236–318 cm; shoulder height: 100–150 cm; weight: 500–960 kg. The two horns are small, typically larger in males. The body is covered in a hairy, reddish-brown skin. Two clear skin folds are present on the body. Sumatran rhinos are mostly browsers, preferring pioneer and secondary-growth plants. They are good swimmers and climbers, able to ascend and descend steep terrain. Gestation is 15–16 months, with an intercalf interval of 3.5 years. Calves remain with the mother for 2–3 years. Courtship is known to be aggressive, with males undertaking courtship chases, leading to copulation. Female Sumatrans are unique in that they are reflex ovulators; the mating act induces ovulation. Males are sexually mature at 7 years of age, females at 4 years. May live to 45 years in the wild. The extensive development of oil palm plantations across its range has converted valuable rhino habitat and allowed poachers access to formerly remote areas.

The Sumatran rhino is polytypic (two or more genetically different species), and three subspecies are known. *D. s. sumatrensis* is found in Sumatra and formerly in Peninsula Malaysia. *D. s. harrissoni* was once found across Borneo but is now extremely rare, most likely functionally extinct. At present only two animals are known to remain. *D. s. lasiotis* was once found across South-East Asia but is now extinct.

The above information on rhino taxonomy and these four living rhino species has been adapted from Dinerstein, E. (2011). Family Rhinocerotidae. Pp. 176-181 in Handbook of the Mammals of the World. Vol. 2. Hoofed mammals *(D.E. Wilson and R.A. Mittermeier, Eds.).*

Factors shaping Asian and African rhino decline

The trade in rhino horns has been traced back as far as 2600 BC. Across tropical Asia, rhinos have been hunted for thousands of years. Over 1,000 years ago, the trade was well established and during the mid to late 1800s, traditional medical demand for rhino horn escalated across China, resulting in increased hunting pressure on wild populations, effectively reducing all three Asian species from most of their former ranges. Globally, the trade in rhino horn has traditionally focused on two main market areas: the first is carved rhino horn handles for *jambiya* (traditional daggers) carried by Yemeni men as a sign of social standing. In 1982, the importation of rhino horn was banned in Yemen, which, unusually, has seen a steady reduction in demand due to the use of culturally acceptable substitutes, meaning Yemen is no longer a major consumer country for illegal rhino horn trade. However, a small but persistent demand remains for rhino horn '*jambiyas*' daggers among northern tribesmen and more affluent young Yemeni men; the second and largest rhino horn market globally is in Southeast Asia. Traditionally, in Chinese medicine, rhino horn is ground into powder and consumed orally. Users argue its use as having curative properties with abilities ranging from fever reduction, hangover relief, rheumatism, gout and stroke. In modern times, a growing misconception that rhino horn can cure cancer has increased demand in Vietnam. Since 2003, Vietnam has become the world's leading importer of legal trophies and illegal rhino horns from South Africa. Increasing economic prosperity has allowed Vietnamese people to afford high-value wildlife products and rhino horn's rarity, builds a powerful status value and prestige within traditional Asian gifting culture. Growing affluence during the 1970's across many parts of Asia and the Middle East, increased the demand for rhino horn. Rising rhino horn prices encouraged a surge in rhino hunting, and consequently- during the period 1970–1987, an estimated 85% of the world's remaining rhino population was lost.

The CITES (Convention on Trade in Endangered Species of Fauna and Flora) ban on the trade of rhino horn has been in place since 1977, where demand can only be met through the illegal market, which is supported and driven by the poaching of rhinos for their horns. An estimated 50+% of illegal and black-market trade in rhino products occurs in Vietnam, along with a suite of other endangered species parts and products ranging from tigers, to bears and the eight species of pangolin (e.g.; *Manis, Phataginus, Smutsie*) (family Manidae), are relentlessly pursued, and are the world's most trafficked mammal to name a few. Despite the ongoing trade ban, poaching continues to rise. High poaching levels are driven by the significant growth in the retail price of horn, from an estimated USD $4,700 per kg in 1993 to a high of around USD $65,000 per kg in 2012. Based on today's Asian black-market, rhino horn is selling for an estimated USD $60,000 per kg. With Asian species, due to smaller horn size and rarity, the price can be significantly higher. Both white and black rhino have two horns. White rhinos have between 3–6 kg of rhino horn; black rhino between 1.5–3 kg. Ongoing illegal demand for rhino horn has driven increased pressure from conservation agencies, especially in South Africa, which has seen an upward trend in poaching, for consideration of a well-managed, regulated legal trade based on using appropriate renewable harvesting methods of horn from live white rhinos. In contrast to Yemen, driven by rising wealth and increasing affluence in Asia, particularly China and Vietnam, demand for rhino horn has spiked. Supporting this rhino horn demand, poachers, often in mobile, highly organised, well-armed and resourced gangs, have targeted rhinos across Africa. For example, between 2006 and 2017, at least 8,355 black and white rhinos were poached in Africa, with the majority in South Africa. This continuing illegal trade has driven different applications of rhino conservation and protective approaches, which authorities and partner organisations must resource, implement, and enforce.

The exponential growth of human populations across Africa and Asia poses an ongoing threat to rhino and other wildlife populations. Outbreaks of civil war have caused social, political and ecological impacts in many ecologically diverse countries, with consequent effects on wildlife and habitat. Historic rhino population estimates are at best educated speculations. For example, in Africa, accurate rhino population recording didn't commence until 1980. It is quite feasible that both Asian and African rhino taxa could have once numbered in the hundreds of thousands, possibly millions. In 1970, an estimated 65,000 black rhino remained across Africa. During the period 1970 to 1992, excessive and intensive poaching saw black rhino numbers drop to 2,300 animals. Today, Africa's black and white rhinos continue to be protected mainly by four range States, South Africa, Namibia, Kenya and Zimbabwe, with 2024 totals of white rhino (17,464+) and black rhino (6,421+). Current estimates for the Asian species are Sumatran (difficult to determine, estimates range between (34–47?), Javan (50–60?), and greater one-horned (4,014+) (International Rhino Foundation State of the Rhino Report 2024).

Rhino reproduction and recruitment challenges

Compared to the recovery of other rhino species, the trajectory for both Sumatran and Javan rhino has been their persistent low populations which, by the 1930s, was in rapid decline across all range countries and spiralling towards extinction. Significant numbers of remaining female Sumatran rhino suffer from compromised reproductive pathology, most likely exacerbated by reproductive isolation from lack of access to potential mates and pregnancy. Nearly half of female Sumatran rhinos captured between 1984 and 1995 suffered the condition. The phenomenon is associated and afflicts many mammalian families, where either a lack of breeding or ability to complete pregnancies to full term causes the condition, which is amplified and particularly detrimental to rhinos.

The lack of breeding success across the few remaining Sumatran populations is clearly at crisis point, and the consolidation of all small, isolated populations into one management unit, supported by intensive captive breeding and rapid introduction of modern state-of-the-art reproductive technology, appears the only way forward. The single remaining Javan rhino population is stable and slowly breeding but remains at risk from several threats ranging from founder effects, outbreaks of poaching, disease risk from domestic stock, to a major tsunami. The establishment of a second population would free up habitat, food resources and promote breeding in the current population.

With ongoing political will, protection and resourcing, greater one-horned rhino numbers continue to trend upwards across India and Nepal. For both African species, ongoing biological management of remaining populations is essential for the maintenance of and to increase rhino reproductive capability in the face of continued high poaching rates.

Rhino protection and conservation initiatives

Over the past 150 years, the establishment of protected areas has been the main approach to support wild populations in their habitat. In recent times the focus on many Asian rhino populations have been to reduce the threat of poaching through the instigation and use of rhino patrol or rhino protection units (RPUs), and, since the late 1990s has been effective in reducing and detecting poaching threats across Africa. In addition to protected areas the large-scale conversion of domestic livestock ranches to focused wildlife and game ranches (due to legislative change and availability of excess animals from protected areas to private owners) has benefitted many species.

Rhino conservancies are another conservation approach used across Africa. Conservancies are typically fenced-off areas of land (up to 1000 km² but can be larger) and encompass a collective of private properties with security provided by the landowners. In recent years, the rise of militarised conservation has expanded across Africa and to other parts of the world. Conservation agencies and private landowners acknowledged the rising threat to wildlife, including rhino from well organised and highly equipped poaching gangs, which warranted a coordinated response.

The reality is species don't suddenly decline or go extinct. There is always a history, a chain of events, today however, preventing extinction depends on human interventions and willing investment. For example, isolated individual Sumatran rhinos are now captured and kept in facilities such as the Sumatran Rhino Sanctuary (SRS) in Way Kambas NP, Sumatra. Appropriate decision-making is often a barrier to conservation initiatives.

In the case of Sumatran rhino, the long-term survival of the species in the wild at present is not helping the species. By bringing individuals together in a managed way i.e., protected fenced facilities, the goal is to recover numbers by a goal of maximising the birth rate which is declining in the wild. A new SRS is being established in Aceh Province in Northern Sumatra, and this will be the third site in Indonesia after Way Kambas SRS (in Lampung Province) and Kelian SRS (in East Kalimantan Province). The new SRS in Aceh is intended to accommodate Sumatran rhinos from the wild in Aceh Province, who remain in increasingly fragmented habitat.

Some real successful examples where such a conservation approach has worked is species such as the Arabian oryx (*O. leucoryx*), American bison or buffalo (*B. bison*), California condor (*Gymnogyps californianus*) and Black-footed ferret (*Mustela nigripes*). All these species would now be extinct if this particularly appropriate intensive conservation response was not applied. So, the key point here is applying the best conservation approach to the need at hand. Ideally, Sumatran rhinos (or *'Badak sumatera'*) are protected in the wild, to do their thing naturally but this is not about being idealistic, it's not reality. The landscape is now so fragmented Sumatrans can't find a mate, they have to contend with oil palm and rubber plantations, roads and human activity, they need intervention; the semi-captive approach enables them to persist, albeit via a so not-perfect scenario but it is working, animals are breeding and producing young. There are many ways to make a change in rhino conservation, some occur with research and militarised protection, others are not so subtle! A positive and true-life example occurred with a guy named Ted Reilly. Ted is CEO and founder of ESwatini's (formerly Swaziland) Big Game Parks. Today, ESwatini has the most exemplary record of rhino protection anywhere across Africa, with only three rhinos poached in the last twenty years, due in major part to Ted's actions. Between 1988 and 1992, ESwatini lost 80% of its rhino population to poachers. The catalyst and turning point for Ted came when he found his favourite black rhino butchered and its horn brutally removed. In a high-risk strategy to get the poaching problem noticed, Ted and his rangers collected the rotting, maggot-infested rhino carcass and dumped it on the lawn outside the palace of ESwatini ruler, King Mswati. A risky approach, the King could have responded decisively and put Ted in jail, exiled him, pick your punishment, however, the carcass dumping was catalytic for the King, who was concerned about totally losing rhinos from his kingdom. Immediately, the King amended the ESwatini Game Act to put even suspected poachers behind bars with no bail. Anyone found guilty of poaching or even attempting to poach a protected species, such as rhino automatically went to prison for a minimum of 5 years, with an option to increase to 15 years, with no option of a fine. Additionally, on top of the prison sentence, the prescribed value of the animal poached has to be paid to the owner. If the poacher is unable to pay, an additional two years is added to the prison term.

The reduction in Eswatini's poaching rate speaks volumes, three animals poached in the last 20 years, go Ted, what a legend, followed closely by King Mswati for showing genuine leadership in the conservation of his kingdom's rhinos. If all African rhino states followed this lead, we would see more rhino. Weak poaching laws and cheap fines are a major weakness in the broader African rhino conservation story, government has to get tougher and put accountable pressure on poachers.

Table of current distribution range, broad description, and present status of the five extant rhino species († denotes extinct, ~ denotes in decline, + denotes increase), as of 2024.

Species	White rhino *Ceratotherium simum*	Black rhino *Diceros bicornis*	Greater one-horned rhino *Rhinoceros unicornis*	Sumatran rhino *Dicerorhinus sumatrensis*	Javan rhino *Rhinoceros sondaicus*
Sub-species	Polytypic *Ceratotherium s. cottoni* (northern white)	Polytypic *Diceros b. bicornis* (south western), *D. bicornis michaeli* (eastern), *Diceros b. minor* (southern-central), *Diceros b. longipes*†	Monotypic	Polytypic *Dicerorhinus s. sumatrensis* *Dicerorhinus s. harrissoni* *Dicerorhinus s. lasiotis*†	Polytypic *Rhinoceros s. annamiticus* † *Rhinoceros s. sondaicus* *Rhinoceros s. inermis* †
Population size	17, 464+	6,421+	4,014+	~34-47?	~50-60?
Current distribution	South Africa, Namibia, Botswana, Kenya, Mozambique, Zimbabwe, Eswatini, Uganda, Zambia	South Africa Namibia Botswana Kenya Tanzania Mozambique Zimbabwe Malawi Angola, Zambia, Eswatini	Nepal India	Indonesia. Sumatra (3 x protected areas only), Kalimantan (few animals)	West Java, Indonesia, only in Ujung Kulon National Park,
Body height (m)	1.5–1.8	1.4–1.7	1.7–2	1–1.5	1.5–1.7
Weight (kg)	1800–2700	900–1350	1800–2500	500–960	1200–1500
IUCN Red List Status	Near Threatened	Critically Endangered	Vulnerable	Critically Endangered	Critically Endangered

Sources used (Emslie et al. 2019; IUCN 2023; International Rhino Foundation State of the Rhino Report 2024; Nardelli & Robovský 2022; Melletti et al. 2025).

Part I—Bibliography

IUCN Red List 2024; IUCN 2024; Barnosky et al. 2011; Ceballos et al. 2007; Verdaadonk 2018; Pálinkás 2018; UNODC 2018; Sayer et al. 2013; Redpath et al. 2012; UN Food & Agriculture 2009; Hoffman et al. 2011; Ripple et al. 2015, 2016; Ceballos & Ehrlich 2002, 2009; Morrison et al. 2007; Fisher 2011; Sandon et al. 2015; Estrada et al. 2017; Zuraina 1982; Ahmad et al. 2014; Roth et al. 1998; Roth 1999; Velho et al. 2012; Rangarjan 2001; Lindsey et al. 2009, 2013; Brasheres et al. 2014; Guriev & Rachinsky 2009; Duffy 2016; Lewis & Alpert 1997; Leader-Williams 1992, 2009, 2013; Cousins et al. 2008; Dinerstein 2003, 2011; Smith et al. 2003; Laurence et al. 2014; IRF 2015; Malhi et al. 2014; Brook et al. 2014; Meijaard 2014; Payne & Yoganand 2017; Courchamp et al. 2007; Harris et al. 2013; Agil et al. 2008; Deng et al. 2021; Prothero, Guerin & Manning 1989; Wall 1989; Qui & wang 2007; Shijie, Qigao & Tao 2022; Prothero 1993:82; Prothero et al. 2016; Tougard et al. 1986; Wilson & Reeder 1993, 2005; Cozzuol et al. 2013; Nowak 1991; Nowak & Paradiso 1983; Norman & Ashley 2000; Groves & Grubb 2011; Emslie & Brooks 1999; Groves et al. 2010; Owen-Smith 1988; Loch 1937; Harper 1945; Hubback 1939; Groves & Leslie Jr 2011; Hermes et al. 2006; Ayling 2012; Cota-Larsen 2010; TRAFFIC 2011; Milliken & Shaw 2012; Nowell 2012a; Rabinowitz 1995; Duffy 2016; Fitzgerald 1989; Schlitter 2005; Loh & Loh 1994; Marshall 2012; Moneran et al. 2017; Biggs et al. 2013; Carmignani 2015; Dean 2018; Knight 2018; Schaffer et al. 2001; Foulds & Spencer 2019; IRF State of the Rhino Report 2024; Nardelli & Robovský 2022; Melletti et al. 2025.

PART II

Getting started

Before I continue, its worth acknowledging that sometimes conversations and small leads can lead you to good opportunities and outcomes. This is certainly what happened for me, looking to start a PhD on one of the most critically endangered species on the planet. In my backgrounding of who's who in the rhino world, I came across Clare Campbell, Director at Wildlife Asia at the time. Clare was pivotal in getting me started, I will always be grateful to her. I explained my idea for my a PhD, Clare was supportive and suggested I contact Inov Sectionov who was based in Java, Indonesia and worked for the International Rhino Foundation as their Indonesian Programme Manager, and had good connections to the Indonesian Rhino Foundation and importantly, Ujung Kulon National Park Authority staff. I connected with Inov, and he suggested I do a short visit to Java, where he would introduce me to people, he felt could help me. Inov and I really clicked and have remained firm friends ever since our initial meeting. Before I knew it, after some permit approvals, I was on my first visit to Ujung Kulon National Park in November 2014.

My Indonesian connection! Inov Sectionov, Indonesian Programme Manager, International Rhino Foundation, author and the late Widodo Ramono, Chair of the Indonesian Rhino Foundation, key players in the Asian Rhino conservation space, and both avid supporters of my studies in Ujung Kulon at the local NGO Yayasan Badak Indonesia (YABI), or Indonesian Rhino Foundation office in Bogor, Java.

Whilst in Java, Inov introduced me to Dr Widodo Ramono, head of the Indonesian Rhino Foundation, or Yayasan Badak Indonesia (YABI) based in Bogor. Widodo was highly respected and well-connected both locally and internationally in the Asian rhino space and was to be a key player in supporting my PhD moving forward; we became close friends through my Indonesian journey. Connecting and building rapport with the Ujung Kulon National Park Authority was pivotal, and Dr Mohi Haryono, the Ujung Kulon National Park Authority Director's approval at the time was critical. Fortunately, we hit it off well and Dr Haryono, would, for the first time ever, allow a researcher access to camera trap footage of rhinos collected by the authority. This gesture helped me enormously. Direct observation of Javan rhinos is difficult at best, my field trips would be time bound and busy, I never had time to go searching for rhinos, as much as I wanted to, so I was extremely grateful to the authority. I found out later many researchers from around the world had tried and failed to get access to the camera trap footage because they just expected to be given it. I never expected this; I wanted to earn the right by getting out in the jungle on a regular basis and learn from the rangers and rhino protection staff.

My next key step was securing an Indonesian foreign research permit, which is no mean feat. Firstly, the Australian Indonesian Consulate in Melbourne has to approve you before moving to the Javan Consulate in Jakarta. This involves checking I'm not a criminal, seeing my CV, work history, academic history, provision of letters of support from the University of Queensland, both the Indonesian and International Rhino Foundations and so on. Once you get the green light in Australia, you need to spend at least a week in Jakarta, sorting stuff there. Unfortunately, the Indonesian Ministries operate autonomously and don't communicate well with each other, so I would have to get independent approvals from the Ministry of Home Affairs, checking I'm not a terrorist/criminal threat, understanding my in situ field work, and involvement of participants, needing approval from the Ujung Kulon National Park Authority and the Indonesian Ministry of Education, Culture, Research & Technology, before finally arriving for final approval at the Ministry for the Environment and Forestry.

I found the Indonesian government bureaucracy quite challenging; officials would often 'lean' on me to pay for approvals, using 'time for approval' levers to induce me to pay extra. Most of the time I pushed back, however, periodically I would have to concede and pay 'extra' to get things moving. In Australia, we don't have this cultural phenomenon, and over time as I had to renew permits and approvals, I became used to this process 'norm'. This is in sharp contrast to the local villagers I got to know over the years, despite poverty, their low and often seasonal incomes, all would routinely help me whenever I needed it, without any expectation of an 'extra' to get things happening.

At this point I must acknowledge the help I received from Deddy, business manager at the Indonesian Rhino Foundation (IRF). Deddy was pivotal in helping me through the complexities of Indonesian visa, permits and KITAS approvals. Once sorted, then I could go to the Ujung Kulon National Park Authority (UKNPA) and show them all is well and get regular access to the park, noting unlike other national parks, at Ujung Kulon you are only allowed inside the park with permit approval, and are always accompanied by four, usually armed, national park rangers or rhino protection staff. Theory is, if someone falls and breaks a leg the other four will carry you out, as there is no road or vehicle access in the park, it's all on foot!

Importantly, Inov introduced me to a close mate, Dewo, who was a commercial driver and knew the roads of Java really intimately. Dewo and I became great mates, he would meet and pick me up from my regular trips to Jakarta and drive me to Bogor, then down to villages near Ujung Kulon. Dewo was pivotal, noting the trip from Jakarta to Ujung Kulon can take up to nine hours. Dewo was a master of finding a way through the madness of Javan traffic, plus he knew all the best places to eat!

Another key player I needed ongoing help from was the late Mohamed 'Aphuy' Syamsudin. Aphuy was head ranger with the Ujung Kulon National Park Authority, could speak reasonable English and would help plan and coordinate my visits into Ujung Kulon. Given Aphuy managed the staff rosters, he knew who was on and off work and could create staff time to help me. The Ujung Kulon National Park rangers and rhino protection staff typically work shifts in the jungle of between 5,7,10,15 to 20 days straight, depending on their role. For me, at each visit, I would typically spend between one to three weeks in the jungle with the boys, plus I would pay them for their time helping as well. Ujung Kulon National Park has approximately 30,000 ha's of broad-leafed evergreen rainforest, with numerous rivers, creeks and wetlands. Average rainfall is three metres per annum, so it rains regularly, you soon get used to doing everything wet! Each day was like undertaking an obstacle course, climbing over trees, buttress roots, rocks, hills, wading rivers, taking canoes into remote areas and the ever-present saltwater crocodile (*Crocodylus porosus* or *'Buaya muara'*) and occasional bull or Zambezi shark (*Carcharhinus leucas* or *'Cucut'*) lurking in every brackish waterway.

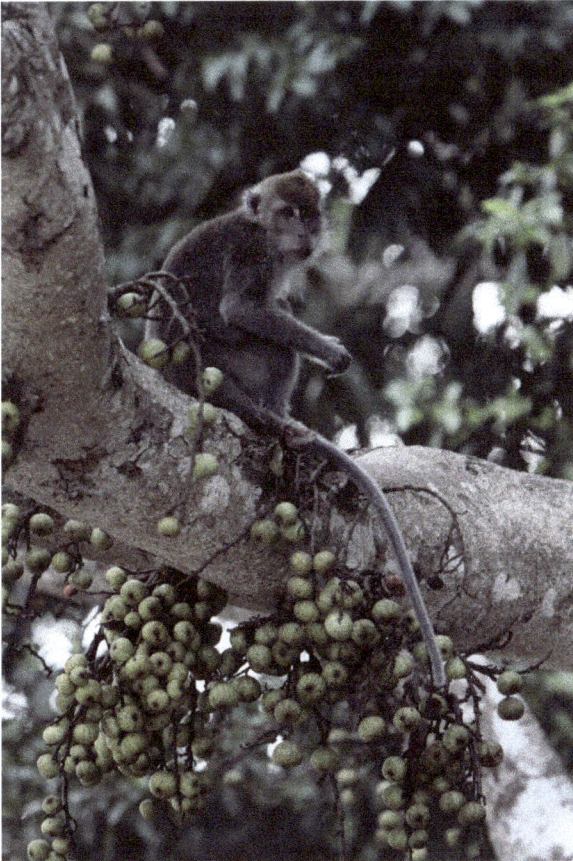

Long-tailed macaque *Macaca fascicularis* or *'Monyet'* feeding on *Ficus* fruit in Ujung Kulon National Park.

Saltwater crocodiles are the largest of the crocodilian species, and regularly patrol the coastal waters around Ujung Kulon. Feeding on a wide variety of prey, including fish, waterbirds, mammals (e.g., pigs) and will readily take carrion. Mated females build a nest of vegetation to lay and incubate their eggs, which are protected by females until they hatch. Tropical disease risk is high as well. Dengue and malaria were common in the community, plus ticks, leeches, an assortment of venomous snakes, scrub itch and *Dendrocinide* stinging trees always trying to nail you but it was awesome!

Over my regular Ujung Kulon visits, I was able to observe and interact with much of its wildlife. Being around when rainforest trees are fruiting is always exciting. For example, I remember on one early field trip a large *Ficus benjamina* or '*ipik*' tree (family Moraceae) was in fruit. Feeding in the uppermost canopy was a family of West Javan gibbons (*Hylobates m. moloch* or '*Owa jawa*') who were calling and swinging madly from branch to branch. Classified by the IUCN Red List (2009) as endangered (family Hylobatidae), Ujung Kulon is one of the few places left that support this rare species. A second endangered subspecies, the East Javan gibbon (*H. m. pongoalsoni*) is found in central and eastern Java. Living in small family groups led by an adult pair, males will actively defend their territories from other males and external threats. Javan gibbons have long fur and are uniformly silvery-grey. This species feeds predominantly on fruit and leaves, with occasional flowers and insects. In early morning and evening this gibbon has a distinctive single-note repetitive call.

Just below them was a troop of Javan grizzled leaf langur (*Presbytis c. comata* or '*Surili*'), classified by the IUCN Red List (2008) as endangered (family Cercopithecidae). A second subspecies, Frederica's leaf langur (*P. c. fredericae*) is found in central Java. These fruit and leaf eaters are very curious. I was able to quietly climb up the tree, leaning back against the main trunk

28

so I wouldn't fall and break my neck, and gently click my fingers, to arouse their curiosity. One curious female climbed down with a baby clinging to her chest and sat on a branch opposite me, only about two metres away, it was amazing, I may have been the first human she had ever directly looked at, it was quite the experience I'll never forget it. Next in the lower levels of the canopy was a large troop of long-tailed macaque (*Macaca fascicularis* or *'Monyet'*) over 30 strong. These primate generalists are ever the opportunists, and a fruiting tree is a prime target. Primates are messy feeders and would often drop pieces of fruit which would be snatched up by ever-vigilant Javan mouse deer (*Tragulus javanicus* or *'Kancil'*) [family Tragulidae]. Living in pairs, these rabbit-sized deer are very nervy and skittish, a much sought-after local delicacy, and given their small stature, are often pursued by birds of prey and the various feline and human predators that roam the forest. It was quite the spectacle, all of these species utilising a different level in the tree at one time. It was worth the watch, and the accompanying leeches that joined me for dinner!

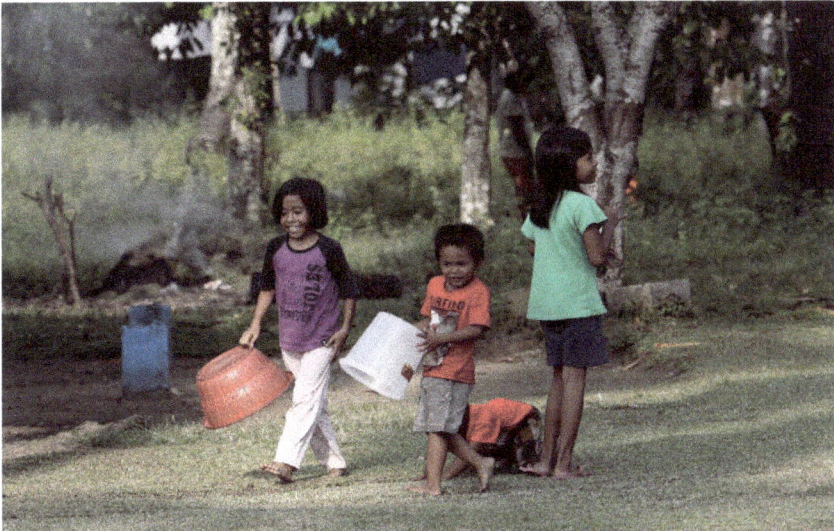

Local kids playing in Taman Jaya, no matter where you are or what country, kids are kids, they love to play and have fun!

Local Taman Jaya teenagers keen for a photo opportunity! These guys came to see me, they wanted help with their geography assignment on Australia. I appreciated their collective initiative, and was very happy to provide some inside knowledge and a photo of a real Australian to show in class!

Importantly, I needed to sort the academic elements of my proposed study, including finding a research supervisor or team of supervisors to support me and get university approval to undertake a PhD. I had recently completed a Masters in Environmental Management, majoring in natural resource management at the University of Queensland in Brisbane, so it was the obvious place to start.

At this point, it's worth mentioning that at the time, I held a senior position as the Land, Biodiversity and Indigenous Program Manager at the Goulburn Broken Catchment Management Authority (GB CMA), based in Shepparton, northern Victoria. A role I continued in for 13 years up until my retirement in September 2022. Given my need for ongoing financial resources to undertake such a venture, my pitch to the university was to undertake my PhD part-time, continue working full-time at the GB CMA and undertake my research work over a six-year period. At the University of Queensland, I approached Professor Salit Kark, who was senior academic at the School of Biological Sciences. Salit, a gifted Israeli academic, was supportive and impressed I'd already visited Indonesia, and had made some important contacts and determined what was feasible. Salit rightly felt I needed a diverse supervisory team, and Dr Duan Biggs, a South African social scientist and Associate Professor Anne Goldizen, an American, with significant animal behaviour and ecology expertise, were approached. After several discussions and various draft research proposals, Salit would become my principal supervisor, and Duan and Anne would support me on elements of my research related to their knowledge and skill base, and be part of my supervisory team. I requested to my supervisory team that I wanted to be self-funded.

I preferred any possible scholarships or university $'s go to the younger generation, plus given the high-risk element of the work in Java, I suspected the Universities' student scholarship/insurance requirements may have been a significant barrier! Ongoing operating risks included: dengue, malaria, saltwater crocodiles, snake bites, charging rhino and banteng bulls, tsunamis, earthquakes and poachers, to name a few! After my initial November 2014 visit to Ujung Kulon, I was already formulating what was feasible regarding my thesis chapter subjects, and what University of Queensland ethics approvals I would need moving forward. Knowing I was going to interact and work with the local community in some capacity, human ethics approval was a given, as well as animal ethics, so I needed to submit research plans for both to the University of Queensland's Behavioural & Social Sciences Ethical Review Committee, and Animal Ethics Committee. Fortunately, my research plans were approved by both committees.

Next step was to speak with the GB CMA about my research proposal and get agreement that I would be saving and using all my annual and study leave for regular visits to Indonesia, plus I offered to deliver regular updates and presentations to GB CMA staff and team on my studies. So, by early 2015, I had everything in place: my Australian Indonesian Consulate and Indonesian foreign research permits to undertake my research activities in Ujung Kulon National Park, a PhD academic supervisory team, my work's approval and, importantly, my family's support. There is no question I wouldn't have succeeded without the support of my partner Tracy, and kids Coen, Daly and Allira, who journeyed with me and had the faith I would get there in the end. I was ready to go and make it happen.

The eventual title of my thesis was '*Factors shaping the conservation of the critically endangered Javan Rhinoceros (Rhinoceros sondaicus)*'.

My seven PhD thesis chapters focused on the following areas:

- Chapter 1—*Introduction;*

- Chapter 2—*Implications of local community awareness to the conservation of the Javan rhino, one of Earth's rarest mammals;*

- Chapter 3—*Protecting an icon: Javan rhino frontline management and conservation;*

- Chapter 4—*Understanding the implications of Arenga palm (Arenga obtusifolia) dominance for the conservation and management of Javan rhino;*

- Chapter 5—*More than just mud: The importance of wallows to Javan rhino ecology and behaviour;*

- Chapter 6—*Understanding an icon: Social behaviour and communication in the Javan rhino; and*

- Chapter 7—*Thesis discussion and conclusion.*

My main working home base in West Java, the rustic Village Prima Homestay in the village of Taman Jaya, situated on the beach and close to Ujung Kulon National Park ranger base and the park itself.

During my regular Java visits, I set myself up in the village of Taman Jaya. Taman Jaya is close to Ujung Kulon National Park, and is the location of the main national park ranger base. I would regularly stay at the Village Prima Homestay. The manager Minggu, and his family were welcoming, and although the roof leaked and the accommodation was basic, it was comfortable and a great base for me to come and go from the national park. The homestay's location was right on the coast, and was an awesome place to recover after long jungle trips, which were physically and mentally exhausting. I always enjoyed the evening calling of Tokay geckoes (*Gekko gecko* or *'Toke'*). It was the perfect place to recharge before coming home to Australia, and excellent for wildlife watching and to witness Sundanese village life.

Around the homestay was a grove of large coconut palms (*Cocos nucifera*) and during the day *Draco* dragons or *'Hap-hap'* would glide between the tall trunks and would flash and display their bib-like dewlaps under their chins. Common across Ujung Kulon, these amazing flying dragons are quite capable gliders. Male and females are of similar size; however, females have pale blue dewlaps under the neck, males have yellow dewlaps with both sexes using for display purposes and communication. Well camouflaged, this species clings to tree trunks and feeds on trails of ants. They're gliding membrane is attached to specialised ribs which can be extended away from the body. In the evening, Large flying foxes (*Pteropus vampyrus* or *'Kalong'*), would fly in to feed on the fruits and nectar of the coconut palms. One of the world's largest flying fox species, with a wingspan of up to 1.5 m, it feeds exclusively on fruits, flowers and nectar. By day, it roosts in colonies, flying out early evening searching for food. Often hunted by locals for bushmeat, this species is classified by the IUCN Red List (2022) as endangered (family Pteropodidae). Javan Sunda colugo (*Galeopterus v. variegatus* [family Cynocephalidae]), would also regularly glide in to feed in the palms. Totally arboreal, local people call colugo *'Tando'* or *'Walang kopo'*. This unusual nocturnal species is a generalist folivore, with a diverse diet including fruit, nectar, flower buds, lichen, and occasionally ants. Typically seen in pairs, females are noticeably larger than males. An inhabitant of tropical rainforest, it prefers areas with tall trees and broad trunks, and aerial space between them to glide. Consummate gliders, this species is able to glide up to 150 metres between trees. This species is found across Southeast Asia. A second species, the Philippine colugo (*Cynocephalus volans*) is found across the southern Philippine archipelago. Java has a rich squirrel fauna (family Sciuridae), including several species that utilised the Taman Jaya palm trees and local vegetation as well. Species observed included, Plantain squirrel (*Callosciuris notatus*), Javan black-striped squirrel (*C. n. nigrovittatus*), and the larger and rarer Javan black giant squirrel (*Ratufa b. bicolor* or *'Jeralang'*) which is classified as Near Threatened on the IUCN Red List (2023). Occasionally, I observed the Javan red giant flying squirrel (*Petaurista p. petaurista* or *'Bajing terbang'*), which tended to do its thing high in the tree canopy, along with West Javan black-eared squirrel (*Nannosciuris m. melanotis*) and West Javan three-striped squirrel (*Lariscus i. insignis*). When I observed a squirrel species, and wasn't quite sure of its identification, I would note down its characteristics and when back in Australia, I'd hit the books and work out what it is. Javan people call small squirrels '*Bajing*'. I have a soft spot for squirrels; they have attitude, plus they never sit still, always on the go and a challenge to photograph! Often when I observed them, they would run vertically down a tree trunk and bark at you, as if to say 'fuck off from my tree', they had spunk!

Java, its people and connection to 'Badak jawa' (Javan rhino)

One of the things that helped me early on in my studies was time spent visiting each of the 19 villages that surround the eastern edge of Ujung Kulon National Park, all of which have some reliance on national park resources. Using motorbikes to get around, Aphuy and I would first meet with the village leader, the '*kepala desa*'. Aphuy would introduce me, and then I would let the village leader know of my plans to undertake a PhD and study the Javan rhino over the next six years. I also explained there would be an opportunity for his village community to help me, and I would be able to pay them for their time and support. Eventually, I would undertake a social survey of the 19 villages, asking each of them about what they knew and understood about the Javan rhino. This work became Chapter 2 in my thesis '*Implications of local community awareness to the conservation of the Javan rhino, one of Earth's rarest mammals*'.

Over the years the villagers got to know me and I them, they called me '*Pak Steve*', the term '*Pak*' is an Indonesian term of respect for older men. I became something of a local novelty, villagers found it amazing that a western 'Australian' person had an interest in their rhino and local wildlife, who kept coming back and was prepared to rough it in the jungle to learn about them. For an exceptionally rare species such as the Javan rhino, understanding local community awareness is critical for the development of future conservation actions. Java is also one of the world's most heavily populated islands, and as of 2019, over 153+ million residents, at a density of 1,196/km², which results in continuous pressure on remaining habitat, wildlife and protected areas. The predominantly Muslim community living near and adjacent to Ujung Kulon NP resides in Banten Province, one of 34 provinces across Indonesia. Banten is the westernmost province on the island of Java, Indonesia. In 2019, the human population of Banten was officially estimated at 14+ million, at a density of 1,200/km², noting a population census is carried out every five to six years. Protected areas and conservation management authorities are increasingly utilising attitudinal studies as tools for evaluating community awareness of the impact of conservation activity. Without the cooperation and involvement of communities who live close to wildlife and protected areas, conservation actions are less likely to succeed.

Community involvement in the management of protected areas correlates positively with protected area policy compliance. Well-resourced and coordinated community-driven activities assist local people becoming key stakeholders in the conservation effort. For example, to protect wildlife in Nepal, the Nepalese government successfully introduced a policy of sharing tourism revenues from protected areas with local communities living adjacent to its reserves. A similar positive result has occurred in West Bengal, India, where improved relations between wildlife management personnel and local villagers had a positive impact on protection and reduced poaching of greater one-horned rhino. Through this approach, authoritie, and the local community work together, supported by rhino awareness programmes, eco-projects and eco-tourism businesses that benefit local villagers, enabling them to reduce their reliance for forest resources.

Around the eastern edge of Ujung Kulon, adjacent to the Gunung Honje Ranges, live the Sundanese (Javan) people that have traditionally used park resources for their livelihood, and in some cases continue to do so. Sundanese society is patriarchal and based on large extended families who provide support and assistance to each other within the broader family unit. The local village is the lowest level of government administration in Indonesia and is the most influential on village life and handles matters of the village through the elected village leader. The inhabitants of these villages are mostly subsistence farmers and fishermen; however not all of their needs can be met by their farming and fishing activities. Local communities are still reliant on national park resources, including firewood, timber and bamboo used as building materials, and various vegetable proteins. Other national park resources provide villagers with a source of income, such as collection of *'jernang'* (a red palm resin used for making dye), bird poaching, wild honey and edible-nest swiftlet (*Aerodramus fuciphagus or 'Wallet'* [family Apodidae]) nest collecting. Many local villagers lack viable alternative livelihoods, so they continue to rely heavily on national park resources.

Edible-nest swiftlets are an interesting species, found along the coast, they nest inside limestone caves and use echolocation to find their nests in the darkness. They build translucent cup-shaped nests made of hardened saliva, and are highly valued and collected by local people. The hard saliva nests are used by gourmet chefs, being the main ingredient of bird's nest soup, a traditional delicacy of Chinese cuisine.

Bird poaching pressure is significant across the park, targeting species such as hornbill (family Bucerotidae). Three species are found in Ujung Kulon, the Oriental Pied hornbill (*Anthracoceros albirostris* or *'Kangkareng'*), Javan Rhinoceros hornbill (*Buceros rhinoceros silvestris* or *'rangkong'*), and Wreathed hornbill (*Aceros undulatus* or *'djulang'*). These large frugivorous birds are hunted for their large beaks and casques. Both the Rhinoceros and Wreathed hornbill have been classified by the IUCN Red List as vulnerable since 2018.

Smaller species such as the brightly plumaged Black-banded barbet (*Psilopogon javensis* [family Megalaimidae]), and Banded broadbill (*Eurylaimas javanicus* [family Eurylaimidae]) are also poaching targets. Fortunately, I was able to observe both these colorful species. I would normally catch them feeding on fruit and insects in fruiting and flowering trees such as *Ficus*, often in the company of larger fruit-chasing species like hornbills.

A Tokay gecko *Gekko gecko* or *'Toke'* on the wall of the homestay. This large nocturnal species, grows between 25–40cm, has adapted well to human habitats, and would actively hunt for insects across villages around Ujung Kulon National Park.

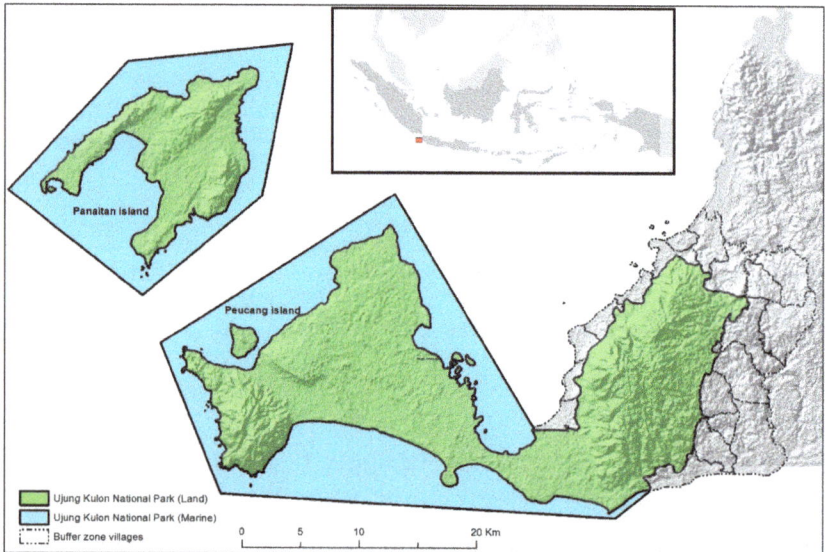

Map of Ujung Kulon National Park, West Java, Indonesia showing the Ujung Kulon National Park Land precinct (green) including Panaitan Island (green) and Marine Protected Area (blue). The eastern section of the map shows the 19 village precinct boundaries (dark dotted lines and grey area). The boxed map above shows the location (red square) of Ujung Kulon National Park in the Indonesian archipelago. Map was created using ArcMap 10.5 software (ESRI).

Given that the Ujung Kulon peninsula has no people living in it, the main area of village and local community activity is centred on the Gunung Honje Mountain region (eastern section of the national park). Ujung Kulon also experiences periodic illegal logging and the tending of domestic livestock, mainly buffalo and goats, on the national park fringes and within the park area itself. A significant and ongoing risk and consequence of the tending of livestock in or near the national park is increased risk of disease being transferred from livestock to wildlife, especially large herbivores such as the endangered Javan banteng (*Bos j. javanicus*), vulnerable listed Javan rusa or Timor deer (*Rusa timorensis russa* or '*Rusa*'), Javan wild pig (*Sus scrofa vittatus* or '*Babi hutan*') and the critically endangered Javan rhino ('*Badak jawa*').

There is some suspicion that anthrax or another infectious agent was implicated in five rhino deaths in 1982, at least two animals in 2002–2003, five in 2010–2013 and two in 2014. This theory is supported by Santiapillai & Suprahman (1986), citing an outbreak of *Septicaemia epizootica*, which killed 50 buffaloes and 350 goats in the neighbourhood of Ujung Kulon in November 1981. As of April 2023, Foot and Mouth disease (FMD) is now listed as endemic across Indonesia, and remains a real risk to both domestic (e.g., buffalo) and native hoof stock (e.g., banteng and deer species), and rhino. To help mitigate this risk, in 2010, authorities launched the 5,100 ha Javan Rhino Study and Conservation Area (JRSCA), sometimes called Suaka Badak Nasional (SBN) or National Rhino Sanctuary (NRS), including installing an 8-kilometre-long rhino-proof fence at the base of the eastern Gunung Honje range to protect the habitat area, exclude domestic stock and keep rhino protected. Between 1979–1980 and again in 2010–2011, the Indonesian Government removed over 300 illegal settlers living within Ujung Kulon's eastern Gunung Honje area. This removal has reduced but not eliminated, ongoing threats due to illegal activities engaged in by local communities, mostly for subsistence reasons.

Since 2010, Ujung Kulon authorities and non-government organisations (NGOs) have utilised local community labour and skills in some aspects of the park's management, which has enhanced the relationship between village communities and national park authorities. Beginning in May 2015, with Aphuy and other national park and rhino protection staff's help, I began survey interviews with each of the 19 local village community leaders. This required Indonesian conservation authority support and an Indonesian interpreter. Cultural protocol dictates consultation through the village leader or 'kepala desa', who speaks for the community. In the event of the village leaders' absence, the village secretary can speak on their behalf.

During each village visit, Aphuy would randomly (note: families habitually sit outside the front of their homes) ask local people whether they would like to participate in a survey on Javan rhino; in most cases, they were pleased and interested in assisting. Only three people (2.28%) of all villagers approached refused to participate, however, in each case they deferred to older members of the family, which is culturally appropriate.

Pre-survey consultation with Ujung Kulon and Indonesian Rhino Foundation (YABI) staff acknowledged the low literacy and limited educational backgrounds of local villagers. It was recommended by a national park staff member the survey questions be kept clear and as basic as possible, and that adult participants be targeted, as they could provide the most informed responses, and culturally, young people if asked would defer to their elders.

The survey questionnaire was first developed in English, and then translated into Bahasa. Questionnaires were piloted on three people, including a rhino protection staff member who came from a local village, as well as the interpreter and a local villager. As a result of the pre-testing and discussions, some questions were deleted, and others modified to improve clarity. During the pilot process, we trialled the questions and the responses together with the interpreter. Additionally, during the pilot, we found that after initial introductions, it was easier for the interpreter to ask participants the questions and record the responses, as this made the process flow more easily.

Before administering the questionnaire, cultural norms were followed, i.e., introduction of the researcher, interpreter, the form and rationale of the questionnaire and an explanation of its intended purpose. All participants signed a research consent form before commencing and additionally signed their questionnaires upon completion. Village leaders would stamp and sign their completed questionnaires with their respective village seals. Participants varied in their times to complete the questionnaire, with an average duration between one to two hours to complete. Under normal travel and weather conditions, in most cases, we could complete three, sometimes four, survey questionnaires each day.

The survey adapted and used Stankey & Schindler's (2005) themes for studying community attitudes and their relationship to the management of rare species, which includes five factors that influence people's attitudes. These themes include knowledge, ethics, perceived risks, spatial, temporal and social context and trust. In this study, I used the model described by Stankey & Schindler (2005) to develop a four-point Likert scale (2–5) for each of the attitude-determining factors, to be able to quantify them. Responses would be ranked from 1 = 0 (don't know), 2 = (no risk) to 5 = (very high risk). Additionally, the survey asked a series of 12 questions about local peoples' opinions on rhino conservation, including five questions requiring a response on a four-point Likert scale. Village leaders were also asked several additional questions relating to their tenure as leaders and village population data, which is a leader's responsibility to record and manage.

Completed questionnaire qualitative data was converted back from Bahasa into English by Aphuy and myself, and both quantitative and qualitative data was entered into Microsoft Excel spreadsheets. The results were analysed in order to identify which factors are important in defining local community attitudes to Javan rhino conservation and to test the hypothesis that community attitude to rhino conservation improves with awareness and involvement in conservation activities. The survey questionnaire used 42 questions (village leader) and 39 questions for local villagers. Twenty questions are based on a Likert scale (2–5) ranking response; the remaining involved qualitative responses. Predictor variables used in the analysis included local community knowledge of Javan rhino conservation status, national park boundaries, regulations, awareness of conservation initiatives, cultural importance and views of risk factors.

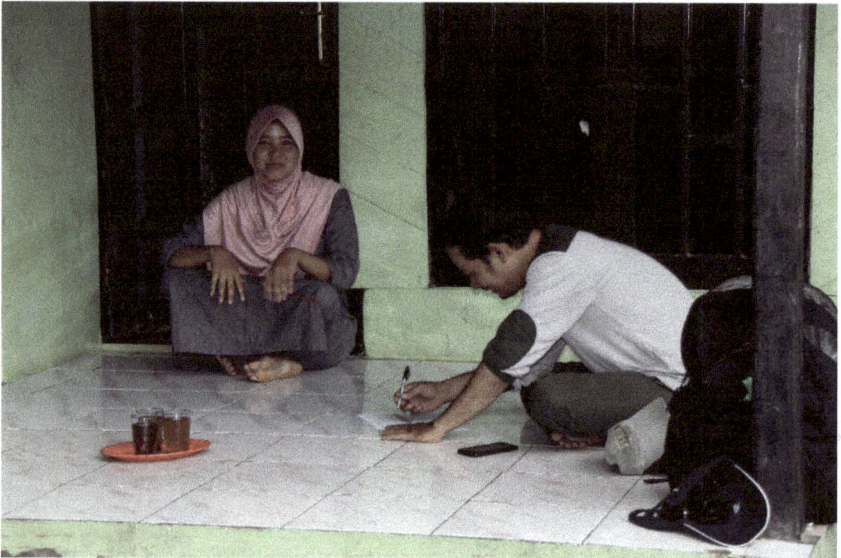

The late Mohamad '*Aphuy*' Syamsudin and villager from Cigorondong, working through my community survey (in Bahasa) to understand local community knowledge of Javan rhino and the conservation effort. Tragically, Aphuy passed away on the 8th December 2021, he was 46 years old.

Illegally grazing domestic buffalo in the eastern Gunung Honje section of Ujung Kulon National Park. Villagers attached loud bells around the necks of their animals, so they can find them in the forest. Along with the disease transfer risk, the loud bell ringing sound would disturb any rhinos in the vicinity. An estimated 6,000+ buffalo live in villages around the park. Rangers and rhino protection staff would regularly move buffalo out of the park.

What did we find out?

Overall, 76 local community members, including 19 village leaders and 57 local villagers, completed survey questionnaires. The sample comprised 53 males (69.7%) and 23 females (30.3%), age range 18–66. Village leaders lived in their villages on average for 33.53 years. The average tenure as village leader was 4.78 years. Local villagers lived in their villages on average for 34.19 years. The population of the 19 villages living around the eastern boundary of Ujung Kulon has grown by 21.55% since 2010. Increasing from 52,599 to 63,936; as of May 2015, a population increase of 11,337. In 2010, the average village size was 2,821; by May 2015, it had grown to 3,365. By May 2020, the average village size was over 4,000.

The survey results highlighted the local community was generally positive about the presence and value of Javan rhino, and having the national park nearby. However, overall community knowledge and awareness of Javan rhino conservation activities and national park regulations and boundaries was low. The most informed communities came from the villages of Ujung Jaya, Taman Jaya and Cigorondong. This may be due to the community being more likely to interact with national park and rhino protection unit staff based at the Ujung Kulon National Park Authority operations headquarters in Taman Jaya and the rhino protection staff bases situated in Cigorondong and Ujung Jaya. Ujung Kulon NP activities, including routine patrolling and conservation management activities such as arenga palm control plant propagation and tree planting, are coordinated out of these bases.

Local villager carrying green rainforest timber on the back of a motorbike collected inside Ujung Kulon NP. This timber is turned into charcoal for cooking. It demonstrates great opportunity exists to educate local community about using other less 'habitat-impacting' energy sources.

National Park and rhino protection staff live in these local villages, increasing communication channels for sharing conservation and park activity information with locals. This was reflected in community knowledge of arenga palm, a major threat to the habitat and food resources of rhino, and with an active conservation management program. The 88% 'do not know' response highlighted this. However, 12% of community that had some knowledge of the palm came from the villages Ujung Jaya, Taman Jaya and Cigorondong, possibly indicating these communities gets more exposure to communication from authorities due to the presence of staff bases compared to villages that do not have staff bases nearby.

As a patriarchal society, the Sundanese (Javan) women, children and young people would naturally defer to the older men in their families. Their village leaders are always men. As a traditional and structured society, we assumed questionnaire responses were based on their real experience or exposure to a question. For example, when asked, 'how interested are your young people in Javan rhino conservation', if they had no obvious knowledge of young peoples' interest, they were reluctant to speak on young peoples' behalf. This appeared to be the case for the significant results to the questions regarding people's opinions of both old and young people on Javan rhino conservation and knowledge of community involvement in conservation activities.

The one-on-one methodology used to survey these communities was accepted by those involved, as has been shown in other contexts, when working with people of low literacy and limited educational backgrounds. It could be argued that some of the results could be biased by participants telling us what we wanted to hear. The diversity of the themes and questions asked should have avoided this bias. People were grateful and pleased to be asked to contribute and it appeared the experience was positive for them. I was pleased when Aphuy informed me, post-survey, that feedback from local community to national park and rhino protection staff on the questionnaire and the research has been positive, which I'm grateful for.

The living conditions in all the villages visited was similar, and all communities faced the same challenges related to their location. Therefore, the sample size (n=76) may be considered large enough to represent all 19 villages. The similarity of the participants' answers supports this notion.

The growing human population around Ujung Kulon is a significant risk, given that there is no additional land available to support this growth. Competition between the national park, rhinos and human settlements will continue, unless viable alternative livelihoods can be seen, which could include increased in-park conservation work. It remains unclear as to how much impact human population growth has occurred, as not all areas of the park see regular patrol activity. national park border areas where they interface with village cultivation and agricultural land are worth examining, noting some form of incremental edge effect into national park land would be occurring and exacerbating habitat decline. Protected area authorities appear to have limited influence on decisions made outside a protected area's administrative boundaries.

The survey participants acknowledged the rarity and uniqueness of the rhino and its protected habitat. However, despite strong intent and claims of wanting to be involved and informed, they essentially remain uninformed of the conservation challenges, their impacts and the management requirements of rhino and the park. When asked about the national park and rhino risk factors, the community response was narrow in context. For example, increased population and better roads and infrastructure 'might' increase the risk of illegal activity. No feedback was given regarding the risks of human population increases and corresponding growth in domestic livestock numbers, which could significantly raise the risk of disease transfer, given that less land is available and park resource use intensifies. This highlights the broad lack of community awareness of the conservation threats.

Opportunities do exist to improve communication channels between authorities and local community. For example, World Rhino Day is actively supported by both authorities and community, and an event is held in Taman Jaya during September each year, and everyone turns up to celebrate. These types of large-scale events can be used to promote and inform local communities of current and intended conservation activity. National park and rhino protection staff have more detailed knowledge and practical exposure to the risks and the management and conservation activities need, so are well placed to influence community within the confines of their staff bases at Taman Jaya, Ujung Jaya and Cigorondong and more widely. It was clear regular visits by authority staff to other villages to share information would be welcomed by local communities. Additionally, authorities could meet with village leaders and local clerics to share concerns and information, which would be a positive and practical way forward. By utilising respected people of influence, who, once appropriately informed and with a solid understanding of the authorities' conservation and management objectives, would be in an ideal position to influence the broader local community.

The support of local people is a critical element for maintaining an ecologically viable and functional protected area. When the community was asked the importance of the national park to community question it elicited a strong response, with repeated reference of its importance to village life, notably provision of water and resources. A community education program that highlighted the benefits forested areas provide beyond biodiversity and habitat preservation outcomes through to benefits such as crop pollination, carbon sequestration and flood mitigation, may be a means of raising awareness and ideally reduce impacts on the resource.

Local communities face many challenges through the remoteness of their location, a mostly subsistence existence (farming/fishing) and poor services. For example, power outages are a common occurrence, with ongoing transport and access issues. The main access road and smaller feeder roads that edge around the national park's boundary quickly deteriorate from the township of Sumur, on the park's north-eastern corner, through to the main national park service entries at Taman Jaya and Ujung Jaya. In extended wet periods, the road network becomes virtually impassable, slowing motorbike, foot and vehicular traffic to slow walking pace. Hence, road conditions dominate and influence village life. The targeting of villages, which are close to the national park but don't reside on the national park's borders would be a valuable exercise. These villages include Sumber Jaya, Ciburial, Cijaralang and Batuhideung. These four villages scored consistently lower, having no knowledge of national park regulations, boundaries, or awareness of conservation activities. Most (70%) of the surveyed villagers who had been involved in conservation activities in some way was positive. However, outside of direct involvement, their overall lack of knowledge of national parks and conservation management is cause for concern, particularly reflective in the poor community understanding of park regulations and knowledge of park boundary responses.

The open question asking if the community would like to contribute or be involved in conservation management planning of Javan rhino and the national park elicited a 100% yes response. This feedback was valuable to authorities wanting to improve community awareness and understanding of their activities and management intent. The responses emphasised, despite involvement in conservation activity, is viewed favourably and community wants to contribute, this does not necessarily correspond with increased awareness. Therefore, the hypothesis that community attitude to rhino conservation improves with awareness and involvement in conservation activities is not supported. Despite this, support was generally strong regarding community interest. All communities were completely united in wanting more regular communication from the authorities.

This study has provided valuable insight into the attitudes and approaches of local communities and the following recommendations are listed for consideration: establish a community reference group in each village. A potential model could include four to six representatives, including the elected village leader as chairperson. The group would meet four times annually and would discuss and take community concerns and issues back to the authorities. Authorities would regularly communicate with these groups. Recommendations that have been identified from this study include the instigation of a social skills training program, incorporating conflict resolution and diplomacy. Village leaders, clerics and rhino protection staff and national park rangers could be targeted for such training and undertake national park boundary and village precinct development assessments. This would include assessment of viable areas for the creation of alternative livelihoods for local people. For example, community forestry, carbon sequestration plantings, rhino food plant plantations, bee keeping (for pollination enhancement and for profit/commodity and options that allow rhino entry, including creating wetlands (possible tourism opportunity?). Through an established community reference group, opportunities to develop projects, source funding and expertise to create alternative livelihoods for local people could be directed to appropriate organisations such as the World Bank.

Establish an intelligence network across the local villages to gather information on illegal encroachment, logging and wildlife poaching activity. This network would also examine current impacts of such activity in the national park, to determine just how large the impacts are and where to direct effort. This network could feed into, or be a component of, the proposed community reference group model.

This study was the first to examine community attitudes and approaches to rhino management across all 19 villages and communities surrounding Ujung Kulon in a conservation research context. The data captured from this study was used to help inform national park managers and conservation planners of local community attitudes and understanding of current conservation activity and assist in identifying future risks, e.g., human population growth, and include community considerations regarding possible reintroductions of rhinos into former historic ranges. Whilst not a social scientist, this local community survey exercise was fun and enjoyable. It enabled me to get real exposure to village life, and get to know the people, as well as share my life and background with those curious to ask, which was often.

Over time, local villagers learnt of my interest in wildlife and would often ask for help removing a snake from a chook pen or home, which I didn't mind, as you never knew what the offending species would be. A reticulated python (*Malayopython reticulatus* or *'Ular sanca batik'* [family Pythonidae]), Javan spitting cobra (*Naja sputatrix* or *'Ular sendok'* [family Elapidae]). Or, villagers would often find and tell me when they had Asian vine snakes (*Ahaetulla prasina* or *'Ular pucuk'* [family Colubridae]) in their gardens. These bright green, pencil-thin, mildly venomous snakes actively chase birds, lizards and frogs in the garden foliage. When disturbed, this species will present the classic S-shaped strike pose, fortunately their venom is not potent. I've talked to a few locals who have been bitten; they said it gave them a mild headache. Interestingly, this snake species is unique in having horizontal pupils, a good diagnostic identifier, as well as their distinctive green colour and size, commonly growing up to 1.8 metres. I regularly caught and relocated this species for villagers, and, fortunately, was never bitten, so I never experienced the expected headache! Also, Asian water monitors (*Varanus salvator* or *'Biawak'* [family Varanidae]) were notorious poultry killers, often raiding chook pens in village communities. Growing well over two metres, these smart lizards were always on the hunt, would readily bite and flick their tails when cornered. Any I caught would be relocated into the national park, along with any captured snakes. In most cases, I carried a pillow slip to put any captures in.

A great example of local community collaboration began in 1996, when the World of Wildlife Fund established a community development program. From 1996 to 2017, this program, and others, engaged communities by involving community members in the park management activities around Javan rhino conservation including rhino monitoring, rhino fecal sampling and arenga palm control. This work, while successful, did not address the root causes of community impact on Ujung Kulon National Park due to their livelihood dependence on the park's resources. In 2017, the focus of community engagement changed to make the community the goal. Community-led processes were established that challenged the local community to identify and assess the problems that they faced in their daily life using the Sustainable Livelihood Assessment method.

As a result of these consultations, it was concluded that the local community shares similar concerns with the park and conservation groups and therefore, real win-win solutions could be developed. Based on the self-identified needs of the local community, an ecological agricultural field school a living food banks field school, a water buffalo animal husbandry field school, and an agroforestry field school have all been established. These field schools have created numerous local champions that have become community trainers helping to spread the ideas and capacity throughout the community. While being community-centered, these programs reduce threats to Ujung Kulon. For example, the living food bank field schools teach women how to grow organic vegetables reducing their need to collect vegetables from the forest. An evaluation of this approach around Ujung Kulon was conducted in 2021, showing positive trends exist that will ultimately lead to positive impacts for rhino conservation.

On one of our last community survey trips, four of us, each on motorbikes were heading back to Taman Jaya. We were riding through the village of Tunggal Jaya, when the lead bike struck and killed a large impressive-looking rooster that ran across the road. I was on the second bike so I witnessed the unfortunate event. An elderly lady emerged from her hut and was devastated by the loss of her rooster. She threw herself on the ground and was wailing uncontrollably. We parked our bikes and I walked over to the woman and asked her if she was okay. Upon hearing my Australian accent, she looked up and said 'Pak Steve' then threw herself at me, crying even more. Aphuy was trying to get a handle on why all the theatrics. It transpired that the now dead rooster was the local 'stud' rooster, '*Makan*' which translates to 'eat', and was well known for his 'service ability'. Villagers from far and wide would drop off their females to the elderly woman and she would place *Makan* and the in 'need of service female' into a bamboo pen, *Makan* would work his magic and the woman would be paid a service 'fee'. So, we had impacted negatively on what sounded like quite a viable business venture! Obviously unable to awaken the dead, we needed a solution. I suggested to Aphuy we should ask the woman if *Makan* has any sons. She immediately pointed to various huts in the distance. Aphuy did some door knocking and eventually found a replacement rooster, showing all the correct *Makan* DNA, i.e., large wattles, good colour, a proud strut that would attract female attention and was impressive in appearance. I was able to converse, and eventually pay a very happy son of *Makan's* owner, 50,000 rupia or roughly $5.00 Australian—problem solved.

The still sobbing but now 'sort of half-happy' owner of the lost *Makan* was grateful, as I handed her the replacement rooster, she squeezed my arm in thanks, as we jumped back on our bikes to head home. This now infamous rooster problem solving did my local reputation no harm, the village telegraph quickly spread that Pak Steve had assisted a local in need, noting Aphuy should have been the acknowledged hero, his Bahasa and door knocking got us over the line. We can only hope the new rooster replacement model has the genes and DNA to deliver as well as his father!

All the local village poultry look very similar to the true wild form, the Javan Red Jungle Fowl (*Gallus g. bankeva* or *'Ayam hutan'* [family Phasianidae]), which was domesticated several thousand years ago, the resulting domestic variant is now annually producing billions across the globe. The natural range of the wild form includes India, Nepal, western Bangladesh, eastwards to southern China, Indochina; southeast into Malaysia, Singapore, the Philippines and right across the Indonesian archipelago. Javan Red Jungle Fowl and its close relative the Green Jungle Fowl (*Gallus varius* or *'Ayam hutan hijau'*) are found across Ujung Kulon. Understandably, they are prized by all the local predators, human and non-human, and I mostly saw them foraging in the jungle only on camera trap, otherwise they were very secretive, with good reason!

I finally finished all the local community survey work in May 2016; next step was to commence surveying all the frontline staff, the Ujung Kulon National Park rangers and rhino protection staff.

Close up of the Asian vine snake Ahaetulla prasina or *'Ular pucuk'*. Note the unique horizontal pupil!

Ujung Kulon, background and history

Located in Western Java, Indonesia, Ujung Kulon National Park (UKNP) is a peninsula protruding from the southwest extremity of mainland Java, to which it is joined by a low isthmus some 1–2 km wide. Ujung Kulon National Park (*coordinates* 6°44'48" S 105°20'1" E), was gazetted in 1980, and in 1992, the park, along with the volcanic Krakatau archipelago, and larger islands including Panaitan, as well as smaller islands such as Handeuleum and Peucang in the Sunda Strait, was Indonesia's first declared UNESCO World Heritage Site.

Ujung Kulon has a total area of 120,551 ha, encompassing 76,214 ha of terrestrial and 44,337 ha of surrounding reef and sea (marine protected area) marine ecosystems. Ujung Kulon supports a diversity of ecosystems, including grassland, lowland rainforest, coastal forest, freshwater swamp forest and mangrove forest habitats. Ujung Kulon represents the largest remaining tract of broad-leaf lowland tropical rainforest on the island of Java.

An area of 35,000 ha in the Ujung Kulon peninsula is the core habitat area for Javan rhinos. The topography of Ujung Kulon is flat to mountainous, with the highest peaks being Gunung Honje (620 m) in the east and Gunung Payung (480 m) in the western peninsula. The peninsula area of Ujung Kulon is interspersed with several rivers, including the Citadahan, Cicakanggalih, Cibunar, Cikesek, Cibandawoh, Cigenter, Cikarang and Cijungkulon. These waterways are important water sources for both rhino and other wildlife, especially during dry periods. Ujung Kulon is managed by the central government through the technical implementation unit of the Directorate General of Forest Protection and Nature Conservation of the Ministry of Environment and Forestry.

The climate of Ujung Kulon is tropical with a seasonal mean average rainfall of 3250 mm, mean temperature range of 25°C–30° C and relative humidity of 65%–100%. The Indonesian archipelago and the Ujung Kulon region, occur in one of the most seismic and volcanically active areas of the world. Famously, on the 27th of August 1883, the nearby volcanic island of Krakatau erupted, sending destructive tsunami waves across the Sunda Straits towards Java. Actual insight into the impact of the tsunamis was recorded by a British ship situated 222 km south of Ujung Kulon on the day: '*Encountered carcasses of animals including even those of tigers and about 150 human corpses... besides enormous trunks of trees borne along by the current*'.

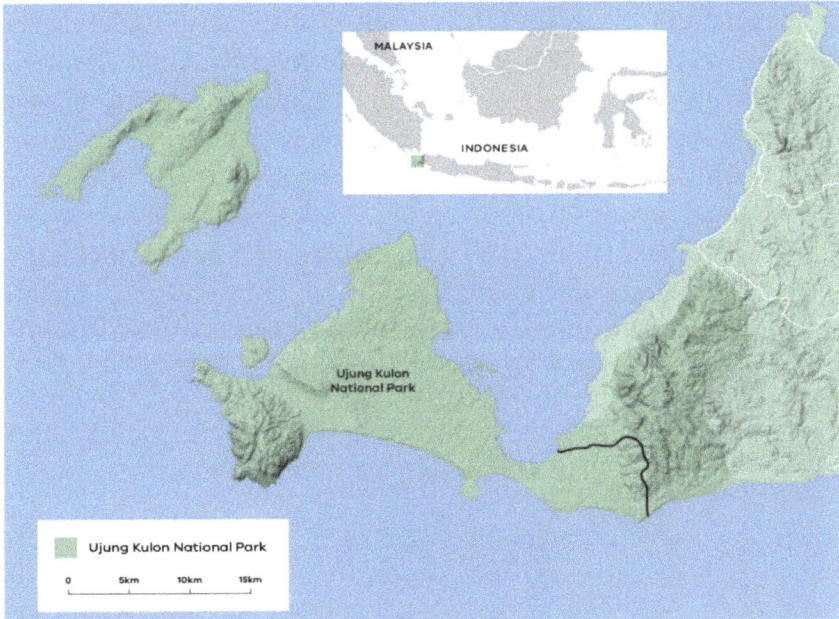

Map of Ujung Kulon National Park, West Java, Indonesia (*coordinates* 6°44'48" S 105°20'1" E) in darker green. The black line shows the location of the 8 km fence erected to exclude domestic stock from entering the park. The large island situated north-west of the Ujung Kulon peninsula is Peucang Island, part of the Ujung Kulon National Park precinct. Map was created using ArcMap 10.5 software (ESRI).

The volcanic explosion of Krakatau in 1883 produced several tsunamis that destroyed the villages and agricultural crops of the coastal areas on the western peninsula and covered the entire Ujung Kulon area in a layer of ash; an estimated 36,000+ people perished. This event saw the total evacuation of the peninsula by humans, thereby creating the opportunity to become a nature refuge for much of Java's flora and fauna, which is now the most intact remaining lowland forest habitat on the island of Java.

The Ujung Kulon region was never heavily populated before or after the 1883 eruption. It eventually recovered from the impacts of the eruption, and some villagers returned. Eventually, in the early 1900s the Ujung Kulon peninsula was abandoned by those returning villagers due to government concerns over outbreaks of malaria and dysentery, and presence of tigers in the area. To this day, it remains unclear just how the 1883 Krakatau eruption impacted on Javan rhino inhabiting the affected Ujung Kulon peninsula area. Most likely the current population came from eastern rhino populations re-colonisation post the Krakatau eruption and remains a risk from founder effects. Even today, you can find evidence of the 1883 Krakatau event. I have found large 'bus-sized' chunks of bleached coral, lying in rainforest habitat, many kilometres from the coast, no doubt torn from coastal reefs, lifted and transported inland by the wave of tsunamis.

Javan rhino killed Ujung Kulon 1908 to 1994

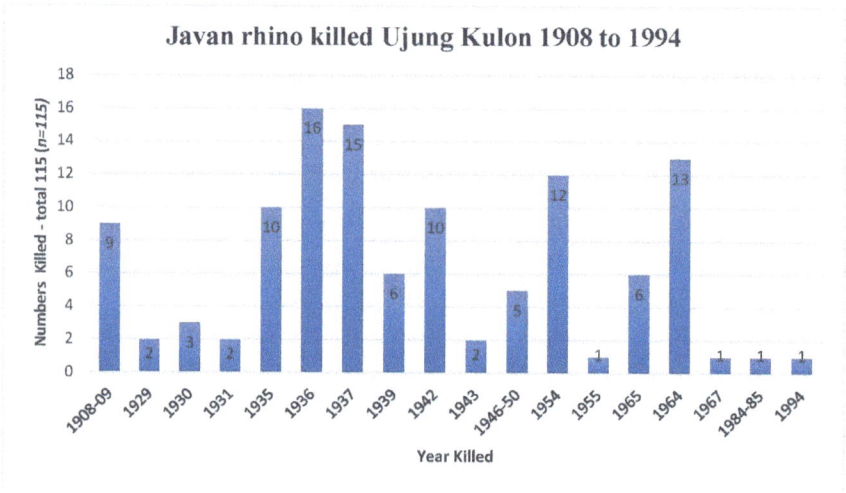

Graph of records of Javan rhino numbers poached in Ujung Kulon during the period 1908 to 1994, when rhino poaching was effectively stopped. Data sourced from historic and modern records including

Loch 1937; Voogd & Siccama 1939; Sody 1941; Talbot 1960; Talbot & Talbot 1964; Groves 1967; Schenkel & Schenkel-Hulliger 1969a, 1969b; Hoogerwerf 1970; PHPA 1982; Sadjudin & Djaja 1984; Nardelli 1987, 2016; Sadjudin 1991; Ramono et al. 1993, 2009; Van Strien & Sadjudin 1993; Lessee 1994; AsRSG 1995; Van Strien & Rookmaaker 2010; Nardelli & Robovský 2022.

Today's population of an estimated less than 60 animals has been isolated since the 1930s, recovering from a 1967 estimated low of 25 individuals, genetic drift, impacted by a small population size, founder effects and bottlenecks. To date, 19 different rhinos have had faecal DNA examined and amazingly, there is still some genetic variation, although small. The 19 animals retain two haplotypes. Collecting rhino faecal DNA is problematic, the dung needs to be less than 3 days old, field staff would always get very excited if they found a 'fresh hot steamer', given it breaks down so quickly, there was always a mad dash to get any found specimens cool and protected! A haplotype (haploid genotype) is a group of alleles in an organism that are inherited together from a single parent. Ideally, the more unrelated single parents there are the better. I suspect over time more genetic diversity will be found in the population—just need to find more 'steamers!

Given the region's seismic and volcanically active status, the risk of an earthquake causing a tsunami remains high. Earthquakes causing tsunamis in the Ujung Kulon region predict the risk of tsunami heights of (>3m) is relatively low (up to 10% of area), however, over longer periods (>100 years), tsunamis of 30 metres are likely. Modelling by Setiwan et al (2017) has identified a tsunami of 30 metres would inundate most, if not all, habitat areas where Javan rhino concentrate. Fortunately, during my visits between 2014 and 2021, only two tsunamis had struck, one in December 2018, caused by an eruption of Anak Krakatoa off the coast; the second in May 2019. I witnessed the devastation caused by the December 2018 tsunami, several months later, which destroyed many local coastal village communities, and killed over 200 people and injured over 800 more. I was able to visit the

2019 tsunami impact area two weeks after it struck. Significant coastal habitat was destroyed, the inland seawater deposition and impact on the rainforest vegetation will take time to recover, on a positive note no rhinos were lost.

Large *Ficus* tree in Ujung Kulon National Park, showing aerial roots, noting these large trees attract many species of wildlife, i.e., frugivorous birds and primates when in flower and fruiting.

Despite a low number of human residents, the Ujung Kulon peninsula was regularly poached, many ignored the 1909 protection decree preventing the killing of rhinos on Java (*Staatsblad van Nederlandsch Indië*, no. 497, 23 October 1909). Rhinos were actively poached up until the early 1990s, when active in situ rhino protection became part of park management. Today, Ujung Kulon authorities' conservation focus is on situ protection of Javan rhino supported by a policy of non-disturbance. The rhino population is actively monitored by national park and rhino protection staff using camera traps, dung collection (for DNA analyses), footprint plaster casting and increasing use of camera trap rhino ID evidence, supported by active patrolling of Ujung Kulon peninsula and coastal areas to search for illegal activities.

Running rainforest stream in Ujung Kulon National Park. When undertaking field work, these cool, fresh rainforest streams were welcome places to drink, rest and soak your aching feet in!

Summary table of conservation authorities and non-government organisations (NGO's) involved in Javan rhino conservation.

Organisation	Role and contribution
International Rhino Foundation (IRF)	Global strategic support and funding resources
Rhino Foundation of Indonesia (YABI)	Administer Rhino Protection Units (RPUs), support rhino monitoring activities (i.e., camera trap recording)
Asian Rhino Project (ARP)/Wildlife Asia	Funding resources for local conservation initiatives and activities
Ujung Kulon National Park Authority (UKNP), Indonesia	National Park management via Ministry of Environment & Forestry
World Wildlife Fund (WWF) Indonesia	Local strategic support and funding resources

IUCN/SSC Asian Rhino Specialist Group	Global strategic scientific support and guidance
Aaranyak NGO—Asian Wildlife Organisation	Strategic support, scientific and research support for biological conservation activities and benefit
Auriga Nusantara NGO	Natural resource management and funding resources for conservation activities and benefit

Rise of frontline management

Managers of threatened species in remote protected areas play a pivotal role in shaping the outcomes of management and conservation programs. The Indonesian Island of Java supports the last remaining population of one of the world's largest surviving mega-herbivores, the critically endangered Javan rhino persists in the wild in one location, Ujung Kulon National Park. Substantial resources are being invested in this single-species management, as it is very difficult to monitor the Javan rhino in the rainforest and to assess whether past and current management actions have been successful. Understanding frontline staff insights into the outcomes of past conservation actions and required future actions are key in enhancing the outcomes of threatened species conservation actions. Study of frontline staff perceptions to Javan rhino conservation, management actions, their outcomes and operating environment began in mid-2016. I surveyed surveyed 22 of 25 rhino protection staff and 14 of 16 national park rangers at their operational bases, asking a series of themed focus questions that allow us to better understand frontline approaches to ongoing Javan rhino conservation and management. This work became Chapter 3 of my thesis, *'Protecting an icon: Javan rhino frontline management and conservation'*.

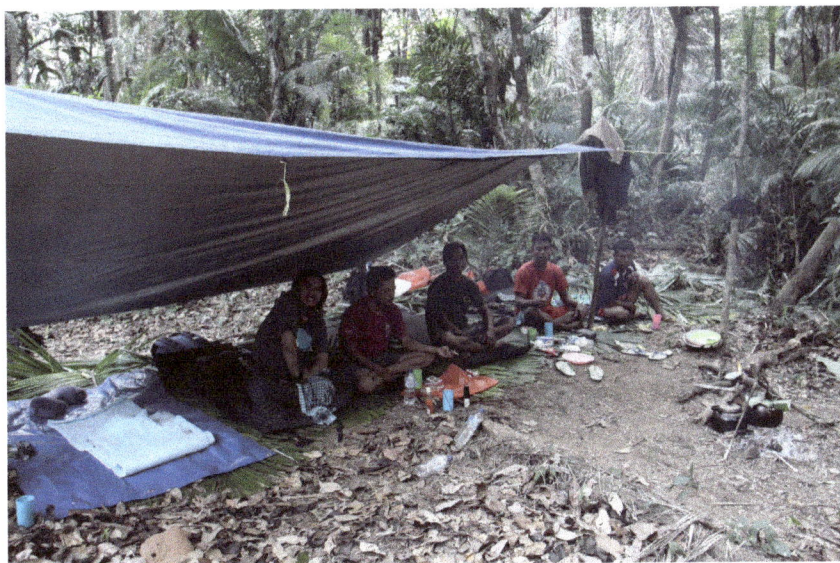

Early morning breakfast with the frontline rhino protection team after a night under the tarp.

While staff perceptions of conservation outcomes were overall positive, there are key anthropogenic threats and challenges that rhino protection staff raised, which are inherent to the survival of the last persisting population. These range from habitat encroachment due to stop human population growth, and efficiency of fencing to transfer of disease from domesticated stock, mainly buffalo and goats, to rhinos.

Work that systematically addresses insights and concerns of on-ground staff in such remote areas can help identify important areas for future conservation actions and threat mitigations to save Javan rhino and other iconic and highly threatened species. The Javan rhino is currently protected by numerous national and international regulations and for many years significant popular and scientific publications have attempted to highlight the species' critically endangered status in Southeast Asia. Despite its iconic name and periodic publicity, scientific studies directed at the many unknown aspects of its biology and ecology, which

61

are fundamental for its survival and recovery, have been slow in occuring. Studies undertaken to date on Javan rhino can be categorised into three areas of focus: population, distribution and conservation; importance of local communities in the management of protected areas and threatened species; and habitat assessment and utilisation.

Over the past decade, many key conservation organisations have become active participants in Javan rhino management and conservation. Collaborative efforts between the authorities and non-government organisations (NGO's) in the national park are focused towards preserving the Javan rhino, protecting its habitat from destruction and fragmentation, improving and supporting anti-poaching activities (active in situ patrolling by rhino protection and national park staff), and reducing in-park illegal resource extraction. Conservation of the last persisting population and its habitat is a major management priority for the species' survival. In Ujung Kulon, and other parts of the world, local participation and regular communication with local community are key in ensuring effective protected area and threatened species management.

Numerous challenges to Javan rhino conservation remain, with many anthropogenic pressures. For example, habitat encroachment due to human population growth and need for farming land to disease risk from domesticated stock, and vulnerability of the remaining rhino population. The field work of frontline staff is critical to the successful management, conservation of the species. However, their perceptions about management and conservation actions and their outcomes have not been evaluated, which may help inform planning future actions. This study aimed to address this gap.

The objectives of this study were to a) identify frontline management operations, including staff recruitment, training and patrol cycles; b) identify the perceptions of frontline staff to Javan rhino conservation, including the current operating and management environment; c) identify risks to rhinos and determine any gaps in conservation approaches; d) examine frontline staff perceptions of local community impacts and their understanding of national park management and conservation activities; and e) use these perceptions and informed opinions to support future management actions that can benefit conservation outcomes for the conservation and management of Javan rhino.

The 1998 instigation of rhino protection units (RPUs) in Ujung Kulon has effectively stopped poaching of rhino for over 30 years but remains an ongoing risk given the small population size. Rhino poaching persisted in Ujung Kulon up until the late 1980s and early 1990s. The Indonesian Rhino and International Rhino Foundations currently employ and manage the Javan rhino protection unit staff and work in partnership with Ujung Kulon rangers, who in turn, are employed by the Indonesian Government's Ministry of Environment and Forestry through the Ujung Kulon National Park Authority. The total global population of the Javan rhinos persists only in this one park. Therefore, management in the region is crucial towards the species' persistence. Any increase in the rhino population requires the strong and continuing protection from anthropogenic pressures such as poaching, harvesting and habitat encroachment.

Rhino conservation is supported by active patrolling of the Ujung Kulon peninsula since 1998, and park environs by rhino protection units and national park staff to identify and control for illegal activities. Five frontline units (four staff each) were operational in Ujung Kulon national park at the time that this study began in mid-2015. Each unit has three members recruited from local communities, and one national park staff member who is authorised to make arrests. Four frontline units operate across the western peninsula area (main rhino population), the fifth unit operates across the eastern Gunung Honje area (Javan Rhino Study Conservation Area or JRSCA). Two marine rhino protection units also now operate around the coastline of the Ujung Kulon peninsula. The Ujung Kulon rainforest landscape has limited accessibility; hence, all in situ patrol activity is currently undertaken on foot, with staff regularly camping out on extended patrols that vary between five and 20 days per month. Patrol tasks are determined by the level of threat as well as assigned and routine activities. Monitoring of the rhino population and other endangered species, such as the Javan leopard (*Panthera pardus melas* or '*Macan tutul*' [family Felidae]) is a core function of the frontline patrol units (rhino protection unit and national park staff) and undertake duties such as camera trap surveillance, rhino track recording and dung collection (for DNA sampling) across the park. Patrol operations of frontline units aim to have staff in the field at most times, with the exception being the December–January monsoon period, when access to most of the park becomes difficult due to heavy rainfall.

During September 2015, 22 of 25 rhino protection unit staff and 14 of 16 Ujung Kulon National Park rangers completed dedicated survey questionnaires and were interviewed by me. The interviews were conducted with national park management and Indonesian Rhino Foundation support and with the assistance of an Indonesian interpreter. The questionnaire was first developed in English and then translated into Bahasa Indonesia. We pre-tested the questionnaire with a rhino protection staff manager, a rhino protection unit staff member and a national park ranger, all of whom came from local villages, as well as the interpreter.

The questionnaire included 42 questions. The first 15 questions focused on determining the rhino protection unit and ranger operating environment such as tenure. The following 27 questions included eight open focus questions related to staff knowledge of community understanding of conservation activities and perceived risks which required the participant to respond on a four-point Likert scale (2–5), noting the 1 value on the Likert scale = 0 (do not know) response. Interviews took approximately 30–40 minutes each and were conducted between 15/9/2015–22/9/2015 with the help of a local interpreter at the Ujung Kulon National Park operations headquarters in Taman Jaya, and rhino protection base offices in the villages of Cigorondong and Ujung Jaya. These three villages are located on the western edge at the Gunung Honje eastern section of Ujung Kulon NP. Staff were interviewed individually, except for one group of three staff being interviewed together due to time constraints and need for these staff to go on active long patrol. For consistency, the same interpreter helped in all interviews.

I used chi-square (χ^2) tests of independence to examine differences in their perceptions of local community views on conservation amongst the frontline staff (rhino protection and national park staff). Then a comparison of frontline (all staff), and specifically rhino protection unit and national park staff responses to the eight Likert scale questions. Analysis predictor variables included frontline staff perspectives of local community knowledge of Javan rhino conservation status, rhino behaviour and ecology, knowledge of conservation initiatives, differences in perspectives of rhino protection staff and national park rangers and views of risk factors.

Getting around Ujung Kulon National Park in the wet via a makeshift, dodgy bamboo creek crossing, these crossings often had resident saltwater crocodiles or *'Buaya muara'* hanging around just to make it interesting!

65

What did we find out?

Overall, the surveyed frontline staff included 36 people, all of whom are male. Staff length of service results for rhino protection staff in their organisation averaged 5.4 years (SD ± 3.75) and for national park staff was 21.9 years (SD ± 8.63).

Seventeen (77%) of the 22 rhino protection unit staff came from villages within the Ujung Kulon precinct (19 villages) while five came from villages outside of the Ujung Kulon area. Eight (57%) of the 14 national park rangers came from the villages Taman Jaya (n = 5), Ujung Jaya (2) and Sumur (1) within the Ujung Kulon precinct, while six of the rangers came from outside the Ujung Kulon area. Most rhino protection staff (86%) were recruited from local villages near Ujung Kulon, including Cibadak (1), Kerta Jaya (1), Kerti Mukti (1), Rancapinang (2), Cigorondong (2), Ujung Jaya (5) and Taman Jaya (6). Four rhino protection staff (14%) came from other areas including Radar Lampung (1), Indramaya (1), Pandelang (1) and Panimbang (1).

The question 'do local community have knowledge of Javan rhino ecology and behaviour' found both rhino protection and national park staff acknowledging community knowledge of rhino was low based on responses on a four-point Likert scale score, 2.71 (no knowledge) to 3.13 (some knowledge) out of 5. Likert responses to the question 'community involvement in conservation activities, such as arenga palm control, being a positive exercise' also produced low results, scoring 2.35 (not important) and 3.36 (some importance) out of 5. When asked, rhino protection and national park staff suggested community involvement in arenga palm control as a way of getting palm leaves for the roofs of their houses. Community, despite involvement in arenga control activities, did not understand the negative impacts of the palm and reasons for its clearance.

Twenty-four staff (67%) were positive about the recently installed rhino fence and its purpose (i.e., to protect rhino from conflict and disease). However, during post-survey discussions, some staff expressed concern of local community regularly illegally breaching the fence to graze buffalo and domestic stock. The rhino protection staff drew statistically positive responses regarding 'if conservation activities such as the newly erected fence and community involvement in arenga palm control work was working' drew less confidence from them compared to national park staff. This may be due to rhino protection staff having more direct involvement in fence protection, breaches of the fence by local livestock, arenga palm control work and dealing with community conflict. National Park staff have broader management issues to contend with, such as park administration and visitor management.

On average, national park staff were more reserved in their responses, which may be related to their years of experience on what is effective and what isn't. Overall, clear differences in perspectives between the national park and rhino protection unit staff were observed. Therefore, our results did support the hypothesis that national park rangers with more years of experience than rhino protection unit staff will have different perspectives on the conservation of Javan rhino.

Section of the 8 km rhino fence in the eastern Gunung Honje section of Ujung Kulon National Park.

Rhino protection staff setting up a camera trap on the edge of a cleared arenga palm site in the eastern Gunung Honje section of Ujung Kulon National Park.

Several threats raised by frontline staff included the expansion of rice fields and gardens, followed by illegal collection of firewood, forest resources, wild honey, birds, fish and grazing of stock. Staff acknowledged human population growth in and around Gunung Honje (eastern edge of the park) and broader West Java was a risk to both the national park and rhino. Interestingly, a mixed response came from staff on the question on what the risks of improved roads and infrastructure to the national park and its wildlife are, with 13 (36%) staff saying illegal activity will increase, while 23 (64%) were unsure of the impacts.

With respect to motivation and training, 86% of rhino protection unit staff joined to protect the Javan rhino, and 64% of national park staff joined to protect the national park and Javan rhino. The training environment was explored, and questions were asked on the benefits and types of training. For example, 100% of staff said the training was beneficial and had helped them, and they had good opportunity to learn a broad range of skills such as navigation and survey techniques. When the frontline staff patrol, operating environment was examined including current patrol cycles, patrol destination determination and observations of Javan rhino and other wildlife. For example, 82% of rhino protection unit staff spent 20 days of every month on active patrol, and 36% of national park staff supported rhino protection units for 20 days per month as well. All staff said they regularly see other wildlife and 78% of staff had observed rhino.

Javan rhino footprint plaster casts of calf, female and male. Camera trapping has largely replaced this practice, which is good given that carrying 50 kg bags of plaster of paris through the jungle to any found footprints would not be fun!

Frontline staff felt that local community members had a substantial impact on Ujung Kulon NP and its resources, including poaching.

For example, 29 (81%) staff said illegal poaching of biota was of concern, 7 (19%) staff were more specific stating poaching of birds, honey, sea turtle, shrimp and rusa deer was an issue. Responses to questions related to frontline staff commonly encountered issues such as poaching and illegal activity, encroachment into the national park and local community conflict were listed in order of concern. When asked about commonly encountered issues such as illegal fishing, bird collecting, wild honey and firewood collection, staff indicated increased protection was needed due to the combined collective impact of these common issues on rhino and habitat.

Conflict with local community was noted by six rhino protection unit staff. Conflict issues included illegal grazing of domestic buffalo, forest timber extraction and community damage to the rhino fence (to allow domestic livestock access). Poaching of Javan Banteng (*Bos j. javanicus*) was noted as an ongoing issue by two of the rhino protection unit staff, and one staff member said rumour of illegal activity was a commonly encountered issue, noting banteng meat is traditionally served at wedding ceremonies. Without education, this practice will continue, given the close proximity of the banteng population.

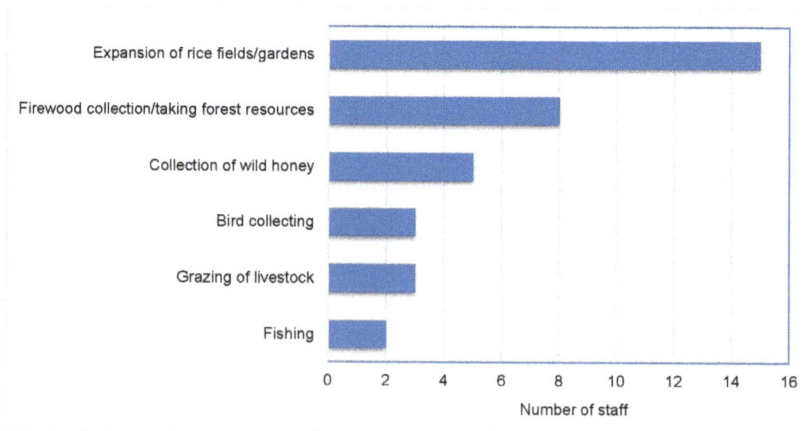

Graph of frontline staff (n=36) perceptions of local community reliance on Ujung Kulon National Park natural resources in order of threat (% of 36 staff perceptions).

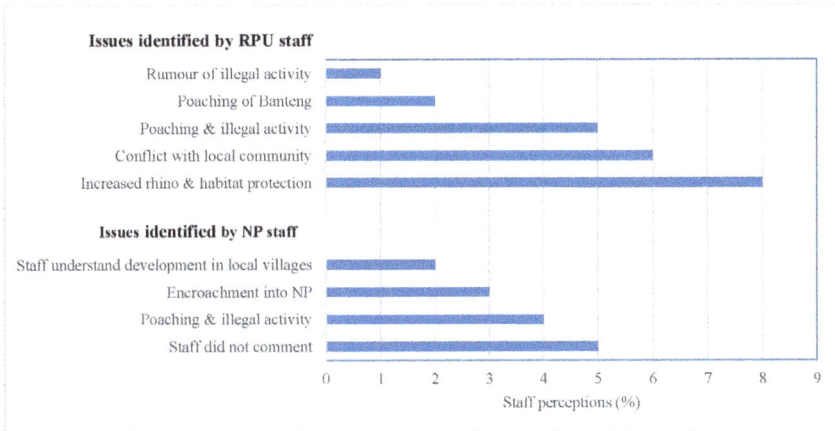

Graph of common issues identified Rhino Protection (RPU) staff in order of concern (% of 22 staff), and National Park (NP) staff (% of 14 staff).

Staff listed competition with other herbivore species such as banteng as a concern. Banteng are listed by the IUCN Red List (2015) as endangered (family Bovidae). This attractive bovid (wild cattle) species, sometimes called '*Tembadau*', is found in decreasing pockets of habitat across Southeast Asia. It remains unclear if banteng is competing with rhino for food and or space, however, recent studies (e.g., Harjanto 2017) indicate territorial competition between banteng and Javan rhino may be occurring. On two occasions I had interactions with banteng bulls, both times in pouring rain. Mostly solitary outside of breeding season, banteng bulls often forage along forest edges, as well as thick rainforest patches. On both occasions I was in dense vegetation, and I literally walked into the bull, due to the rain we didn't hear each other, the animal was as shocked and surprised as I was. Fortunately, each time the bull snorted in protest, then turned and ran in the opposite direction, leaving a trail of flattened vegetation behind it. Guess I need to practice diving to my left or right, as banteng bulls are known to charge when disturbed!

Banteng groups were often accompanied by pairs of Javan green peafowl (*Pavo muticus* or '*Burung Merak*'). Classified by the IUCN Red List (2009) as endangered (family Phasianidae).

71

Over my six years, I only observed them a few times. In each case they were associating with small mobs of females with calves. Following a mob of banteng is a viable feeding strategy, no doubt the moving banteng would disturb many insects which the peafowl would pick off. I suspect they would also pick off external parasites, such as ticks from the banteng as well. The Javan green peafowl is a rarer relation of the common Indian or Blue peafowl (*P. cristatus*) which is often found in semi-captive conditions across the world. Javan myna (*Acridotheres javanicus*) would also use banteng as a moving food source. I would often observe them running across a banteng's back looking for ectoparasites. Starlings and mynas (family Sturnidae) the world over are consummate opportunists and will readily use large herbivores as mobile food kitchens.

Many of these wildlife encounters happened when I was by myself, as typically I'm with a minimum of four rhino protection staff or rangers. I would be left alone when the boys had to make camp, have a smoke and start a fire to boil the kettle. Normally, any in vicinity wildlife would head for cover if they heard 4–5 guys trampling through the jungle, so being on my own even for short periods often bore wildlife encounter fruit.

Human-wildlife conflict is an ongoing concern and acknowledged as a challenge to conservation objectives worldwide. Globally, the extent of these conflicts and interactions varies considerably. Negative interactions occur when humans and wildlife compete for food, resources and space. This often results in either the killing of wildlife, death or injury to people, crop damage and associated destruction, property damage and losses of livestock. Effectively engaging local communities and influencing them to embrace conservation initiatives in such environments is no easy task.

Globally, rhino populations continue to be threatened by human population growth, habitat loss and ongoing development in and around rhino habitat. For example, Nepal, despite recently celebrating its fourth year of zero poaching and significant increase in its rhino population, has moved to increase its cross-border alliances, sharing intelligence and experiences to share responsibility with other rhino-range countries given ongoing threats. Nepal is a country with acknowledged high biodiversity values with 23.24% of its land mass in protected areas and approximately 29% of its forested land is managed by community forestry practices. Despite Nepal's significant conservation successes, conflicts still remain between wildlife and the human population and strategies need to be adaptive to adjust to limited resources for both wildlife and people.

Frontline staff acknowledged the current conservation and management approach was working positively. Despite this success, staff raised multiple challenges that remain for conservation inherent to the survival of the small persisting rhino population. Rhino poaching was not identified as a major threat, understandable given over 30 years of frontline patrolling in reducing this threat. Several gaps and key areas for conservation action were identified, including threat mitigation, aimed at reducing the identified risk of disease transfer and increased support to community education and awareness programs.

This study has highlighted that whilst a conservation program can be viewed as effective, the value of frontline staff input into conservation management is an asset, offering insight that may reduce future risk impacts and improve conservation objectives. Frontline staff acknowledged the inception of rhino protection units and working partnership with the Ujung Kulon National Park Authority, is meeting the needs of rhino protection. Staff attributed this success to regular patrol cycles and high awareness of such in local communities. Despite this success, staff noted challenges remain, notably natural resource competition. This concern over natural resource competition and use is also documented at a higher strategic level by rhino range countries. For example, the Strategy and Action Plan for the Conservation of Rhino in Indonesia (Rhino Century Program 2007-2017), is the Indonesian Government's official conservation policy for the country's rhino populations. The issue of balancing such objectives and the needs of local community is challenging.

Frontline staff residing in local villages can inform and educate local community through their presence. For example, community involvement in Javan rhino conservation work such as arenga palm control, was noted as being a positive exercise, however, staff identified a need for increased education and awareness to community of the conservation benefits to the clearing of arenga palm. Given the focus of patrolling is in core Javan rhino habitat areas, it remains unclear as to how much impact human population growth is occurring in areas of the park that see little regular patrol activity. The national park border areas where they interface with village cultivation and agricultural land is worth examining, noting an incremental edge effect into national park land would be occurring and exacerbating habitat decline.

Despite ongoing issues with illegal settlements in the national park, none of the staff commented on this as a threat or issue. The combination of limited law enforcement, intelligence services and poor penalty outcomes for offenders was viewed by staff as a frustration to their work and an ongoing risk to rhino conservation. This frontline management frustration is not uncommon in many rhino range countries. For example, in Mozambique, strict penalties for rhino poaching and possession of rhino horn are virtually non-existent due to weak legislation and soft penalties, and poaching as a crime is considered only a misdemeanour offence.

Staff cited the biggest threat and risk to Javan rhino was disease from domestic livestock, and most staff noted the importance of the new fence as a preventative structure. The disease risk is well documented, as Ujung Kulon National Park experiences periodic tending of domestic livestock, mainly buffalo and goats on the national park fringes and within the park. Diseases have been linked to past Javan rhino deaths, including *haemorrhagic septicaemia*, anthrax and *trypanosomiasis*. The Department of Animal Disease and Veterinary Public Health at Bogor University, Banten Province authorities were surprised to discover a high prevalence of *trypanosomiasis surra* in 87% (91 individuals) of the buffalo population. Anthrax, *Haemorrhagic septicaemia* and *Brucellosis* were not found in this testing. The prevalence of *trypanosomiasis surra* in the water buffalo population is of major concern given this result occurred in just one tested village area, with the other 18 villages yet to be tested. An escalated potential risk of cross-infection to Javan rhino and banteng populations remains.

A well-managed vaccinated domestic buffalo population around Ujung Kulon would minimise disease spread to Javan rhino. The disease risk highlights concern from rhino protection staff on the question of 'will the fence make a difference to Javan rhino conservation' and identified the ongoing issue of the need for increased community compliance regarding domestic stock fence breaches. This could be addressed via increased enforcement, supported by an education and awareness program highlighting the risks of disease impacts on local wildlife, including rhino.

Multiple communities neighbouring Ujung Kulon face daily challenges owing to the remoteness of their location, living a mostly subsistence existence (e.g., farming and fishing) and enduring poor socio-economic services. For example, power outages are a common occurrence, coupled with ongoing transport and access issues. The main access road and smaller feeder roads that edge around the national park's boundary quickly deteriorate with distance from the township of Sumur. In extended wet periods the road network becomes virtually impassable, slowing motorbike, foot and vehicular traffic to slow walking pace. Hence, road conditions dominate and influence village life.

The growing human population around Ujung Kulon is a significant risk given there is no additional land available to support this growth. Competition between the national park, rhinos and human settlements will continue, unless viable alternative livelihoods can be found, which could include frontline conservation work. Staff acknowledged that coming from a local village and its proximity to Ujung Kulon offered opportunities for local people to be potentially employed as a frontline member of either rhino protection units or the national park staff. Nearly 70% of staff stated coming from a local village did assist their duties, without elaborating why, the remaining 30% of respondents were unsure in responding to this question. However, on the related question regarding if community ever assisted staff with intelligence gathering re poaching or negative activity in the park the response was 100% yes. We suspect some staff preferred to respond with an unsure response given sensitivity around local people who they share a village and possible relationship with, and having to implicate them for undertaking in illegal activity. Staff did acknowledge there was strong importance placed on the involvement of local community in conservation activities such as arenga palm control. Those staff would be well placed to influence local community not only regarding the benefits to locals gaining work but also the work itself and its role in assisting the conservation of Javan rhino and their habitat.

National Park and rhino protection staff live in these local villages, increasing communication channels of sharing conservation and park activity information with locals. The outcomes of this study can be directed to increase conservation actions that deliver improved outcomes for frontline management of this highly threatened mammal and provide a model for other species with focal protection units and located in areas around which rural human populations are active.

Summary table of frontline (rhino protection unit (RPU) and national park (NP)) staff recruitment and training question responses (n = 36).

Questions	Staff comments	No & % of frontline (RPU & NP) staff responses
What attracted you to become part of the RPU/UKNP team?	To protect Javan rhino	19 (86%) RPU staff
	Joined for money	2 (9%) RPU staff
	To learn about rhino	1 (4%) RPU staff
	Protect rhino and NP	9 (64%) NP rangers
	Proud to serve	2 (14%) NP rangers
	Joined for reliable job, protect marine areas and help community	3 (21%) NP rangers
How were you recruited?	Via application and offered positions	28 (78%) via application and eventual selection
What training have you completed?	Navigation, survey techniques, survival, physical education, intelligence gathering, community outreach, protection, tourism guiding, GIS, patrol, animal behaviour, DNA sample collection (dung), plant propagation, leadership (Level II), wildlife and habitat management, first aid, field camera technology and recording	8 (22%) had applied and were offered positions

Note: all frontline staff were given the opportunity to undertake training across the suite of skills-based subjects on offer and to specialise in areas of interest |
| How has it (training) helped you on the job? | Increased knowledge, opportunity to study and learn | 100% of all frontline staff said their training has helped them on the job |

Summary table of frontline (rhino protection unit (RPU) and national park (NP)) staff to patrol operating environment and observations of wildlife, including Javan rhino (n = 36).

Questions	Staff comments	No & % of frontline (RPU & NP) staff responses
What is your current patrol cycle and how long do you go out for?	20 days per month	18 (82%) RPU staff
	15 days per month	4 (18%) RPU staff & 5 (36%) NP rangers
* RMU (rhino monitoring unit—in situ remote camera management team)	5 days per month (RMU)*	3 (21%) NP rangers
	10 days per month	2 (14%) NP rangers
	7 days per month	2 (14%) NP rangers
	5 days per month (marine patrol)	10 (71%) NP rangers
How is the patrol destination determined?	By level of threat as well as assigned and routine duties	100% of staff stated this
Do you ever see Javan rhino, if yes in what situation?	Seen in forest, or in wallow, sleeping, wallowing, swimming and standing	28 (78%) of staff said they had seen rhino
What was the animal doing?	Observed behaviours, walking, feeding, one observation of rhino feeding on salt sprayed vegetation on the beach	8 (22%) of staff said they had not seen rhino yet
Do you ever come across other wildlife, if yes which species?	Banteng Bos j. javanicus, Javan leopard Panthera pardus melas, Javan gibbon Hylobates moloch, Dhole Cuon alpinus sumatrensis, Javan langur Presbytis c. comata, saltwater crocodile Crocodylus porosus and Javan fishing cat Prionailurus viverrinus rizophoreus	100% of staff said yes, they regularly come across many species

Summary table of frontline staff perspective of current conservation approach and impact (n = 36)

Questions	Staff comments	No & % frontline staff responses
In terms of poaching activities what do you find is the most common issue you come across?	Staff interpretation of biota is bush meat (e.g., monkey, deer, wild pig) and vegetable material (e.g., bamboo, forest fruits, fungi). Staff noted community relied on NP resources in some way	29 (81%) of staff said illegal poaching of biota 7 (19%) of staff stated poaching of birds, honey, sea turtle, shrimp and rusa deer
Does coming from a local village assist your duties?	Coming from a local village and its proximity to the NP offered opportunities, e.g., activities such as arenga palm control	25 (69%) of staff that came from local villages said yes but in most cases did not elaborate why 11 (31%) of staff were unsure
Given no rhinos have been poached since 1994, why do you think the rhino protection (RPU) program has been successful?	Active patrol work, increased monitoring, intelligence networks and socialisation with community has helped	100% of staff attributed this to regular patrol cycles and high awareness of such in their local communities
Is there anything you believe the RPU units could be doing that they are not doing now?	Combination of limited law enforcement, and poor penalty outcomes for offenders was viewed by staff as a frustration and risk	100% of staff acknowledged the current management structure and approaches were working and meeting the needs of rhino protection

What do you see as the biggest threats to Javan rhino moving forward?	Disease risk from domestic stock to rhino	19 (53%) of staff
	Human population growth, consequent need for land and loss of habitat	8 (22%) of staff
	Need for stronger penalties for illegal activities as ongoing threats	7 (19%) of staff
	Decline in rhino genetic variation as an ongoing threat	2 (5%) of staff

The value of frontline staff insight into conservation management and effectiveness offers practical exposure to the issues perspective and real insight that may reduce future risk impacts and improve conservation outcomes, especially when species are in high risk of extinction and located in remote areas. One of the key challenges facing managers of frontier protected area and conservation areas is the way natural resources are managed within central government systems. Since 2000, the Indonesian Government has decentralised and allocated much of the responsibility for the management of natural resources to local provinces and districts. The high priority given to economic growth in Indonesia, has led to policies driven by local short-term economic growth objectives, with little consideration to conservation needs. This has resulted in substantial increases in encroachment into protected areas, including some conversion of protected land into agricultural land. Based on frontline staff responses, I provide recommendations for management of rhinos in Java.

The research identified that local communities should understand (and preferably own) the conservation objectives as outlined by authorities. An ongoing community education and awareness program will assist in building this understanding. The 2016 instigation of a dedicated four-person community engagement unit is an important step to building stronger links and awareness in local communities. As acknowledged by more than half of frontline staff, the ongoing risk of disease from domestic stock to Javan wildlife is significant. The instigation of an annual domestic stock vaccination program across all 19 villages in the Ujung Kulon precinct is warranted.

Supporting this action, undertaking regular soil and faecal analyses to identify the presence, location, and type of pathogenic agents both within local villages and the national park and development of an emergency plan in the event of a disease outbreak. Additionally, an education and awareness program be instigated to highlight the risks and benefits to both domestic animals and local wildlife of such an initiative. As a biosecurity/disease outbreak measure, a stock fence to be built with gates across the narrow isthmus area (1.5 km wide) separating the peninsula from the eastern Gunung Honje area of the park which can be closed off in the event of a disease outbreak. This fence would at least contain any disease outbreak from infiltrating the main peninsula rhino population. Outside of a disease outbreak, the fence would remain open to allow natural movement of animals.

Regular risk assessments should be undertaken by authorities to review current and future risks and assess their ability to respond to conservation issues. A risk assessment would also include a review of staff training needs. A long-term strategy to create buffer zones around Ujung Kulon should be examined. Buffer zones would create areas that could be used by, for example, community's water buffalo, thus reducing the illegal use of Ujung Kulon for wallowing and grazing.

This work provides the first study of frontline staff perspectives and insight of Javan rhino conservation and management. Beyond frontline staff, key responsibilities of surveillance, monitoring and protection of Javan rhino and the park. The value of this study is threefold. Firstly, participants can provide frontline assessment of current approaches and threats. For example, staff acknowledgement of the fence as a preventative structure and the associated risk of disease spread from stock to rhino remain high-risk concerns. Secondly, this information can be used by authorities and conservation planners to improve and prioritise management actions. Thirdly, given that interviewed staff live in local communities, understand local community impacts and insight may reveal opportunities to improve relationships and develop conservation-based programmes with local community input. This holds true for not only Ujung Kulon rhino protection and national park staff but also for protected area management in similar contexts elsewhere. This study has highlighted that whilst a conservation program can be viewed as effective (e.g., rhino poaching has been stopped), the value of frontline staff input into conservation management is an asset, which has offered unique insight that potentially reduce future risks and ultimately achieve conservation objectives.

My work on the frontline management was rewarded with the peer-reviewed publication of a paper in *Oryx* journal in 2021. Titled 'Wilson, S.G., Biggs, D. & Kark, S. (2021). *Protecting an icon: Javan rhino frontline management and conservation. Oryx*, August/September'. I was fortunate in April 2018 to visit Way Kambas National Park in Lampung Province, Sumatra. Within Way Kambas is the Sumatran Rhino Sanctuary (SRS). Set up in 1996, this sanctuary encompasses 250 ha of rainforest habitat, divided into 10 paddocks, and one rhino is managed as an individual in its own paddock, each with a lock-up area and chute in which the rhinos get used to coming daily for food. Each paddock has natural habitat, including wallowing sites, which Sumatrans love to indulge in. The Sanctuary's ten rhino residents receive round-the-clock veterinary care and nutrition. Importantly, through this approach we are able to learn more about them, what their needs are, and train the next generation of field staff, rangers, rhino protection staff, veterinarians and conservation planners moving forward. This small population is the core of a managed breeding and research programme that is intended to promote the species' population growth, while also establishing a genetically diverse 'founder' group that could be used as a source of animals to repopulate former habitats. This applied management system has worked well. Animals can be protected, observed, monitored and even undertake ultrasound examinations, therefore providing timely information when to pair animals or isolate due to pregnancy. The facility was set up by the International Rhino Foundation in partnership with local NGO Yayasan Badak Indonesia (YABI), or the Indonesian Rhino Foundation, which currently manages the SRS, the Indonesian Ministry of Environment and Forestry, Way Kambas National Park and Taman Safari International.

The facility now provides a semi-wild home to the only reproductively viable captive Sumatran rhinos in the world. To date there have been four successful births at the facility, noting a female calf was born in September 2023. I felt very privileged and grateful to spend time and talk rhino conservation with the veterinarians and field staff at the facility in the park, and view the now ten well-looked-after Sumatran rhinos, while visiting with my eldest son Coen, it was a real treat.

Coen, an archaeologist, is studying early hominid stone tool assemblages in South Africa for his PhD at Latrobe University in Melbourne, so it's always special to spend time with him, especially when we are in the field. My second son Daly, is a talented artist, no apologies for the bias! In 2020, Daly drew for me the detailed image of an adult pair of Javan rhinos presented in this book. Daly's original rhino drawing work now sits framed, and in pride of place on a wall in our family home. I smile every time I see it, and regularly brag to anyone that will listen how artistically talented my son is! As for me, I have absolutely zero artistic talent but that's okay. My extended family more than makes up for what I lack. Guess I missed that side of mum's DNA but I did score the motion and travel sickness gene, thanks mum!

Going on patrol with the frontline guys in Ujung Kulon was always a positive experience and I always learnt stuff. It was fun to rough it, sleeping under a tarp, cups of tea in the pouring rain—what's not to love! I remember one hot night camping out, I had my head torch on and was making notes under a mosquito net, when a foot-long Asian forest centipede (*Scolopendra subspinipes* or '*kelabang*' [family Scolopendridae]) was sharing my space under the net! These multi-legged guys have a nasty debilitating bite, fortunately I was able to gently move it back into the jungle and on its way. I do consider myself lucky, I tend not to jump or overreact when these encounters happen, Yes, I was definitely surprised and on guard but my immediate thought was bloody hell, that multilegged beast is on steroids, and I suspect he or she has the extra venom to size ratio as well, pity it's too dark to take a joint selfie! So, for all you terrified centropodes out there, my words of wisdom are, understanding it's probably easier said than done, if you stay calm, be careful and don't 'jump' at the sight of such a critter and you won't get tagged!

After many years of sleeping it rough, I worked on the theory; I was probably better off 'not' knowing what crawled over me while asleep in the field! Normally I would carry a small tarp to keep me off damp ground, and a bedroll to sleep on, noting whatever you took into the field you had to carry, always aiming to keep my pack as light as possible. In the more remote areas of the park, the boys have set up several semi-permanent field camps. These camps are essentially bamboo structures, with above-ground bamboo benches for sleeping and sitting, pots and pans hanging up for cooking and a large tarp pitched over the top to keep the rain at bay, not exactly the Hilton but semi-comfortable. To be honest, you would need to see a bookie to bet on which was more comfortable, sleeping on the ground vs bamboo slats!

What worked for me was, at the end of most days I was dog tired, so sleeping rough comfortably or not wasn't an issue. When on patrol, all the boys would carry coils of nylon fishing line in their shirt pockets, usually only 2 to 3 metres in length. They either had a piece of cheese or a plastic lure as bait, they would regularly catch bream or garfish from a local tidal creek, which was added to our staple rice dish or two-minute noodles, along with some added edible fungi collected at the end of each day.

One of my 'out on patrol' challenges was my weight. I'm an average middle-aged Australian model, of around 90+kgs compared to the lighter Sundanese/Javan ranger and rhino protection staff model which sat around 60–70 kg at best. This often-presented challenges as I would regularly 'test' the strength of giant bamboo poles tied together and used to cross gullies, rivers and creeks. What would normally happen, is all the Javan lightweights would skip across first, then they would line up, smirk and watch and wait for me to cross. One wet morning, when it was my turn to cross, I got to the middle section of a crossing on a deep dry gully, the bamboo poles snapped and I fell. Remarkably, I fell over two plus metres straight down, I landed firmly on my feet! The boys were all looking down at me and said, 'Pak Steve you ninja.' I replied, 'no bloody lucky!' I can only surmise the physics worked in my favour, i.e., weight of me, my pack, camera gear and the fact I didn't fall forward or backwards, were in balance? My theory anyway, importantly nothing broken, it certainly gave the boys something to chuckle about Pak Steve the ninja!

Normally when going on patrol, the frontline staff and I would have a catch-up and discussion about what their needs were vs what my needs were. For example, the boys often needed to put fresh batteries in a number of camera traps, or download camera trap memory cards. I often needed to revisit a cleared arenga site, checking for rhino activity and signs, measure re-growth, or re-examine a new wallow I'd found, where I didn't have time to record the details from on my last trip. These discussions often occurred with a cup of tea around an early morning fire, listening to the dawn chorus of a family of Javan gibbons or *'Owa jawa'*. I always enjoyed the early morning jungle wake up, as we packed up, broke camp and headed off. It was to the sounds of a waking jungle, the growing intensity of bird calls and the shuffle of sun skinks (*Eutrophus multifasciata* or *'Kadal pohon'* [family Scincidae]) emerging from the leaf litter to capture the first rays of sun, charging their batteries in readiness for a day of insect catching. Seeing this activity always put a positive spin on the day. Occasionally, the marine patrol unit would take us out and drop us off in the north-east section of the park, which saved us considerable walking time. During these trips out I always enjoyed sitting on the bow of the boat watching iridescent flying fish do their thing at speed, almost lapping the boat. The Indonesian flying fish (*Cheilopogan kaptoptron* or *'ikan terbang'* [family Exocotidae]) was the main species we regularly observed, noting 18 species are found across Indonesia, from a total 64 species globally. Flying fish are an amazing piece of design evolution, with enlarged pectoral fins, they have evolved an ability to 'glide' at speed between 25–100 metres, no doubt an advantage when trying to elude predators from above and below. Sometimes the schools would be over 100 strong, all leaping out of the water at different times and gliding at speed, when they were about, I never tired of seeing them, it was always amazing to witness.

Part II—Bibliography

Janečka & Janečka 2018; Khairani et al. 2018; Save the Rhino international 2016c; Acharya et al. 2016; Harjanto 2017; Lessee 1994; Ramono et al. 2009; Worldometer 2019; Statistics Indonesian Banten Province 2019; Van Merm 2008; Santiapillai & Suprahman 1986; IFRC Report 2013; Stankey & Schindler 2005; Ministry of Forestry 1995; Indonesian Ministry of Forestry 2010; Nardelli 2016; Haryono et al. 2015; Van Strien & Rookmaaker 2010; Schenkel & Schenkel-Hulliger 1969a, 1969b; Setiwan et al. 2017; Sody 1941; 1959; Hoogerwerf 1938, 1970; Fernand et al. 2006; Collette & Parin 1995; Strange 2012; Nardelli & Robovský 2022.

PART III

Ecology of Javan rhino, what do we know?

The Javan rhino uses a broad variety of habitat types including rainforest, riverine and swamp forest habitats. There are no Javan rhino in captivity. The Javan rhino population is actively monitored by national park and rhino protection staff using camera traps, dung collection (for DNA analyses) and footprint plaster casting, supported by active patrolling of the Ujung Kulon peninsula to search for illegal activities. The Ujung Kulon population has been subject to many population trends since the early 1900s. Investigations into locating other potential habitat sites for Javan rhino have been ongoing, with an aim of increasing numbers and securing a buffer around existing habitat and rhino populations.

The Indonesian Rhino Conservation Action Plan has set a goal of 'creating conditions conducive to, and then actually developing, and increasing viable populations of Javan rhinos in the wild.' The aim of the action plan is to increase the current wild population by 20% and relocate small groups to other suitable areas. Due to its isolation, rarity and protected status, our knowledge of Javan rhino ecology, biology and behaviour has remained limited. In essence, the Javan rhino is a solitary, mobile, generalist browser that uses its bulk and reach to move foliage into its reach. Its preferred habitat is open or tree-fall areas containing primary lowland and secondary broad-leaf evergreen rainforest. Javan rhinos prefer to eat the leaves, shoots and twigs of woody species, with little to no known consumption of grass or herbaceous species. Early studies by Hoogerwerf (1970) suggested Javan rhino are highly dependent on the shrub and sapling layers found in secondary vegetation. The highest densities of Javan rhino are found in or adjacent to coastal areas, where it is presumed most of its mineral requirements are provided through the consumption of salt-sprayed vegetation, halophytic plants (e.g., mangroves) or by drinking sea or brackish water which has been observed. I would regularly find Javan rhino tracks in the sand along beaches, presumably they entered the saltwater to drink or to remove parasites. Male rhinos separate themselves spatially and temporally through olfactory (scent/odour) communication using dung, urine and the understudied pedal scent glands to convey scent signals.

Several habitat assessment and utilisation studies have been undertaken since the late 1960s (e.g., Schenkel & Schenkel-Hulliger 1969a, 1969b; Hoogerwerf 1970). Wallowing, the immersion of the body in water or in mud, is a widespread behaviour among large mammalian herbivores. The core function of wallowing is for heat regulation. Other viable reasons for wallowing include reduction of sun damage, removal of ectoparasites, skin conditioning and olfactory advertisement by impregnating the skin with the urine-rich mud or water of the wallow. The consequent odours that emanate from wallowing rhino is then spread throughout the habitat as mud on saplings and vegetation, and is presumably recognised by others. Javan rhino across Ujung Kulon National Park regularly use wallows or '*Kubangan*' that are often well concealed by rainforest vegetation. In dry periods, to reduce heat stress Javan rhino will use tidal waterways, muddy wallows, riverbanks and emersion in rivers and creeks. In most cases I was able to find wallowing sites, detecting them via mud on trees and vegetation, sometimes following a muddy track though rainforest, and 'rub marks' on trees close to the wallow, from entering and emerging rhino.

Adult male Javan rhino in rainforest habitat. Rhino horns (males only), which vary in size and shape, and along with body scars and differences in eye wrinkles can be used to identify different animals. (Image: Stephen Belcher/Minden Pictures, with support from the Ujung Kulon National Park Authority, and Indonesia's Ministry of Environment and Forestry).

Sympatry with other species and predation

The interspecific interactions of Javan rhino with other species are poorly studied. Javan rhino in Ujung Kulon are sympatric (share the same habitat) with other large herbivores such as Javan banteng, barking deer or red muntjac, Javan or Timor deer and Javan wild pig. These are potential competitors for forage and space. Both the Bali tiger (*Panthera tigris balica*) and Javan tiger (*P. t. sondaica*) were declared extinct within the last 50 and 20 years, respectively. The extinction of an apex predator from an ecosystem is significant. The consequent changes to trophic levels may cause unknown effects that have implications for many of the endangered species in Ujung Kulon National Park including Javan rhino. Since the extinction declaration of the Javan tiger in 1980, the predator-prey relationships of Javan leopard (*Panthera pardus melas* or *'Macan tutul'* [family Felidae]) and Javan dhole Cuon (*alpinus sumatrensis* [an Asian wild dog species] or *'Anjing hutan'* or *'Adjag'* [family Canidae]) in Ujung Kulon may have altered and their relationship to Javan rhino and other large herbivores is not understood and worthy of study. The IUCN Red List, lists both the Javan leopard (2021) and Javan dhole (2015) as endangered. Although no records of tiger, leopard, or dhole predation on Javan rhino calves are cited, the predation of greater one-horned rhino calves by tiger is a regular occurrence in Rajiv Gandhi Orang National Park, Assam, India. This predation effect on greater one-horned rhino calves by tiger was also reported in Kaziranga National Park, Assam, India.

Aside from humans, an adult Javan rhino, as with other rhinos, has no regular predators. Interestingly, I have observed on camera trap, a large Javan dhole pack attacking a small herd of Javan banteng in rainforest habitat. They eventually were able to isolate a female with a young calf which they ultimately overpowered and killed. I also observed on camera trap a pair of Javan dhole following an adult male Javan rhino in the jungle, the rhino was well aware of their presence and would periodically turn around and chase the dogs, who would hang back then follow again. Following a large mega-herbivore may be a viable hunting strategy for the dhole, a large rhino would disturb the undergrowth and vegetation, possibly making small animals i.e., reptiles or small mammals move from their hiding places and be snapped up. Dholes occupy a similar ecological niche to the African wild dog (*Lycaon pictus*). They are smart, work as a team and are able to take down animals much larger than themselves due to their collective co-operation.

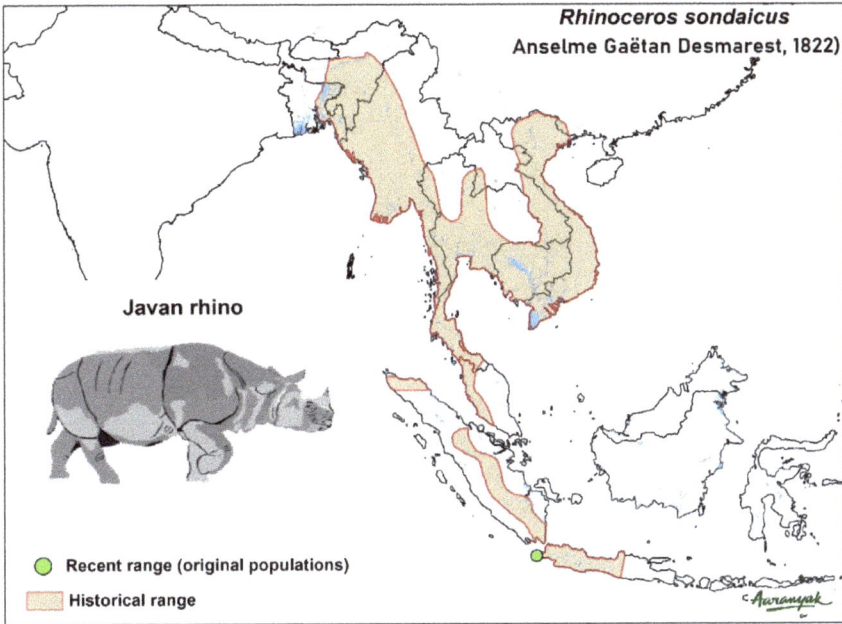

Map of Javan rhino *Rhinoceros sondaicus* current and historical distribution range (red shape) (Map: Courtesy © *Aaranyak* GIS team)

The Javan rhino is currently protected by numerous national and international regulations and for many years significant popular and scientific publications have attempted to highlight the species' critically endangered status in Southeast Asia. Despite its iconic name and periodic publicity, scientific studies directed at the many unknown aspects of its biology and ecology, which are fundamental for its survival and recovery, have been slow to happen. Outside of the conservation industry, the broader public is mostly unaware of its history, rarity and challenges. Javan rhino studies to date can be categorised into three areas of focus: population, distribution and conservation; importance of local communities in the management of protected areas and threatened species; and habitat assessment and utilisation.

Over the past decade, many key conservation organisations have become active participants in Javan rhino management and conservation. Collaborative efforts between the authorities and non-government organisations (NGO's) (eg., YABI) in the national park are focused towards preserving the Javan rhino, protecting its habitat from destruction and fragmentation, improving and supporting anti-poaching activities (active in situ patrolling by rhino protection and national park staff) and reducing in-park illegal resource extraction.

Status in the wild

The entire population of Javan rhino today are found in the wild only in Ujung Kulon Nation Park, West Java, Indonesia. Up until recently the population was 76, 37 females (comprised of 25 adult females, eight sub-adult females and four female calves), and 39 are male (comprised of 29 adult males, seven sub-adult and three male calves), recovering from an estimated low of 25 individuals in 1967. However, and seriously concerning, between 2019–2023 poaching events saw 26 animals killed, which has seen the population plummet. One bright note: a calf was born in March 2024. Otherwise, the current situation is dire. The Javan rhino population has been actively monitored by national park and rhino protection staff since 2012 using camera traps (currently 140 camera traps are operating). Across the park 35 quadrats have been established, each contains 4 cameras, which is starting to help develop a clear idea of the population demographics. The population has been isolated since the 1930s and given genetic drift due to the small population size, founder effects and bottlenecks. It remains remarkable that the population still retains two haplotypes (two genetically unrelated individuals). The single remaining Javan rhino population is stable and breeding but remains at risk of from several threats such as outbreaks of poaching, disease risk from domestic stock and a major tsunami. Field staff believe the current population is divided into three populations: east (JRSCA area, includes the 8 km rhino fence), west and south. Staff suggest these populations rarely mix, due to habitat and food plant constraints caused by large areas of monoculture arenga palm (*Arenga obtusifolia*). The suggested three-population theory is certainly an area worth investigating. Importantly, the establishment of a second population would free up habitat and food resources and promote breeding in the current population. Investigations into locating other potential habitat sites have been ongoing, with an aim of increasing numbers and securing a buffer around existing habitat and rhino populations.

Status in captivity

Over the years captive-breeding programs have been repeatedly proposed for Javan rhino but to date no action has ever been undertaken. Javan rhino are not currently kept in captivity. Considerable knowledge exists about the history of captivity and the captive husbandry of other species of rhino.

Throughout their early history, zoological institutions across the globe collected individuals of unusual species for their menageries, which were very in vogue at the time. I would imagine a Javan rhino would have been a significant display prize. They were captured and kept as best they could. Virtually nothing is known about the captive husbandry of Javan rhino but at least 27 individuals have been held in captivity (e.g., Reynolds 1960, 1961; Rookmaaker 1998, 2005, 2011, 2018, 2019). The last known captive Javan rhino lived at the Zoological Gardens in Adelaide, South Australia, from 12 April 1886 to 4 February 1907 when it died; it was exhibited as a greater one-horned rhino for most of its 20 years, 9 months and 15 days in captivity (Reynolds 1960; Rookmaaker 1998). Hoogerwerf (1970) noted this animal was purchased in Singapore during January 1886 for £65, by the Adelaide Zoo Director R.E. Michen. At the time the animal was estimated to be 18 months old.

Museum specimen of the last Javan rhino held in captivity. This male specimen which died in 1907 at the Zoological Gardens in Adelaide, South Australia, is held at the Adelaide Museum, in South Australia (Image: Courtesy Janice Mentiplay-Smith).

Subspecies and distribution

The Javan rhino, formerly occurred from north-eastern India, Bangladesh, Myanmar, Thailand, Lao PDR, Cambodia, Vietnam, through Peninsula Malaysia to Sumatra and Java and possibly China but generalised overall distributions published in the past were likely overstated (Rookmaaker 1980). The Javan rhino is the only known species of rhino to have occurred in the Sundarbans, the extensive mangrove biome of India and Bangladesh. The species' exact historical distribution is unclear, in part because early accounts failed to distinguish rhino at the specific level, due to partial sympatry with the other Asian rhino species, the greater one-horned rhino (*Rhinoceros unicornis*) and Sumatran rhino (*Dicerorhinus sumatrensis*) (Groves & Leslie Jr. 2011).

The Javan rhino is polytypic (two or more genetically different subspecies) and three subspecies of the Javan rhino are recognised: *Rhinoceros s. sondaicus* Demarest, 1822, *R. s. annamiticus* Heude, 1892 and *R. s. inermis* Lesson, 1836. Now extinct, *R. s. inermis* formerly occurred in north-eastern India, Bangladesh and Myanmar. *R. s. annamiticus* formerly occurred in Vietnam, Lao PDR, Cambodia and eastern Thailand; the last remaining animals were discovered in 1988 and were restricted to the Cat Loc area (Dong Nai province) of Cat Tien National Park in Vietnam. The Javan rhino was once common throughout lowland Vietnam, with high numbers present during French colonial times (1859-1956). Tragically, *R. s. annamiticus* was declared extinct in Vietnam in 2011. Javan rhino *R. s. sondaicus* formerly occurred in Thailand, Malaysia and Sumatra. Interestingly, about 12,000 years ago they occurred in Borneo, and about 2,000 years ago, in parts of southern China.

Today, the taxon's only surviving Javan rhino population resides at one location in Indonesia's Ujung Kulon National Park (UKNP), western Java, Indonesia, where the conservation of its habitat is a crucial management priority. Although historical population numbers of the Javan rhino are unknown, there is historical evidence suggesting they were once common in parts of their distribution, such as that from Dutch tea planters in Indonesia who viewed Javan rhino as a pest and hunted them during colonial times. Bounties were paid in Java, between 1746–1747, a reported 60 Javan rhino were hunted, and between 1747-1749, an additional 526 Javan rhinos were hunted and 80 Javan tigers were killed (Sody 1959; Hoogerwerf 1970).

The Javan rhino's former distribution across many countries meant the species was called many different names in other languages, these included: Indonesian (Malay & Sundanese): *baduk or badak jawa*; Javanese: *warak*; Indian (Hindi): *gainda*; Bengali: *gonda*; Naga: *kyeng, kyan-tsheng and kyan-hsin*; Laos (Burma): *meeza, het*; French: *rhinocéros de la Sonde, rhinocéros de Java*; Spanish: *Rinoceronte de Java*; German: *Java-Nashorn*; Dutch: *Javaanse neushoorn*; Chinese: 犀牛 *Xīniú;* Vietnamese: *con tê giác*; Thailand: แรด - *raaet* (Horsfield 1894; Hoogerwerf 1970; Van Strien et al. 2008; Groves & Leslie Jr. 2011). The species' scientific name has changed many times since its discovery.

Former scientific names include: *Rhinoceros javanicus* Geoffroy Saint-Hilaire & Cuvier, 1824; *Rhinoceros camperis* de Blanville in Griffith, Hamilton-Smith & Pigeon, 1827; *Rhinoceros javanus* (incorrect subsequent spelling) Cuvier, 1829; *Rhinoceros camperii* (incorrect subsequent spelling) Jardine, 1836; *Rhinoceros sivalensis* Falconer & Cautley, 1847; *Rhinoceros nasalis* Gray, 1868; *Rhinoceros floweri* Gray, 1868; *Rhinoceros frontalis* von Martens, 1876; *Rhinoceros karnuliensis* Lydekker, 1886; *Rhinoceros karnuliensish* (incorrect subsequent spelling) Lydekker, 1886; *Rhinoceros sivasondaicus* Dubois, 1908; *Aceratherium boschi* von Koenigswald, 1933; *Rhinoceros s. sinhaleyus* Deraniyagala, 1938; *Rhinoceros javanensis* Barnard, 1932; *Rhinoceros sondaicus simplisinus* Deraniyagala, 1946; *Rhinoceros sondaicus floweri* Groves, 1967; *Eurhinoceros sondaicus* Heissig, 1972; and *Rhinoceros sondaicus guthi* Guérin in Beden & Guérin, 1973. The generic name *Rhinoceros* means nose (*rhino*)-horn (*ceros*) in Greek, and the specific name *sondaicus* references the Sunda Islands (=Java) with the Latin locality suffix "*icus*" (Groves & Leslie Jr. 2011).

Species descriptive notes

Few measurements and limited baseline data are available on the body characteristics of wild Javan rhino. Head and body length: 305–344 cm; shoulder height: 150–170 cm; body mass: 1200–1500 kg. Horn: male Javan rhino have a single nasal horn, averaging 20–25 cm, and females typically lack horns. Javan rhino have upper and lower incisors being hypertrophied (body part excessively enlarged) and tusk-like. Males use their tusks to control breeding females; females use their tusks to deter males. The flanks and shoulders of adult females often have slash marks from mating encounters with males. Javan rhino gestation is unknown but presumed to be about 16 months like the greater one-horned rhino (*R. unicornis*). Javan rhino have a single offspring per pregnancy, and birth intervals are thought to be 4–5 years. Body colour is grey, with the distinctive mosaic-like pattern on the skin, with pronounced skin folds as in the greater one-horned rhino but adult males lack the distinctive 'bib' and deep neck folds of the former species. It may live to 40+ years in the wild. Javan rhino possess pedal scent glands (cutaneous glands in their feet) but how they use them in their communication repertoire remains unclear. Body hair is limited to the ear-fringes, eyelashes and tail-brush. The upper lip is long, flexible and prehensile in appearance. Dental formula is i2/2, c 0/0, p 3/3, m 3/3, total 32; deciduous dental formula is i 2/2, c 0/0, m 4/4.

The above Javan rhino descriptive notes have been adapted from Dinerstein, E. (2011). Family Rhinocerotidae. Pp. 178-181 in Handbook of the Mammals of the World. *Vol. 2. Hoofed mammals (D.E. Wilson and R.A. Mittermeier, Eds.*), and *Groves & Leslie Jr. (2011), formative work in* Mammalian Species 43(887):190-208, *Rhinoceros sondaicus* (Perissodactyla: Rhinocerotidae).

Close up of adult male Javan rhino, they utilise creeks, rivers, mangrove swamps and wallows to keep cool. Only males have horns, typically have broader heads and are bulkier in body shape. Females lack horns and have a narrower head shape, and are less bulky compared to males. (Image: Stephen Belcher/Minden Pictures, taken with support from the Ujung Kulon National Park Authority, and Indonesia's Ministry of Environment and Forestry).

Ujung Kulon habitat

Ujung Kulon National Park (UKNP) is located on the Gunung Paying peninsula on the southwestern end of mainland Java, to which it is joined by a low isthmus 1–2 km wide.

The 35,000-ha Ujung Kulon peninsula provides the core rainforest habitat for the remaining Javan rhino population. The rainforest vegetation is a complex mosaic of dense primary or old secondary broadleaf evergreen forests including palms, bamboo, and Zingiberaceae (ginger family, e.g., *Amomum*) and young, open secondary broadleaf evergreen forest, with shrub jungle interspersed with arenga or sugar palm.

The landscape ecology of the park was described in detail by Hommel (1987) as having three distinct landscapes: limestone plateau (arenga palm slopes and dissected plateaus); coastal plains (sandstone beach ridges and sand dunes) and *Dendrocinide* beach ridge and sand dunes. Coastal and intertidal areas also support significant mangrove and swamp forest habitat. Five mangrove genera are known in Ujung Kulon, including *Avicennia* or *'api'* (family Verbanaceae), *Sonneratia* (family Sonneratiaceae), *Rhizophora, Bruguirera* or *'bogem'* (family Phizophoraceae) and *Nypa* (family Arecaceae, subfamily Nypoideae). The unique Nipa or Mangrove palm (*Nypa fructicans*), is also found along the Ujung Kulon rivers and estruarine waterways.

I regularly observed long-tailed macaques (*Macaca fascicularis* or *'Monyet'*) feeding on fruiting palms. The Cigentur River, situated on the north coast of the park, has healthy stands of Nipa palm. Indonesians call Nipa palm, *'bobo'; 'buyuk';* or, *'nipah'.* Mangrove habitats are great places to see wildlife, especially if your tolerant of sand flies, mud and stifling humidity. One day I was with the boys in a nice patch of dense rainforest looking for active rhino wallowing sites about 300 metres from the coast. In the distance I could faintly hear the high-pitched screams and wails of what sounded like a group of smooth-coated otter (*Lutrogale p. perspicillata* or '*berang-berang*'). I told the boys I wanted to check this out and follow the screams to the coast, they all smirked thinking Pak Steve can't help himself, and nodding in agreement, sat down for a rest, while I walked off and honed in on the screams. Eventually finding them, I managed to climb over some mangrove roots and sat quietly in the mud for 10 minutes watching a very vocal raft of six smooth-coated otters from about 20 metres away before they eventually swam away. The group were actively hunting in and amongst the mangrove roots and branches, noisily splashing and diving catching crabs. Once they caught a crab, they would emerge from the water and sit on a mangrove branch and eagerly crunch away on their catch. Any otters that caught more than one crab would tuck the 'extras' under their armpits in readiness for crunching once the first crab was dispatched, it's a very innovative behaviour I was rapt to observe.

Smooth-coated otters are a large species growing between 7–11 kg. In Ujung Kulon, they work the mangrove swamps and coastal wetlands, feeding on fish, crustaceans (e.g., crabs, shrimp), shellfish, frogs and insects. The IUCN Red List (1996) classifies the species as vulnerable (family Mustelidae). Found across the Indian subcontinent and Southeast Asia, this species is rarely seen. I only observed them on this occasion, and despite the friendly sandflies, it was special to see them doing their thing. The rangers mentioned Asian small-clawed otters (*Aonyx cinereus*) are also found in the park but in small numbers. Asian small-clawed otters are the smallest of the 12 species, growing between 2–4 kg and are classified as vulnerable on the IUCN Red List (2020), unfortunately I never saw any on my visits.

When otters aren't around, these mangrove swamps are alive with mudskippers. Inhabiting tropical and subtropical habitats, there are 24 known species (family Oxudercidae). The Indonesian mudskipper (*Periophthalmus gracilis* or '*ikan gelodok*') is common in Ujung Kulon's coastal areas. Always fun and comical to watch, these amazing 'character' fish are able to feed and interact with each other out of the water, providing they can stay moist. With an ability to breathe through their skin, known as cutaneous air-breathing, they are able to utilise the tidal extremes that often occur in mangrove habitats. Amphibians also have cutaneous air-breathing capability as well.

The invasive but native arenga palm, locally known as 'langkap', is an evergreen, cluster-forming species that grows rapidly up to heights of 16 metres. The dominance of arenga palm across Ujung Kulon is influencing rhino habitat use through plant succession and negatively affecting rhino foraging areas. It is estimated up to 60% (>18,000 ha) of the peninsula is covered by arenga palm. By mid-2016, my next PhD chapter and target included working on understanding the impact of arenga palm on Javan rhino. Additionally, any visits to Ujung Kulon meant I had to continue setting future PhD work up to maintain momentum, which included allowing time for jungle searches of Javan rhino wallows, to record and map their location and characteristics. This work eventually became Chapter 5 in my thesis titled 'More than just mud: The importance of wallows to Javan rhino ecology and behaviour'.

Javan rhino habitat preference in Ujung Kulon is determined by a broad suite of biophysical factors, including sensitivity to human disturbance. While vegetation and elevation are important determinants of rhino habitat, their influence is strongly modified by proximity to water, mineral salt (e.g., ocean salt-sprayed vegetation) and especially habitat conditions that favour the maintenance of long-term wallows. Both male and female Javan rhino regularly use freshwater wallows in Ujung Kulon that are often concealed by rainforest vegetation (rarely bamboo) and are relatively evenly spaced. In Ujung Kulon, wallows are generally 3–5 metres wide, 6–7 metres long and 50 cm from the water's surface to a mud layer of 50–75 cm deep. Javan rhino wallow, on average, 0.7–0.8 times/24 h. Multiple Javan rhino will visit the same wallow, even together, and they urinate in them to the point that they can be 'smelt dozens of metres away by an odour reminiscent of that of a large quantity of horse dung'.

Based on and adapting Ammann's (1985) descriptions of wallows recorded in the Ujung Kulon peninsula, and my investigations of wallows from the 5,100 ha eastern Gunung Honje region of Ujung Kulon, situated at the base of the Gunung Honje massif (620 m), two wallow types were identified:

Mud wallow—clay based and contained mud to a depth averaging 14 cm (mean 14.31; SD ± 6.08). Rhino using and leaving the wallows were clearly coated with a film of mud. In mud wallows, animals were observed on video to periodically shake their heads and necks, presumably enabling mud to penetrate the deep skins folds.

Water wallow—characterised as holding water to depth averaging 18 cm, (mean 18.31; SD ± 10.90). Water wallows often had a soft base of mud that would be stirred up and mixed with active use. Rhino using and leaving the wallows were clearly coated with a film of water, and the skin was clearly darkened by immersion in water.

Two male greater one-horned rhinos wallowing in Chitwan National Park, Nepal. Notice the frogs resting on the rhino's body, a great place to catch flies and bugs from!

Eventually, by the end of 2020, I had found, spatially recorded and analysed 35 wallows in the eastern Gunung Honje section of the park. The following common wallow characteristics are noted. For example, wallows are often created at a mean elevation of 31.77 m (SD ± 10.05), in slightly sloping areas. The rear of the wallow was often dug out from a bank or edge that enabled the wallow to be enlarged and expanded as necessary, horn marks in banks were often observed. The soil being latosolic (highly leached due to heavy rainfall) and clay-based meant run off during rain helped maintain a level of water and mud in the wallow. Shade at the wallow site was important because it influenced the temperature of water and mud, and the percent cover averaged 75% (mean 75.14; SD ± 27.04). The dominant over storey shade plant was arenga palm (*Arenga obtusifolia*).

Wallow size depended on either single or multiple users, the latter often being many years old due to persistent use. The largest wallow I recorded was 8 metres long by 7 metres wide; mean length was 3.69 m (SD ± 3.12), mean width was 3.17 m (SD ± 3.37). Mud and water depth varied according to prevailing climatic conditions. All members of the family Rhinocerotidae have a requirement to wallow in mud or water to protect their skin from sun damage, remove ectoparasites and for thermoregulation (Dinerstein 2003). Javan rhino need to wallow regularly throughout the year. Access to wallows is therefore a critical element of Javan rhino habitat.

Table descriptions of eight (n=8) behavioural patterns exhibited by Javan rhino at wallows and recorded on camera trap videos 2011–2016. Adapted from Hazarika & Saikia (2010) descriptions.

Behaviour category	Description
Non-breeding	
1) Feeding	Behaviour associated with consumption of vegetation or water and techniques for intake of different vegetation types.
Drinking	Rhino would place its mouth in water and suck it into its mouth. Drinking often occurred soon after entering a wallow, flehmen (lip curl/facial grimace) was often displayed post-drinking by both sexes, presumably in response to other rhino scent in the wallow.
Geophagy	Soil licking or ingestion of soil by rhino in habitat. Observed on two occasions in wallows. In both cases the animal licked and appeared to eat soil from the edge of a wallow. Often followed by a flehmen response.
Browsing	Browsing was the only form of food intake observed and involved consumption of leaves and small twigs from understorey vegetation. Observed using their prehensile upper lip to either bring leaves from standing vegetation directly into their mouth or to pull a branch down and then strip leaves along the length of the branch. Animals would 'taste' leaves, either eating or moved on.
2) Locomotion	Behaviour that resulted in the rhino moving from one place to another.
Walking	Slow movement from one place to another, using the alternate fore and hind limbs simultaneously.
Entering water/ wading through water/mud	Entering water/wading through water/mud was characterised by movement from dry land into a mud or water body.
3) Comfort	Behaviour that gave relief to the rhino, related to energy levels or relief from ectoparasites and/or the sun. Comfort behaviour was sometimes characterised by a lack of motion within the body.

Resting	Lack of physical activity, rhino lying or sitting down in the wallow.
Sleeping	Rhino lying in a recumbent position on their hunches and being in a relaxed state (i.e., ears not alert and erected, eyes closed).
Rubbing	Vigorous rubbing of a section of the rhino's body or head against a tree stump or tree trunk.
Mud and water wallowing	Rhino lying or standing in the wallow. Either motionless while in the wallow or when lying down, often moved/ rolled to cover themselves in mud. Wallowing rhinos periodically shake their heads allowing mud and water to penetrate the skins folds on the neck.
4) Vigilance	Behaviours suggesting 'alertness'. Included raised head, scanning with the eyes and head, erect ears and swivelling of ears, likely to determine the source of sound disturbance. Solitary females and females with calves demonstrated this behaviour the most.
5) Investigating environment	Scanning of surrounding environment and sniffing the ground, vegetation and any structure either while stationary or while walking along. Tracks leading into and away from wallows were often investigated via sniffing the ground and vegetation.
6) Calls (vocalisation)	Call sound or sounds emitted by rhino.
7) Smelling/ sniffing	Males would smell/sniff and call a 'sniff-huff' when close to females in wallows. Mud on structure e.g., tree stumps, trees/vegetation would be smelt/sniffed presumably in response to scent left by other animals.
8) Breeding (courtship)	Courtship took place between adult male and female before mating.
9) Touching	Males approaching females in wallows would lightly touch females with nostrils and lips, and sometimes their horns. A flehmen response would often occur soon after touching.

Table of Peninsula rhino population wallow camera trap video behaviour observation results 2011–2015 (n = 68 videos).

Variable	Result		% of records
Season (Wet = Nov–May), (Dry = June–Oct)	Wet season (n=51)		75%
	Dry season (n=17)		25%
Habitat where observation occurred	Wallows (n=8 locations), (n=68)		100%
Vegetation type where observation occurred	Open broadleaf evergreen (n=4)		6%
	Dense broadleaf evergreen (n=17)		25%
	Open broadleaf evergreen/arenga palm (n=45)		66%
	Dense broadleaf evergreen/arenga palm (n= 2)		3%
Number and descriptor of calls (vocalisations) recorded at wallows	Calls (n=157)		80%
	Call descriptor (n=7), sigh, lip vibration, short pant, long hiss, bleat, sniff-huff and snort		
Behaviour category, no. and percentage of behaviours recorded at and near wallows on camera traps (2011–2015)	Non-breeding		
	Feeding	Drinking (n=6)	9%
		Geophagy (n=2)	3%
		Browsing (n=3)	4%
	Locomotion	Walking (n=4)	6%
		Entering/wading through water/mud (n= 3)	19%
Note the percentages are based on the % of video clips for a particular behaviour against the total 68 video clips reviewed	Comfort	Resting/standing/sitting (n=5)	7%
		Rubbing (on structure) (n=5)	7%
		Wallowing (mud/water) (n=68)	100%
	Vigilance (n=4)		6%
	Investigating environment (n=4)		6%
	Flehmen response (n=3)		4%
	Non-breeding play (n=4)		6%
No. of observations (n=70) and sex of rhinos at and near wallows	Solitary male (n=1)		31%
	Solitary female (n=17)		25%
	Female & sub adult calf > 2yrs (n= 1)		31%
	Female & calf < 2yrs (n=2)		3%
	Male & female (n=4)		6%
	Male, female & calf (n=5)		7%
Distance from coast where observation occurred (km)	Mean 1.81; SD ± 1.47		
Distance from nearest waterway from where observation occurred (km)	Mean 0.22; SD ± 0.19		

105

Other species directly observed using wallowing sites and on camera trap video include Javan wild pig (*Sus scrofa vittatus*), Javan or Timor deer (*Rusa timorensis russa*) and Asian water monitor (*Varanus salvator*). I analysed 137 remote camera trap videos (recorded between 2011 and 2015) and 255 videos (recorded in 2016) and discovered that wallows are important communication hubs for Javan rhinos.

In late 2018, along with my partner Tracy, I was able to visit Chitwan National Park in Nepal. During this trip I was able to observe the wallowing behaviour of greater one-horned rhino, the congeneric (same genus) and closest relative of Javan rhino. I found greater one-horned rhino, like Javan's used wallows as a shared resource and as a communication hub. Wallowing rhinos love to urinate in their wallows, to put it mildly they seriously stink! These stinking masses attract many bugs, and in Nepal I often observed large numbers of local frog species using the wallowing rhino's body as a launching place to catch flies and bugs from.

During my time searching for wallowing sites in Ujung Kulon, I would often 'bump' into some interesting local wildlife. The most exciting encounter is meeting a king cobra (*Ophiophagus hannah* or '*Ular lanang*'). King cobras are the world's longest and largest venomous snake, growing on average between, 3 to over 5 metres in length. Recently an animal was found in Thailand that measured 5.85 metres! I would love to meet and photograph that guy or girl! Their diet is predominantly other snakes, including its own species. Found across Southern and Southeast Asia, this species is uncommon and rarely seen, and has been classified as vulnerable on the IUCN Red List since 2010 (family Elapidae).

Over my six years visiting Ujung Kulon, I observed king cobra only on two occasions, both in similar circumstances. Interestingly, king cobras are the only snake species that builds a nest, using leaf litter which females collect and pile up with their tail. They usually build the nest and lay eggs inside, between March and May, often nesting at the base of trees. A key fact is these nesting sites are actively defended! So, when I would walk through a forest clearing and see a pile of leaf litter at the base of a tree, I would proceed with caution! Fortunately, my cobra 'meetings' were on the edge of a rice paddy and along forest edges, most likely when the snake was out hunting. When confronted or disturbed the snake would hold its ground and stand up well over a metre in front of me, following my every movement, emitting an unusual low sounding 'hissing growl' and always making sure it's 'famous cobra hood' was visible and facing me while I was taking a wide berth around it!

King cobras are one of the most significant wildlife encounters I had in Ujung Kulon, they didn't move out of the way just because I was there, and why would they. Both animals I observed were well over 4 metres in length, their bodies as thick as your arm and with no fear of Australians or I suspect anyone else, they deserved that right! The main snake species I was always mindful of is the Javan or Indonesian spitting cobra (*Naja sputatrix* or '*Ular sendok*'). This species is naturally nervy and very defensive when disturbed, and can accurately spit venom, which is expelled via special grooves in each of their fangs. Each stream of venom joins and is accurately, and almost always aimed at your face and eyes. Highly variable in colour, and common, this species feeds on frogs, reptiles and small mammals, and grows between 1.3–1.8 metres in length. Fortunately, despite several encounters I was never sprayed with venom.

My work in the Javan rhino wallowing space was rewarded with a peer-reviewed publication of a paper in *Pachyderm* journal in 2020. Titled 'Wilson, S.G., Hockings, G., Deretic, J.M., & Kark, S. (2020)'. *More than just mud: The importance of wallows to Javan rhino ecology and behaviour. Pachyderm, 61, 49–62.*

Hidden active in-use Javan rhino wallowing site deep in rainforest habitat in Ujung Kulon National Park.

Healthy rainforest habitat in the core peninsula (western area) of Ujung Kulon National Park.

Table of comparison of all five rhino species wallowing behaviour and type of wallow used.

Species	Wallow type used	Behaviour	References
Javan rhino *Rhinoceros sondaicus*	Mud and water wallows in forest, also rivers and riverbanks (dug out muddy banks) during dry periods when wallows may dry up	Daily use (up to 6 hrs), year-round wallowing (based on camera trap observations), often rests in shade near coastal areas, benefitting from onshore breezes and cooler temperatures	Schenkel & Schenkel-Hulliger (1969a, 1969b) Hoogerwerf (1970) Ammann (1985) Rahmat (2007) Hariyadi et al. (2010) Groves & Leslie Jr (2011) Dinerstein (2003, 2011) Santosa et al. (2013) Wilson (2021)
Greater one-horned rhino *Rhinoceros unicornis*	Rivers, also in riverine forest, mud and water wallows, also ox-bow lakes, large water bodies and smaller narrow creeks	Daily wallowing peaks (up to 8 hrs) during monsoon period (June–September), less frequently during so in dryer hot periods (mid-Feb–mid-June), remains within 2km of water	Laurie (1978, 1982) Laurie et al. (1983) Dinerstein (2003, 2011) Hazarika & Saikia (2010)
Sumatran rhino *Dicerorhinus sumatrensis*	Needs clean mud wallows	Daily use (5–6 hrs) year-round wallowing activity will utilise number of wallows in home range	Groves & Kurt (1972) Van Strien (1985) Ng et al. (2001) Dinerstein (2011)
White rhino *Ceratotherium simum*	Waterholes, mud and water wallows, will also use sandy areas and dust baths as well	Ability to go without wallowing for several days, also keeps cool by resting in shade or ridge crests utilising cool breezes, may wallow during heat of the day, more active in cloudy conditions	Groves (1972) Owen-Smith (1973, 1975, 1988) Pienaar (1994) Dinerstein (2003, 2011)
Black rhino *Diceros bicornis*	Muddy depressions, pools, will also use sandy areas and dust baths as well	Ability to go without wallowing for several days, also keeps cool by resting in shade or ridge crests utilising cool breezes	Goddard (1967) Joubert & Eloff (1971) Hillman-Smith & Groves (1994) Dinerstein (2003, 2011)

Map of the eastern Gunung Honje section of Ujung Kulon (5,100 ha), showing where I found and identified 35 wallows (green squares). Map was created using ArcMap 10.5 software (ESRI).

Table of Eastern Gunung Honje Javan Rhino Study Conservation Area (JRSCA) Ujung National Park wallow characteristics (n=35).

Variable	Results
Wallow length (m)	Mean 3.69; SD ± 3.12
Wallow width (m)	Mean 3.17; SD ± 3.37
Wallow water depth (cm)	Mean 18.31; SD ± 10.90
Mud depth (cm)	Mean 14.31; SD ± 6.08
Number entry/exit points	Mean 2.62; SD ± 0.68
Percentage (%) shade cover	Mean 75.14; SD ± 27.04
Elevation (m)	Mean 31.77; SD ± 10.05
Permanent wallow (n=27)	77% (defined as existing in environment beyond climatic conditions, in active use)
Temporary wallow (n=8)	23% (defined as existing in environment only when conditions allow i.e., enough rainfall)

110

Plant species recorded at wallow sites Note: FP denotes rhino food plant	*Arenga obtusifolia, Callamus sp, Salacca edulis* (FP), *Leea sambucina* (FP), *Vitex pubescens* (FP), *Amomum coccineum* (FP), *Spondias pinnata* (FP), *Donnax cunnaeformis* (FP), *Phrynium parviflorum* (FP), *Dillenia obovate* (FP), *Barringtonia gagantostachua* (FP), *Anadendrum microstachyum* (FP).
Distance from coast (km)	Mean 0.64; SD ± 0.52
Dominant vegetation type	Complex mosaic of **1.** Dense broadleaf evergreen forest—primary or old secondary forest including palms, bamboo, Zingiberaceae (ginger family e.g., *Amomum*), and **2.** Open broadleaf evergreen forest—young, open secondary forest, with shrub jungle (Hoogerwerf 1970).

Movements and home range

Data are limited but I suspect dominant male Javan rhino are probably territorial like the greater one-horned rhino. In Ujung Kulon, the highest densities of Javan rhino are found in the western peninsula area of the park, and adjacent to coastal areas, presumably where most of mineral requirements are provided through the consumption of salt-sprayed vegetation and halophytic plants (e.g., mangroves) or by drinking sea or brackish water, which was been observed by field staff. Groves (1982) calculated the density of Javan rhino in Ujung Kulon at only 0.14 individuals/km^2, and later Ammann (1985) found densities of 0.47–0.51 individuals/km^2.

Table of home-range sizes reported in literature for the five living rhino species.

Species	Sex	Size	Reference
Black rhino	♀	2.59–90.6 km²	Goddard (1967)
Diceros bicornis	♀	12.5–47.3 km²	Kiwia (1989)
	♂	2.59–51.8 km²	Goddard (1967)
	♂	69 km²	Kiwia (1989)
Greater one-	♀	20 km²	Laurie (1982)
horned rhino	♂	(2–4 km² core)	
Rhinoceros		3–4 km²	
unicornis	♀	12–15 km²	Groves (1972)
	♂	2–8 km²	Laurie et al. (1983)
Javan rhino	♀ (no calf)	10 km²	Schenkel & Schenkel-
Rhinoceros	♀ (with calf)	2–3 km²	Hulliger (1969b)
sondaicus	♂	20 km²	
	♀	2.61–8.4 km²	
	♂	12.5–26.4 km²	Ammann (1985)
	♀	14.20 km²	
	♂	105.53 km²	Setiwan et al. (2017)
Sumatran rhino	♀	10–15 km²	Van Strien (1986)
Dicerorhinus	♂	30 km²	
sumatrensis	♀	2–3.5 km²	Groves & Kurt (1972)
White rhino	♀	9–20 km²	Owen-Smith (1975)
Ceratotherium	♂	97 km²	van Gyseghem (1984)
simum	♀	0.75–2.6 km²*	Owen-Smith (1975)
	♂	30 km²	Van Gyseghem (1984)
	♀	12–15 km²	Groves (1972)

* Denotes breeding territories

Javan rhino appear to wander extensively, particularly males; Ammann (1985) estimated that they travelled 0.4–3.8 km/24 h. Like earlier observations by Ammann (1985), a study by Setiawan et al. (2017), using a large dataset of camera video clips discovered strong evidence that home-range size varied between males and females and across seasons. Females on average maintained the smallest home-ranges (14.2 km²) during dry seasons, typically June–July, and their home ranges overlap extensively. Male home ranges on average were the largest (105.5 km²) during the period from dry to wet season, usually September–October. Seasonal female home ranges were on average one-half the size of males.

Dispersal and activity patterns

During poor plant growth periods, home-range sizes of Javan rhino fluctuate and change, most likely expand, and such periods potentially limit population density. As highly mobile generalist browsers, and not being restricted to certain plant species, Javan rhino can adapt by moving and seeking alternative food plant species during lean periods. Under a variety of prevailing conditions, Javan rhino can experience shortages of specific nutrients caused by periodic reductions in certain nutritionally valuable plant species. For example, *Zanthoxylum rhetsa* (Indian prickly ash) is a rhino food plant species known to be high in protein (17.11%), fat (1.94%) and energy (3.667 k/cal/kg). Studies (e.g., Haryono et al. 2016) estimate Javan rhino moved 1.4–3.8 km in their home ranges each day. The proximity and access to wallows are important given Javan rhino need to wallow daily. Proximity to coastal areas was considered important by Setiawan et al. (2017) who found that Javan rhino mostly occurred in coastal areas in Ujung Kulon, presumably due to cooler conditions and access to salt-sprayed mineral-rich vegetation. Camera trap data showed Javan rhino were active throughout the day and night, with peak activity occurring between 1500 and 1800 hours, and less so between the hours 0600 and 1500 hours. Although the activity patterns differ from one individual to another, observations indicated that the Javan rhino can spend up to 30% of the time in wallows to thermoregulate and interact with other animals.

Feeding ecology

Vegetation in Ujung Kulon is greatly affected by microclimate conditions. The Ujung Kulon National Park Authority conducts regular microclimate assessments by measuring temperature and humidity in several parts of Ujung Kulon that represented specific locations of Javan rhino's known habitat (ranges). Recorded ambient temperatures were as low as 20°C and as high as 28°C, and relative humidity varied from 80% to 100%. In addition to rainfall, temperature and humidity, water availability and soil types play crucial roles in shaping the vegetation structure in Javan rhino habitat.

Javan rhino use feeding grounds known locally as *'rumpang'*. These feeding grounds are spread across the peninsula of Ujung Kulon and are often used as one of the indicators of habitat suitability. Quality of feeding grounds is described based on size and diversity of food plants. As generalist browsers, Javan rhino feed on a broad variety of plant species. As mega-sized, hind-gut fermenters (perissodactyls e.g., horses, tapir's, rhinos), Javan rhino can consume small quantities of low-quality forage throughout the day and survive under conditions that similarly large, bodied ruminants (e.g., water buffalo) might not get adequate nutrition for their daily requirements. Hind-gut fermenters can extract more nutrition from smaller quantities of food than ruminants.

The Javan rhino in Ujung Kulon consumes mostly undergrowth plants. At least 12 food plant species are identified as good sources of energy (calorie), fat and protein. Javan rhino have been recorded (Ammann 1985) to prefer plant species including *Spondias pinnata, Amomum* sp., *Leea sambucina* and *Dillenia excelsa* that made up 44% of the 190 plant species consumed. It is worth noting these are pioneer species that appear rapidly after disturbances (e.g., tree fall or storm damage) and in successional habitats.

Analyses of the nutritional quality and digestibility of food plants of Javan rhino by Hariyadi et al (2016), showed that *Spondias pinnata* or *'kedongdong'* had the highest calcium (4.70 g/100 g) and *Hibiscus tiliaceus* had the most phosphorus (0.3 g/100 g). *Leea sambucina, Dracontomelon puberulum, Amomum megalocheilos, Spondias pinnata, Zanthoxylum rhetsa, Diospyros macrophylla* and *Ficus hispida* were the most palatable. Known Javan rhino food plants *Dracontomelon puberulum, Zanthoxylum rhetsa, Diospyros macrophylla* and *Ficus hispida* contained much higher levels of protein, fat and energy than many of the other highly palatable species. These observations highlight the need for variability and availability of these plants in home-ranges of Javan rhino and the importance of having a diverse these balanced diet. In addition to the diversity of food plants in the *'rumpang'*, the quality of wallows or *'Kubangan'* is an important part of the ecology of Javan rhino. Furthermore, the habitat quality will also be determined based on the type of salt lick/wallow/water. Wallow and water sources can be differentiated into permanent and temporary depending on the availability of water. Permanent wallows have water throughout the year, while temporary wallows only have waters during rainy season. About 70% of wallows in Ujung Kulon appear temporary.

Analysis of mud and water samples from various wallows in Ujung Kulon showed that wallow mud and water contained calcium and potassium, minerals elemental in the formation of skeletal tissue, activation of enzymes and maintenance of the integrity of cell walls. Under a variety of prevailing conditions, Javan rhino can experience shortages of specific nutrients caused by periodic reductions in certain nutritionally valuable plant species, which can influence home-range size and potentially limit population density.

Reproduction and growth

Reproduction in rhino species depends on a female's hormone production where oestrogen, progesterone, luteinizing and other hormones are produced sequentially, creating reproductive 'cycles'. Cycling females are considered capable of pregnancy. There have been no studies on the actual cycles in female Javan rhino, so the cycles are modelled using that of the closely related greater one-horned rhino measured in urine, saliva and faeces of captive individuals. The mating process requires overlap of male and female home ranges. Cycling females spray urine as chemical signals that can be recognised by male rhino. Based on video and camera trap data, female and male rhino engage in courting rituals consisting of wallowing and walking. I observed Javan rhino courtship behaviour on video camera trap, where the male used his head to touch a female on her head and used his horn to rub under the neck. The female responded with open-mouth displays and rubbing back against the male. Touching was gentle and non-agonistic and presumed to be a prelude to mating. During courtship, males approach females with repeated *'short-pant'* calls. Female responds with a repeated *'moo-bray'* call. There is an indication that aggression between (competing) males often occurs during this process. Video and camera trap data from Ujung Kulon show that courting activities conclude with intercourse between the male and female rhino. It remains unproven, however plausible, that Javan males would engage in mate guarding behaviour.

I suspect, older, experienced and possibly past their reproductive prime males could be excluding younger and more sexually potent males from getting access to willing females. There remain significant data gaps, especially in understanding the reproductive repertoire of Javan rhino due mostly to lack of direct observation. There is a need for active management of Javan rhino to keep population densities lower and at more productive levels. For female rhino, the age at first reproduction can be an impediment given it takes time for a population to rebound and respond. A study by Dinerstein (2003) estimated the greater one-horned rhino female's age at first breeding in one population at 7–7.5 years, and presumably Javan rhino have similar ages at first breeding.

With low numbers, only a few Javan females may be reproductively active at any given time. Presumably, Javan rhino longevity as in other rhino species might compensate for the slower population recovery time, or at minimum reduce the disadvantage compared with the rebounding ability of many small mammals. Under ideal conditions and in good habitat, Dinerstein (2003) suggested a rhino could produce a calf every 2.5 years. The current lack of accurate knowledge of Javan rhino age at first breeding and interbirth interval is a significant data gap and worthy of investigation.

There are consequences for threatened species such as Javan rhino with long birth intervals that lower the reproductive rate (long gestation) and their recovery. The management issue of older, possibly infertile dominant males consorting with females to the detriment of younger more fertile males, reducing the birth rate is also worth considering. The Javan rhino population in Ujung Kulon, based on camera trap recordings, shows a trend of growth, as indicated by several rhino births recorded. For example, in 2019 the population structure of Javan rhino in Ujung Kulon based on camera trap identification was 28 adult males (41.2%), 23 adult females (33.8%), 8 young males (11.8%) and 9 sub-adult females (13.2%). This suggests that the composition of adult and sub-adult females increases to 47% of the population after 15 years. Assuming that each female needs 4 years from mating to bearing the second calf, reproductive capacity of sub-adult and adult females can be calculated. Rough estimations suggest that one sub-adult female will have about 13 years of productivity, while an adult female will have 6 years. Given the 4-year reproductive cycle, a sub-adult female will be able to give birth to 3.25 calves throughout her lifetime, and an adult female, 1.5 calves. In other words, an adult female will have about one-half the capability to bear offspring compared with a subadult female.

Based on field records and observations, time required for individual Javan rhino to grow from one age class to the next is as follows:

1) infant to juvenile takes about 2 years;
2) juvenile to subadult takes about 2 years; and
3) subadult to adult takes about 4 years.

These benchmarks can be used to project population growth under ideal condition. If an annual infant cohort has a 1:1 sex ratio and if each infant has a 100% survival rate, one-half of juveniles each year will increase the numbers of sub-adult females that are then able to breed. Demographic analysis from video and camera trap data shows that the population of Javan rhino in Ujung Kulon consists of mainly adults that could result in 1% population growth per year.

Social behaviour and communication in mammals

The class Mammalia represents a highly variable range of social systems, coupled with diversity of social complexity, behavioural flexibility, brain size and cognitive ability (e.g., Silk 2007; Clutton-Brock 2009; Isler & van Schaik 2009; Ricklefs 2010). The variation of social organisation can broadly be defined via three basic types: adult individuals can either lead a solitary existence, form a bond or relationship with the opposite sex by forming pairs, or they associate with two or more partners forming groups.

Despite ongoing threats, as genuine megafauna, the large size of modern rhino has two significant advantages: a strong defence from predators (as adults) and ability to survive on coarse low in nutrient vegetation. For the family Rhinocerotidae the most stable and social bond amongst extant rhino species is between a female and calf. Typically, males are solitary, separating themselves spatially and temporally through olfactory communication using dung and urine to convey scent signals. All five living rhino species are polygamous and polyandrous, with both males and females seeking multiple mates (Owen-Smith 2004). Intraspecific courtship and mating behaviour (e.g., male combat) are known to be aggressive, intense and often violent in all five species (Dinerstein 2011). Mammals communicate primarily in three main forms: using visual, vocal (calls) and/or olfactory signals (dung, urine, scent gland secretions).

Communication, the method by which animals convey information to each other, is the bond that holds animal societies together, facilitating reproduction, conveying information on identity, status, mood and intentions. Communication behaviour includes a significant proportion of the behavioural repertoire across animal taxa and is a major driver of species biology, affecting the evolution of life histories and genes. In most mammal species, olfaction (scent/odour) is the primary form of communication, with information passed via urine (e.g., spray or stream); dung (e.g., faeces or droppings); or specialised scent glands (e.g., pre-orbital [facial] and pedal scent glands [feet]). Olfactory communication provides many advantages. Chemical scent signals allow a clear indicator of the depositors' characteristics. For example, female house mice (*Mus musculus*) have the detection ability to determine the health status of males from urinary scents and amazingly, can identify and show preference for non-parasitised males (Cavalieres & Colwell 1995).

In Madagascar, male ring-tailed lemur (*L. catta*) use scent gland secretions to promote their genetic qualities (Charpentier et al. 2008) allowing females to make suitable mate choices. A major advantage is that olfactory communication ensures that information remains available long after the sender has moved away. For example, Linklater et al. (2013) discovered that black rhino dung was still effective in stimulating investigatory behaviour 32 days after deposition. Olfactory signals can also provide spatial information, for example, territory ownership and dominance or movements of a significant individual such as a dominant male. A study by Bhattacharya and Chakraborty (2016) suggested greater one-horned rhino dung and dung piles (middens or heaps) not only scent mark territories but they also communicate the reproductive state of individuals.

Social behaviour in the Javan rhino

There is a lack of ecological and behavioural knowledge for most of the world's threatened mega-herbivores. Understanding the application of such behavioural knowledge can increase the likelihood of conservation program success, as shown for example, where knowledge of social structure and behaviour has informed conservation actions for elephants and rhinos (e.g., Pinter-Wollman 2009; Shannon et al. 2013; Dutta et al. 2015).

My interest in Javan rhino social behaviour and communication, led to my work on Chapter 6 of my thesis, *'Understanding an icon: Social behaviour and communication in the Javan rhino'.* Given the small remaining population, it is important to better understand the species' social behaviour to plan and assess management actions, including relocation options. The primary aim of this study was to examine the social behaviour of the Javan rhino, the forms of communication used by the species and the value of using camera trap data for conservation.

I analysed 137 remote camera trap videos (2011–2015) from the peninsula area and 255 videos (2016) from the eastern Gunung Honje region of Ujung Kulon in this study and confirmed wallows as important communication hubs for the Javan rhino. Altogether 11 behavioural patterns were categorised, and these were related to their daily activities.

This work has expanded our knowledge of Javan rhino vocalisation, identifying eight vocalisation descriptors with the first ever sonograms via 55 recordings comprising 196 individual vocalisations. The information collected can help monitor the species and enhance its persistence. Research on Javan rhino behaviour and communication has been limited due to their rarity, cryptic nature and highly protected status.

During my studies, camera trap data showed that male and female Javan rhino have a mostly solitary existence. Female Javan rhino with young maintain the strongest social bond and social interaction. Adult male Javan rhino regularly visit wallowing sites to monitor visiting females for sexual receptivity and thermoregulatory purposes. Solitary Javan males and females would periodically drink and taste soil or mud at wallows, often followed by a flehmen response. Female Javan rhino with calves were noticeably vigilant when approaching wallows, particularly if a male was present; females often would not stay, and both the female and calf would call and vocalise their nervousness in these situations. Adult females with calves do not appear to form associations with other individuals regardless of sex and age. Adult females without calves are mostly solitary. Sub-adult males might form groups of two individuals, and these pairings might occupy peripheral areas of dominant male home ranges. Presumably, sub-adult males form these groupings to increase their ability to detect and be protected from dominant males. Sub-adult greater one-horned rhinos are known to form loose associations living around the edges of a dominant male's territory. The social structure of Javan rhino likely has similarities to other rhino species, particularly the greater one-horned rhino. For example, adult males of the other four species are usually solitary outside of breeding events. Historically Javan rhino may have lived in more social and group behaviour settings than the current low wild numbers indicate, and current grouping behaviour is likely marginalised relative to what it once was.

The subspecies *R. s. inermis* once occurred in large numbers. Sody (1959) wrote in 1884 it was '*yet plentiful in the Sundarbans*'; and between 1860 and 1870 in Assam, Pollock '*shot there 44 to my own gun, and probably saw some 60 others slain, and lost and wounded fully as many as I killed*'. Burton (1951) noted its presence in the Sunderbunds up until the late 1800s; however, by January–February 1892, De Poncins (1935) estimated 3–4 animals remained.

Javan rhinos are naturally attracted to early successional habitats (e.g., tree-fall or storm-damaged areas) maintained by local disturbance regimes; this is reflected by early colonists who saw rhinos as pests in their gardens and tea estates. Human-rhino conflict and interactions have been well documented, as early as the 1700's. Bounties were paid in Java because of crop depredation; bounty records between 1st September 1747 and 14th January 1749 showed that 526 *R. sondaicus* and 80 Javan tigers were killed, causing suspension of the bounty system because of its exorbitant cost (Sody 1959; Hoogerwerf, 1938, 1970). Horsfield (1824) wrote '*the rhinoceros lives gregarious in many parts of Java, it is not limited to a particular region or climate, but its range extends from the level of the ocean to the summit of mountains of considerable elevation*'. Java was clearly viewed as a place to source rhino horn, records from as far back as the T'ang Dynasty, 618–906 AD, mention the export of rhinoceros horn from Java (e.g., Sody 1959; Hoogerwerf, 1938, 1970).

Vocalisation (calls) in rhinos

While there have been studies on vocalisation and communication in many large mammal species, such as elephants (e.g., Wood et al. 2005; Venter & Hanekon 2010), much less is known about vocalisations for the family Rhinocerotidae, and almost no information has been collected to systematically record and learn about vocalisation in Javan rhino.

For the family Rhinocerotidae communication via vocal and olfactory signals (e.g., dung, urine, pedal scent glands) are prominent as they have an acute sense of hearing and scent detection but relatively poor eyesight. All five rhino species vocalise (hereafter called 'call') in various categories including puffing, snorting, growling and harmonic calls. Based on limited research Javan rhinos are considered the least vocal rhino species (e.g., Hazewinkel 1933; Schenkel & Schenkel-Hulliger 1969a, 1969b; Hoogerwerf 1970; Ammann 1985). This suggests that the conception that the Javan rhinos have a very limited repertoire of calls could be due to its geographical remoteness, small numbers and very limited research on the species, in contrast, the Sumatran rhino is considered the most vocal (e.g., Muggenthaler et al. 1993, 2003; Dinerstein 2011; Groves & Leslie Jr. 2011), producing more call signals over time than any other species of rhino.

Field studies (e.g., Hazarika & Saikia 2010) of the greater one-horned rhino have identified a range of 10 calls including snorts, honks, bleats, squeak-pant and a moo-grunt commonly used by mothers and calves. At least five different types of call have been recorded in black rhino (e.g., Spellmire 1981; Budde & Klump 2003). White rhino considered the most social rhino species, and are known to have the broadest vocal repertoire out of all rhino species whose calls have been studied bio-acoustically (e.g., Muggenthaler et al. 1993, 2003; Budde & Klump 2003; Policht et al. 2008). All rhinos have part of their vocal range at or below 20Hz, thus they are producing infrasounds. Sounds below the level of human hearing are considered to be 'infrasonic'. An average adult human hears sounds between 20Hz and 16,000Hz, infants can hear to 20,000Hz in their early years. Currently, our knowledge of Javan rhino social structure, behaviour and communication has been restricted to a few historic accounts mostly from the 1900s (e.g., Hazewinkel 1933; Schenkel & Schenkel-Hulliger 1969a, 1969b; Hoogerwerf 1970; Ammann 1985). For example, Schenkel & Schenkel-Hulliger (1969a, 1969b), suggested Javan rhino were mostly solitary, independent, or were 'loosely associated nomads'.

Initial work by Ammann (1985) described five distinct Javan rhino calls, including *'neigh'*, the *'loud blowing whistle'* of Schenkel & Schenkel-Hulliger (1969a, 1969b); *'bleat'*, a contact call between mother and young; *'snort'*, made separately or in a series; *'shriek'*, a possible response to a threat; and *'lip vibration'*, or *'whinny'* similar in sound to that made by horses. Hoogerwerf (1970) believed that the majority of audible sounds, such as loud sniffing, snorting and puffing, have *'without exception ... an unpleasant note to them and can often be heard over several hundred metres.'* Hazewinkel (1933) was of a similar opinion, describing *'low growls'*, *'savage sniffing'* and *'snorting'*, and *'short, intermittent barks'*. Dinerstein (2011) notes individual white rhino is known to use subsonic or advanced ultrasonic communication like elephants. Other species of rhino are known to produce infrasounds (greater than 20 Hz, inaudible to humans).

Vocal and olfactory signals are considered important for communication amongst rhinos; however, their vocal communication has only been investigated to a limited extent to date. A goal of this study was to systematically document the range of calls in the only remaining population of the Javan rhino for the first time. By relating this information to the social and spatial dynamics of the Javan rhino, I hope to help inform management actions to assist conservation of the species. Given historical and modern accounts of Javan rhino vocalisations, I have no doubt the vocal repertoire is much larger than what has been described to date.

How do Javan rhinos communicate?

The Javan rhino conveys information with conspecifics (its own species) via vocal (call) and olfactory (scent/odour) signals including using dung, spray urination and pedal scent gland secretions. It remains unclear if Javan rhino deposits dung in the same spot in piles or middens, early accounts suggested they did (e.g., Sody 1959; Ammann 1985). However, Schenkel and Schenkel-Hulliger (1969b) and Hoogerwerf (1970) didn't believe they did. Because rhino have poor eyesight, they rely on vocalisations, urine, dung deposits and scent to communicate with conspecifics, it is reasonable to assume that Javan rhino call vocabulary can be expanded with further research and investigation, particularly in the still understudied area of Javan rhino courtship and reproductive behaviour.

Both sexes use a flehmen response. The flehmen response is a prominent mammalian behaviour mostly displayed by male hoofed ungulates (perissodactyls e.g., horses and artiodactyls e.g., deer) and felids (family Felidae, e.g., tiger) but poorly understood aspect of reproductive behaviour. On camera trap I have observed this behaviour more frequently in males than females during encounters. A flehmen response occurs when an animal curls back its upper lip, exposing its teeth and usually inhales with closed nostrils. These mouth and facial movements facilitate the transfer of scent particles (pheromones) and other scents to the jacobsen's or vomeronasal organ in the roof of the mouth. During flehmen response it appears as if the animal is grinning or grimacing. Therefore, it appears the core function of flehmen is intraspecific communication. Based on my camera trap video observations, dung deposits communicate information on individual identity and generate investigation from other rhino, including sniffing and periodic flehmen responses.

All my in situ forest observations to date, we have found dung depositions in a variety of situations such as in water, at feeding sites, occasionally on trails and randomly in the habitat but never in the same spot or in a latrine. Social behaviour increases at wallowing sites due to the increased chances of communicating, meeting and interacting with other rhino given wallows are often a shared habitat resource. My camera trap observations indicate a male Javan rhino delivers a single back-foot kick immediately after defecation, presumably to spread the scent and impregnate the foot, it remains unclear if females perform the same behaviour.

Adult greater one-horned rhino swimming in the early morning mist like a submarine on the Rapti River, in Chitwan National Park, Nepal. We quietly observed this animal from a canoe.

Our 'submarine' adult greater one-horned rhino standing up after a swim in the early morning mist on the Rapti River in Chitwan National Park, Nepal. I have this image blown up and framed on the wall at home, I've always loved this image.

White rhino for example, defecate communally in dung piles or middens, where individuals leave olfactory signals and obtain information left by other individuals. Territorial male white rhino are also known to kick dung with their back feet immediately after defecation. During a seven-day visit during 21/09/2018–27/09/2018, to both Chitwan National Park (27°30'0"N, 84°20'0"E) and the adjacent Andrauli Community Forest, near Megauli, Nepal (27.58°30'0" N, 84.21°20'0"E), I observed and recorded the congeneric (same genus as Javan rhino) greater one-horned rhino dung middens in both riverine forest and *Saccharum spontaneum* (family Poaceae) grassland habitats. Most rhino dung middens I observed during my September 2018 visit had germinating seedlings of *Trewia nudiflora* coming through. The rhino fruit tree *Trewia nudiflora* (family Euphorbiaceae), local Nepali name '*bhellur*' is a common riverine forest tree and is also found in pockets of trees occupying *Saccharum* grassland areas established through germination in rhino dung middens. Greater one-horned rhino regularly feed on the fallen fruit which ripens during the monsoon period June–September. *Trewia nudiflora* is not the only plant species to take advantage of dung middens as sites of germination and establishment.

A study by Dinerstein (1991b) recorded 38 species including four trees, five grasses, sixteen shrubs, six herbaceous plants, and seven herbaceous climbers growing at greater one-horned rhino dung middens. Interestingly, after six years (2015–2021) of examining Javan rhino dung in the field, including older depositions, I never observed any plant or seed germination activity occurring, maybe I was just unlucky! A study of the defecation behaviour of the greater one-horned rhino by Bhattacharya and Chakraborty (2016) found 86% of dung middens were situated along major movement pathways. They also discovered single dung depositions were often placed near major pathways, eventually over 80% of these depositions would become dung middens. Greater one-horned rhino is stimulated to defecate by the sight and scent of previously deposited dung and dung middens. This indicates there are clear communication benefits to placing dung deposits in locations where rhinos will investigate.

During my study I only periodically detected Javan rhino dung on movement pathways or tracks, in most cases it was random deposits found in a variety of locations. Other rhino species including white rhino and black rhino also tend to place dung middens in locations frequented by other rhino such as travel pathways, near waterholes and territorial boundaries. This dung midden placement in prominent locations suggests territorial marking, most likely by dominant males, however, both sexes and different age classes are known to use middens also. I suspect dung middens are used not only as territorial markers by dominant males but also as communication hubs. However, just how the different age and sex classes of rhino use middens is a worthy research investigation across all three species (white, black and greater-one horned) that utilise middens in their behavioural repertoire.

An Indochinese rat snake *Ptyas korros* or '*Ular picung*' in the jungle foliage of Ujung Kulon. Found across Southeast Asia, this common, non-venomous species grows to 1.8 metres and feeds on frogs, small mammals, lizards, birds and bird's eggs. I often saw this species.

Behavioural studies (e.g., Owen-Smith 1973; Rachlow et al. 1998; Kretzschmar et al. 2001; Marneweck et al. 2018) have suggested that sex is identifiable via odour. For example, a study by Linklater et al. (2013) discovered both sexes of black rhino examined male dung more frequently than female dung suggesting they were able to determine the sex of conspecifics (same species) from dung odour. Interestingly, animals may also be able to identify the actual age of the depositors via the signals of dung, urine and scent marks. Additionally, Linklater et al. (2013) suggested black rhino are able to identify the dung of adult animals greater than six years old and from sub-adults two to four years old from scent signals alone. Common scent organs found across the Order Artiodactyla (e.g., deer, antelope, giraffe, pigs), and shown to be confined to the genus *Rhinoceros* (Javan and greater one-horned rhino) among the Order Perissodactyla are pedal scent glands (cutaneous glands in their feet). Dinerstein

(2011), suggested pedal scent gland secretions are used to mark territory, home-range and presence. Oestrus females may also be detected by males from scent deposited from pedal scent glands. I support Dinerstein's view. I suspect pedal scent glands are used by both sexes, and may leave an olfactory trail to guide a potential mate, signal reproductive status, an in-oestrus female, or signal dominance, a dominant male could be targeted by a receptive female.

I have observed Javan rhinos urinating in wallows which helps impregnate their bodies with distinctive odours, and males investigating the ground closely near wallows and in rainforest. My observations on camera trap showed Javan rhino would spend considerable time getting mud all over their bodies, especially in their skin folds, which would maximise cooling and increase presentation of scent.

During our visit in September 2018 to Chitwan National Park, Nepal, my partner Tracy and I undertook an early morning (pre 6 am) canoe trip down the Rapti River, it was amazing. We saw many greater one-horned rhino just resting and cooling off in the gentle current of the river. A heavy mist was hanging over the river and we paddled up to a swimming rhino that looked like a submarine just cruising on the surface, it was barely disturbing the surface as it swam. When it reached the shallows, it stood up, spun around, snorted in protest and looked at us from only a few metres away, I was able to take the images above. A wildlife encounter we will never forget! Beyond vocalisation, the 'pub' version of rhino communication is, the boys use 'cologne', the girls use 'perfume'. For example, the boy's scent might say, 'I'm top horn pick me, the girl's scent might say 'okay, follow me and you might get lucky' or, 'no, I'm not interested but, if you behave, I'm happy to share this wallow'. All messaged through scent infused dung or scented urine-soaked mud or vegetation. Not exactly Chanel No. 5, but it does work! In close proximity both sexes would use vocalisations to infer their intentions in a similar way.

Summary table of Javan rhino camera trap video data (2011–2016)

Total no. video clips	Year video recorded	Clip duration (min)	No. clips with calls	Call clip duration (min)
6	2011	3.0	5	2.5
45	2013	22.5	13	6.5
32	2014	16.0	8	4.0
54	2015	27.0	15	7.5
255	2016	127.5	14	7.0
Total 392		183.5	55	27.5

Note: no camera trap data was collected by authorities during the 2012 period.

Summary table of camera trap video Javan rhino call descriptor data (2011–2016).

Call descriptor	No. individual calls	Call frequency band width (Hz–kHz)
Short pant	65	100 Hz–12 kHz
Sigh	32	100 Hz–12 kHz
Snort	2	100 Hz–12 kHz
Sniff-huff	48	100 Hz–14.5 kHz
Long hiss	6	100 Hz–11.5 kHz
Lip vibration	5	100 Hz–5 kHz
Bleat	34	100 Hz–4.5 kHz
Moo-bray	4	100 Hz–12 kHz
Total 8	196 (157 at wallows, 39 in forest)	

Note: no camera trap data was collected by authorities during the 2012 period.

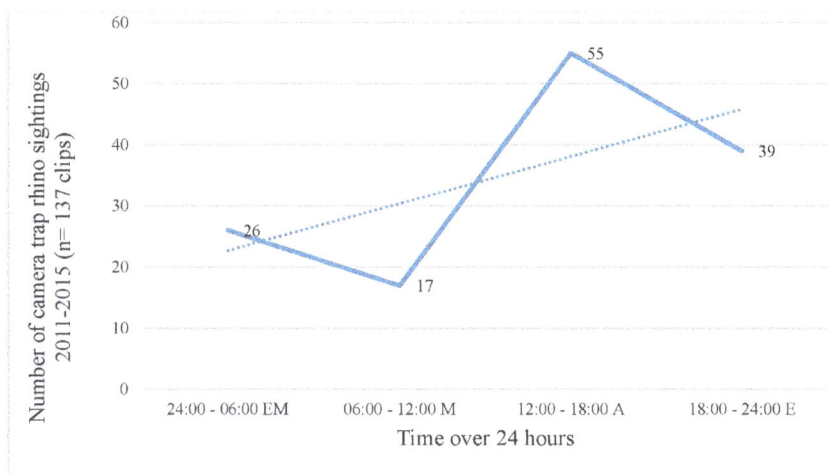

Line graph of Javan rhino activity patterns (time over 24 hrs) EM (early morning); M (morning); A (afternoon); E (evening) of animals from the peninsula area of Ujung Kulon NP.

Using camera trapping in the study of behaviour and conservation

The advent and use of camera trap technology has improved the opportunity to record more animal behaviours. Camera trapping can be a cost-effective, non-invasive method of studying rare and elusive species. Camera traps have been used in Ujung Kulon since 2010 to estimate the population size and structure of the Javan rhino; the most cryptic of all rhino species. The camera traps reduce observer bias, and can operate for extended periods in remote locations and during seasons where access to field sites is limited. They also provide time and location-specific records of multiple species' presence. Camera trapping is particularly useful when studying medium to large terrestrial mammals, as well as critically endangered species that have a very small population size and are therefore difficult to locate in the field.

Direct observation of Javan rhino is extremely difficult due to its rarity and remote rainforest habitat, plus they are naturally vigilant

131

to any disturbance by sound or movement. With exceptional hearing, this species regularly showed 'awareness' of cameras but was not spooked by them. I suspect they could hear the quiet camera mechanism sound emitted when filming. Otherwise, catching them unaware of your presence is extremely unusual! Therefore, camera traps are a valuable remote sensing tool for studying Javan rhino behaviour in the wild.

An obvious weakness in camera trap use is the reliance on the animal being in the cameras field of view, so many behaviours would be missed. All rhino calls were recorded using Bushnell 8-megapixel Trophy CAM HD™ cameras as part of an ongoing monitoring program used by UKNP managers to monitor Javan rhino populations and other endangered species. Across the Ujung Kulon peninsula, 140 cameras have been permanently strategically placed in 35 quadrats, each with 4 cameras, to best capture rhino activity, and each quadrat has been given a coded number and letter, for example, 34AQ.

Each camera was set at a height of 1.7 metres, then angled 10 degrees to cover a field of view out to 5 metres. To reduce disturbance to the rhinos and other animals, the cameras were placed high above rhino eye level with a downward angle that enables capture of details of rhino behaviour. The video camera footage was provided to the author by the UKNP Authority and Indonesian Rhino Foundation due to their clarity of imagery. No camera trap video data was collected by authorities during the 2012 period. Due to the low, dispersed population, access to clear imagery and reliance of animals to move in front of cameras is quite difficult.

The calls and behaviours were captured after reviewing 137 camera trap videos recorded between 2011–2015 examining rhinos occupying the peninsula area of Ujung Kulon and 255 camera trap videos recorded during 2016 from the eastern Gunung Honje area of the park. The cameras were programmed to record sound and imagery both day and night when an animal is in the field of view. The camera video records in 30-second intervals whilst an animal remains in camera vision.

Ujung Kulon NP rangers and rhino protection unit staff collect and download camera memory cards each month (while on routine patrol), except for December and January when the whole park area becomes inaccessible due to monsoonal conditions. In this study, all rhinos were identified only to determine their sex due to individual identification limitations of the video clips.

The Ujung Kulon NP Authority monitors the rhino population across the national park using its network of permanent video cameras and has built up a considerable database of each individual rhino and its identification characteristics. Each video was converted into a sound file using Adobe Audition CC 2015 to create a sonogram of each identified call. The video file was opened in Adobe Audition, sample type was then converted and a sample rate of 32,000 Hz was used with Channel to Mono and Bit Depth of 16 bits. The files were originally recorded in stereo at a sample rate of 48,000 Hz with a 32-bit depth. The file was converted to a mono sample at 32,000 Hz with a 16-bit depth to show the vocal characteristics more clearly.

Calls were then sampled by using the cursor to measure length and frequency of the rhino's vocal. Headphones with a noise-cancelling function are used to listen to calls to ensure good quality sound. A video of the sound recording was made using Microsoft Office PowerPoint and then the video of the rhino was attached to this using Adobe Premiere. The sample rate indicates the number of digital snapshots taken of an audio signal each second and determines the frequency range of an audio file. The higher the sample rate, the closer the shape of the sound wave is to the original waveform. The bit depth determines the dynamic range of the sound wave. Amplitude is shown as intensity of either grey scale or colour. I acknowledge the recorded frequency bandwidth may vary due to the bandwidth range being a function of the recording volume (which could vary based on the rhino distance to the camera trap microphone).

Sonograms of each different call were identified using Adobe Audition CC 2018. Calls were compared to the video vision to ensure they were correct, isolated and saved as wav. files into a new window within Adobe Audition. Individual calls were then opened in Raven Lite 2.0.0™ showing the time (sec) and frequency (kHz) scales. These calls were then converted to a colour scale for clarity and snipped using the snipping tool in Microsoft Office 2016. Images were saved as jpeg files.

Collected data from each video included gender of rhino, age, date, time of day, location, call type, duration of call (sec), frequency of call and behavioural activity. Animals can be identified through several criteria (Griffith 1993), which has been verified as best for use. For example, presence of horns (males only) or absence of horns (females). Horn length in Javan rhino male's averages 25 cm. The sample rate indicates the number of digital snapshots taken of an audio signal each second and determines the frequency range of an audio file. The higher the sample rate, the closer the shape of the sound wave is that to the original waveform. The bit depth determines the dynamic range of the sound wave. Amplitude is shown as intensity of either grey scale or colour. Spectrograms enable a three-dimensional plotting frequency against time, and are useful tool for presenting and visualising sounds. I also used and modified Hazarika & Saikia's (2010) ethogram model developed for the congeneric (same genus) greater one-horned rhino to identify and present the range of behaviours seen on the camera trap videos.

A table has been provided presenting a description of all behaviours seen (e.g., Stevenson & Poole 1976), as well as a flowchart (behavioural catalogue) adapted from Hazarika and Saikia (2010); Cinková and Bičík (2013) and Hockings (2016). Chi-squared (χ^2) tests were used to determine whether there were temporal and seasonal differences in the frequency at which Javan rhino were captured on the camera trap videos. To test whether there was temporal variation, the categories Early Morning (EM, 24:00–06:00), Morning (M, 06:00–12:00), Afternoon (A, 12:00–18:00), and Evening (E, 18:00–24:00) were used. To test for seasonal variation, I used wet season (November–May), and dry season (June–October) observations. I also examined the frequency of sightings in four vegetation types: open broadleaf, dense broadleaf, open broadleaf/arenga palm and dense broadleaf/arenga palm forest. I considered test statistics as significant with P values < 0.05. Additionally, chi-squared (χ^2) analysis was used to determine whether there was any significant statistical variation in the number and frequency of use of vocal descriptors (calls) used.

This was undertaken for each year of camera trap video recordings e.g., 2011. A total of 196 individual calls (2011–2016) were examined. In the peninsula area of Ujung Kulon, I identified several behaviours from 137 videos taken during (2011–2015). Fifty-five video recordings comprising 196 individual calls, identifying eight individual call descriptors with accompanying sonograms (a first for the species), were developed after reviewing 392 camera trap videos (2011–2016), 137 from the peninsula area and 255 from the eastern Gunung Honje section of the park. I identified eight call types from the audio-video data and categorised these in a manner consistent with terms used by previous researchers (e.g., Schenkel & Schenkel-Hulliger 1969a, 1969b; Ammann 1985).

The following eight sonograms identify and describe the characteristics of these new calls:

Sniff-huff. The sniff is a short nasal inhalation, followed by an exhaled huff. Used by both sexes, often used when investigating the environment i.e., sniffing vegetation, or possible scent trails left by conspecifics. Frequency band width range is shorter than the snort or sigh, and ranges between 100 Hz–14.5 kHz, with most calls lasting less than half a second (e.g., 0.2–0.5 sec). Average based on dataset = 0.379 seconds, n=48, mean 0.322; SD ± 0.104.

Bleat. Low-intensity contact call made by calves to females. The bleat call is short, clear and often repeated. Repeated bleats appear to imply urgency or uneasiness i.e., calf wanting to suckle, vocalising vulnerability, or seeking a contact or acknowledgement response from the mother (e.g., sigh or lip vibration). Frequency band width range = 100 Hz–4.5 kHz, n=34, mean 0.293; SD ± 0.091.

Snort. A strong exhaled loud call may infer vocal dominance from adult male or female. The frequency band width range varies between 100 Hz–12 kHz, with a single vocal lasting more than one second (e.g., 1.148 sec), n=2, mean 1.148.

Short pant. A short, often repeated air-sounding call. Circle (brown) indicates soft whistle sound at start of call. May be a contact/ acknowledgement call, possibly infers sexual or dominance status. Recorded only in males to date. The frequency band width range varies between 100 Hz–12 kHz, with most repeated calls lasting less than half a second (e.g., 0.1–0.3 sec). Average based on dataset = 0.260 seconds, n=65, mean 0.278; SD ± 0.122.

Long hiss. An extended single, strong, air-sounding, almost ear-piercing call. May infer a warning/message i.e. I'm with calf or I'm non-reproductive. Only recorded in adult females near approaching males to date. The frequency range varies between 100 Hz–11.5 kHz, with the single call lasting more than half a second (e.g., 0.7–0.8 sec). Average based on dataset = 0.754 seconds, n=6, mean 0.754; SD ± 0.114.

Moo-bray. A repeated single 'bleat-like' call exhibited by the female during courtship. Frequency band width range varies between 100 Hz–12 kHz, with repeated calls lasting on average based on dataset = 0.596 seconds, n=4, mean 0.596; SD ± 0.041.

Sigh. An exhalation call, longer in duration to lip vibration, slow and softer in emphasis, comfort-like and may be used as an acknowledgement, i.e., female response to calf bleat or infers comfort, i.e., resting in a wallow. Lip vibrations occasionally follow the sigh call. Sighs appear to be used mostly as single calls. The frequency range varies between 100 Hz–12 kHz, with most calls lasting less than one second (e.g., 0.2–1.056 sec). Average based on dataset = 0.610 seconds, n= 2, mean 0.685; SD ± 0.285.

Lip vibration. Softer than snort, may be a contact response i.e., from female to calf, or indicate comfort, i.e., when feeding. Lip vibrations appear to be mostly single calls, rarely repeated and may be called after a snort or sigh call. The frequency range varies between 100 Hz–5 kHz, with calls lasting less than one second (e.g., 0.7–0.8 sec). Average based on dataset = 0.810 seconds, n=5, mean 0.987; SD ± 0.166.

Social interaction and behaviour recordings

Altogether 11 behavioural patterns were categorised, and these were related to their daily activities. Additionally, within each behavioural pattern, 11 sub-categories of behaviour were identified. A flow chart behavioural catalogue of both non-breeding and breeding behaviours was developed. The 137 (2011–2015) peninsula area videos (30 sec) = 68.50 minutes of footage. Forty-three videos contained social behaviour with more than one animal = 31.38%, 55 videos contained calls = 40.1% and 100 videos contained only one animal = 73.0%. The 255 (2016) eastern Gunung Honje region videos (30 sec) = 127.50 minutes in total.

Videos taken between (12/11/2016–16/12/2016) recorded the following behaviours: 14 calls, 5.49%, nine (n=9) walking, 3.5%, drinking (n=1), 0.03%, standing (n=2), 0.07%, feeding (n=1), 0.03%, rubbing (on structure), 1.5% and wallowing (n=244), 95.6%. A total of 137 videos were viewed of recorded rhino activity at both wallow and forest areas. Eight wallow sites captured 68 videos, 49.6%, and 23 forest sites captured 69 videos, 50.4%.

Description of behavioural patterns adapted from (Hazarika & Saikia 2010) exhibited by Javan rhino recorded on 137 camera trap videos (2011–2015) in the peninsula area of Ujung Kulon NP.

Behaviour category	Description
Non-breeding	
1) Feeding	Behaviour associated with consumption of vegetation or water and the method for intake of different vegetation types.
Browsing	Involved the consumption of leaves and small twigs from understorey vegetation. Used prehensile upper lip to either bring leaves from short standing vegetation directly into their mouth or to pull a branch down and strip leaves along the length of the branch.
Geophagy	Soil tasting or ingestion of soil by rhino in habitat. For example, was observed on two occasions in wallows. In both cases the animal licked and appeared to eat soil from the edge of a wallow. Followed by a flehmen response.
Drinking	Often drink water when first entering a wallow, may be for thirst, however some animals display a flehmen response. Known to urinate in wallows to impregnate their scent, any new animal entering a wallow could be stimulated to use a flehmen response.
2) Locomotion	Included any behaviour that resulted in the rhino moving from one place to another. The most commonly seen locomotion sub-category was walking.
Walking	Slow movement from one place to another, using the alternate fore and hind limbs simultaneously.
Galloping	Rapid movement from one place to another, where at a point both fore and hind limbs are not touching the ground.

Entering/ wading through water/ mud	Entering or wading through water or mud by the movement from dry land into a body of water or mud.
3) Comfort	Behaviour that showed relaxation or relief to the rhino, whether related to energy levels or relief from ectoparasites and/or the sun. Comfort behaviour patterns were sometimes characterised by a lack of motion within the body.
Resting	Resting was characterised by the lack of physical movement and the rhino was either sitting down or standing motionless.
Rubbing (on structure)	Vigorous rubbing of a section of the rhino's body against a tree stump or tree trunk. May be a form of scent marking, for example, after leaving a wallow impregnated with scent-laden mud and water.
Mud/water wallowing	Rhino lying or standing in the wallow. Animals were either motionless while in the wallow or when lying down often moved and rolled about to cover themselves in mud or water. Rhinos periodically shake their heads allowing mud and water to penetrate the skins folds on the neck.
4) Vigilance	Behaviours which suggested a heightened sense of 'alertness'. Including raised head, scanning with eyes and head, erect ears and moving of ears, likely to determine the source of sound heard.
5) Investigating environment	Scanning of the surrounding environment and sniffing of the ground, either while stationary or while walking along. Sniffing ground could possibly be related to searching for food as suggested by Hazarika and Saikia (2010), with their inclusion of foraging behaviour in their description of feeding behaviour.
6) Defecation	Defecation is rapid and was not on a heap of previous defecation (midden) as has been recorded for other species. Animal gives a single quick back leg kick of the dung post-defecation, presumably impregnating dung on the feet and spreading dung odours.

7) Spray urination	Recorded on two occasions by adult males. May infer male dominance? Unclear if females spray urinates? Involves urine being sprayed backwards across the ground and on vegetation up to and across a three-metre arc.
8) Flehmen response	Recorded on three occasions, twice by adult males and once by an adult female. A flehmen response was displayed after drinking water from a wallow and tasting mud. Rhinos periodically urinate in wallows and impregnate their scent on their bodies.
9) Play behaviour	Only recorded between mothers and young or sub-adult calves. Characterised by play sparring between mother and calf (on both dry land and while in a wallow), young calves running around while the mother fed or displayed vigilant behaviour and mothers and calves running and spinning around to come back together.
10) Non-breeding vocalisation	Several different calls were recorded including a 'bleat' call produced by calves to their mothers, a 'sigh' response by the mothers, a 'sniff-huff', 'short-pant', 'long hiss' and 'snort', 'lip vibration' call made by both sexes.
Breeding	
11) Courtship	Courtship behaviour was seen between males and females and is related to seeking/choosing a mate.
Touching	Male used his head to touch a female on her head and used his horn to rub a female under the neck. Female responded with open-mouth displays and rubbing back against the male. Touching was gentle and non-agonistic and presumed to be a prelude to mating.
Breeding vocalisation	Males approach females with repeated 'short-pant' calls. Female responds with a repeated 'moo-bray' call.

Behaviour Cataloguing of Javan rhino

Non-Breeding

Breeding

1) Feeding
- Browsing
- Drinking
- Geophagy

11) Courtship
- Touching
- Smelling

2) Locomotion
- Walking
- Galloping
- Entering water
- Wading through water/mud

3) Comfort
- Resting
- Sleeping
- Rubbing (on structure)
- Mud wallowing
- Water wallowing

4) Vigilance

5) Investigating environment

6) Defecation

7) Spray urination

8) Play behaviour

9) Vocalization (call)

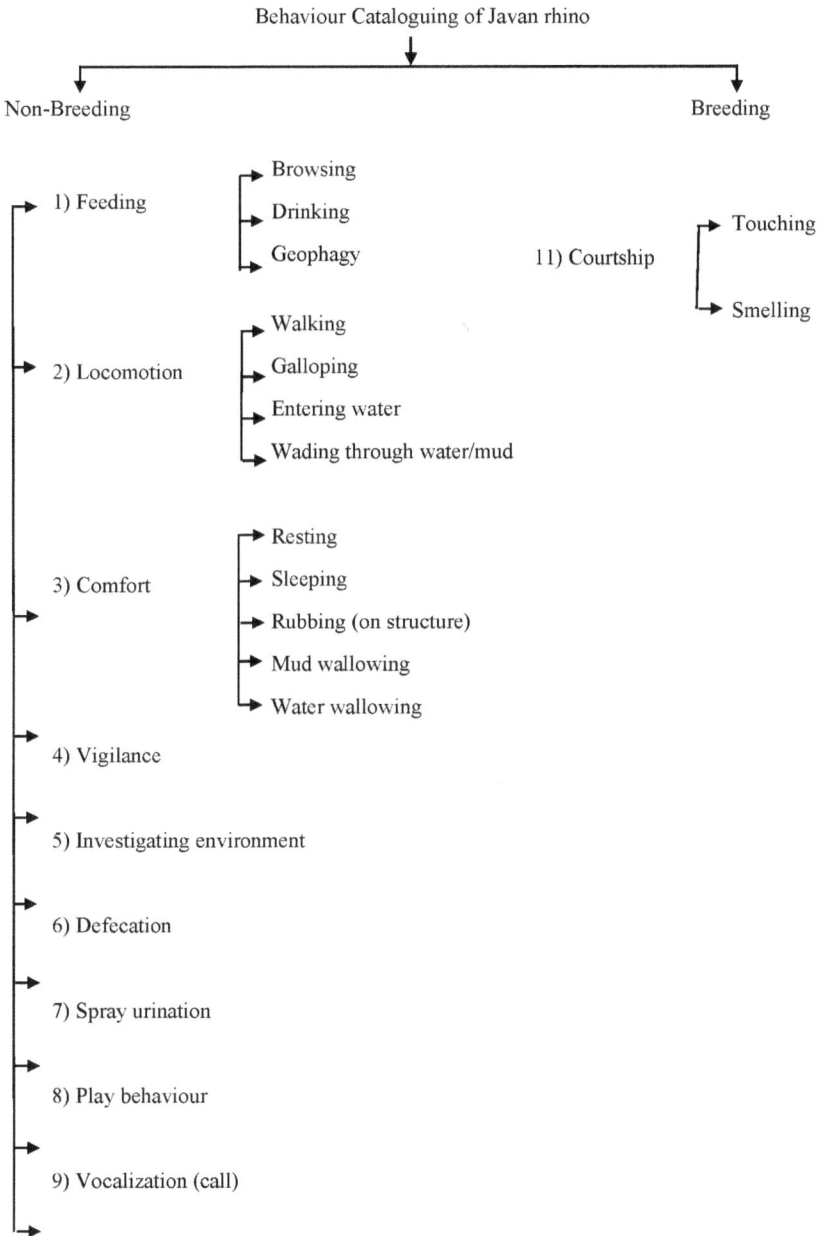

Flowchart of behavioural categories for the Javan rhino. Adapted from Hazarika and Saikia (2010), Cinková and Bicik (2013) and Hockings (2016).

Summary table of Ujung Kulon (western) peninsula rhino population video behaviour observation results 2011–2015 (n = 137 videos).

Variable	Result		% of no. video clips
Season (Wet = Nov–May), (Dry = June–Oct)	Wet season (n=73) Dry season (n=64)		53.28% 46.72%
Habitat where observation occurred	Wallows (n=68) Forest (n=69)		49.6% 50.4%
Vegetation type where observation occurred	Open broadleaf evergreen (n=23) Dense broadleaf evergreen (n=49) Open broadleaf evergreen/arenga palm (n=55) Dense broadleaf evergreen/arenga palm (n=10)		16.78% 35.76% 40.14% 7.29%
Number of individual (vocalisation) calls recorded	Calls from 55 (n=55) videos, comprising 182 (n=182) individual calls (peninsula), 14 (n=14) from eastern Gunung Honje area. Total 196 (n=196)		
Behaviour category, no. and percentage of behaviours recorded on camera traps (2011–2015), n=137 clips	Non-breeding		
	Feeding	Browsing (n=3) Drinking (n=8) Geophagy (n=2)	2.18% 5.83% 1.45%
	Locomotion	Walking (n=64) Galloping (n=1)	46.71% 0.72%
		Entering/wading through water/mud (n=15)	10.94%
	Comfort	Resting/standing/sitting (n=9) Rubbing (on structure) (n=7) Wallowing (mud/water) (n=67)	6.56% 5.10% 48.9%
	Vigilance (n=16)		11.6%
	Investigating environment (n=20)		14.5%
	Defecation (n=1)		0.72%
	Spray urination (n=2) Flehmen response (n=3) Non-breeding play (n=4) Non-breeding calls (n=51) Breeding		1.45% 2.18% 2.91% 37.2%
	Courtship	Touching (neck, chin and head rubbing) (n=1), 0.72% Call (short pant, moo-bray (n=4), 2.91%	

No. of observations (n=138), social context and sex of rhinos	Solitary male (n=72)	52.55%
	Solitary female (n=28)	20.43%
	Female & calf (n=26)	18.97%
	Unknown sex (n=2)	1.45%
	Male & Male (n=1)	0.72%
	Male & female (n=4)	2.91%
	Male, female & calf (n=5)	3.64%
Distance from coast where observation occurred (km)	Mean 1.71; SD ± 1.11	
Distance from nearest waterway from where observation occurred (km)	Mean 0.31; SD ± 0.30	

The wallow sites recorded increased calling and greater diversity by rhinos, including 157 individual calls compared to 39 calls by rhino in forest. Presumably, this is due to increased opportunities to interact with conspecifics at wallow sites, an often-shared habitat feature. For example, at wallows the number of different call recordings, dataset = 16, averaged, mean 3.2; SD ± 1.643.

In forest the number of different call recordings, dataset = 5 averaged, mean 1.25; SD ± 0.5. In forest individual calls recorded included *'sniff-huff'* (n=26), *'short pant'* (n=9) and *'moo-bray'* (n=4). In wallow individual calls recorded included, *'short pant'* (n=58), *'bleat'* (n=23), *'sniff-huff'* (n=15), *'sigh'* (n=30), *'lip vibration'* (n=5), *'snort'* (n=2) and *'long hiss'* (n=6). The statistically significant χ^2 result for the number and frequency of vocalisation (calls) recorded in 2015, may have been due to the uneven observed total data set (n=25) comprising four call descriptors, the largest being *'sniff-huff'* (n=12), *'short-pant'* (n=7), *'lip vibration'* (n=2) and *'moo-bray'* (n=4). The expected or average figure was 6.25.

Table of observations (n = 42) of social behaviour of Javan rhino recorded on camera trap videos (2011–2015) in the peninsula area of Ujung Kulon NP.

Clip # Date Time of day	Location	Gender	Behaviour
MVIV 04,5,8,9,36 03/01/2011 10:02–10:58	Water wallow	Adult female, male calf < two yrs, adult male	Female with calf in wallow, calf bleats, female calls a 'long hiss', male approaches wallow calling a repeated 'short pant', male approaches female produces a flehmen response, all settle together in wallow
MVIV 08,11,12,68 31/03/2013 19:08–20:50	Water wallow	Adult female with male calf < two yrs	Female calls a repeated 'sniff-huff', enters wallow, drinks water and produces a flehmen response, calf at edge of wallow repeats a 'bleat' call, both animals settle and rest in wallow with eyes closed
MVIV 10,11,12,13, 14,15,41 01/04/2013 02:21–02:24	Water wallow	Adult female with male calf < two yrs, adult male	Female and calf enter a wallow, female calls a repeated 'sniff-huff', calf 'bleats', female and calf head rub each other and begin wallowing. Male approaches wallow calling a repeated 'short pant', all animals settle together in wallow
MVIV 05, 6 14/04/2013 22:06–22:07	Water wallow	Adult female and sub-adult male calf and adult male	Female and calf approach wallow with adult male present. Female calls repeated 'sniff-huffs', adult male responds with 'short pants. Female and calf leave, adult male remains then emerges from wallow
MVIV 39,40,47 23/05/2013 16:27–16:34	Mud wallow	Adult female with male calf < two yrs, adult male	Female enters wallow, drinks, produces a flehmen response and call a 'lip vibration'. Male calf enters behind female, both lay down and rest, then wallow and head rub each other
MVIV 12 19/07/2013 17:51	Forest	Two sub-adult males	Two sub-adult males walking in forest together, no agonistic behaviour was observed
MVIV 4,5,6 25/11/2013 18:56–18:58	Mud wallow	Adult female and sub-adult male calf	Female and sub-adult male calf wallowing together, with occasional head rubbing behaviour

MVIV 20 03/04/2014 23:54	Forest	Adult female with female calf < one yrs	Female with young calf sits down, calf calls a repeated 'bleat', tries to suckle, female sighs in response
MVIV 61 12/10/2014 08:25	Forest	Adult female and sub-adult female calf	Female with sub-adult female calf enter forest clearing, demonstrate vigilance behaviour, then walk off
MVIV 89 27/11/2014 11:00	Mud wallow	Adult female and sub-adult female calf	Female with sub-adult female calf leave wallow, calf calls repeated 'bleats', female 'sighs' in response, both show vigilance behaviour
MVIV 007 09/03/2015 17:27	Forest	Adult male and adult female	Adult male and female in courtship display. Male neck rubs and rubs horn under the chin of female. Male calls a repeated short pant, female play bites male, has open mouth and repeats a 'moo-bray' call. Courtship was gentle and non-agonistic
MVIV 023,25 05/06/2015 03:33–03:34	Forest	Adult female and sub-adult unknown calf	Female with calf stands in forest, showing vigilance behaviour, then both walk off
MVIV 10,11,12,13 24/06/2015 16:26–16: 29	Mud wallow	Adult female with female calf < two yrs, adult male	Female and calf leave wallow, female calls a repeated 'sniff-huff', both animals stand and show vigilance behaviour, calf calls a repeated 'bleat'
MVIV 08 27/07/2015 15: 17	Forest	Adult female and sub-adult female calf	Female with calf walking in forest
MVIV 4,3,5,7,8,9 07/08/2015 13:15–13:26	Forest	Adult female with female calf < one yrs	Female with young female calf enter forest clearing, showing vigilance behaviour, then walk off

145

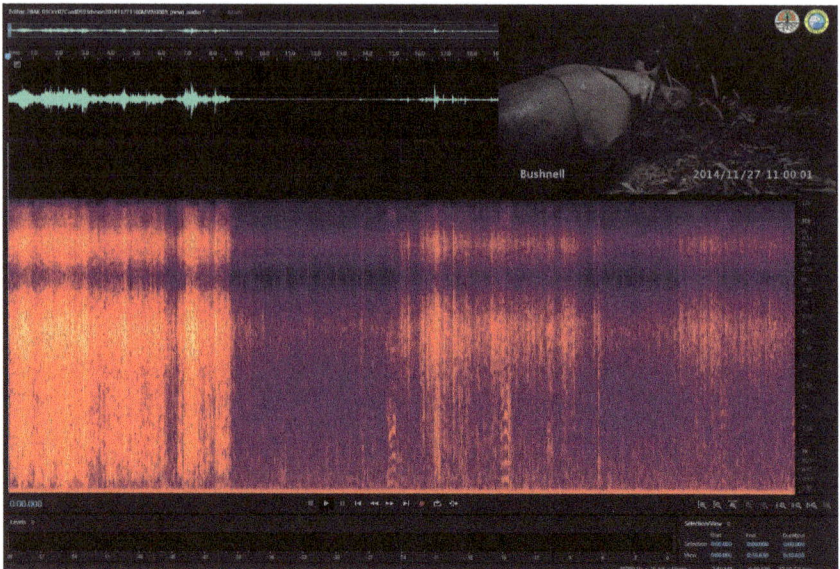

Example of a spectrogram. Emerging from a wallow, a Javan rhino calf, following its mother, vocalises (calls); the mother calls in response. The segmented vertical bands represent the call, wide bands indicate longer call duration, taken from camera trap video recorded on 27th November 2014. (Night 11.00 pm). Spectrogram was created using Microsoft Office PowerPoint, then the camera trap video (courtesy of the Ujung Kulon National Park Authority, and Indonesia's Ministry of Environment and Forestry) is attached using Adobe Premiere. GBCMA's Jo Deretic put this spectrogram together, thanks Jo Jo!

Sonogram images of eight rhino vocalisations (calls) include: *sniff huff, bleat, snort, short pant, long hiss, moo-bray, sigh and lip vibration.* Sonograms were created using Adobe Audition CC 2015.

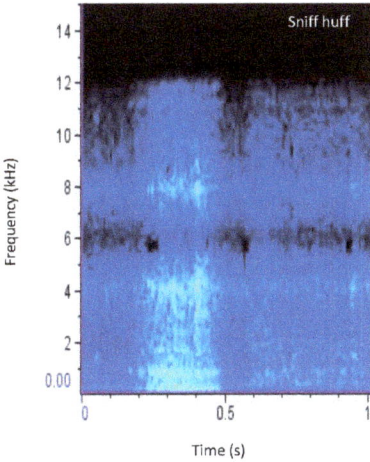

Sniff-huff. The sniff is a short nasal inhalation, followed by an exhaled huff.

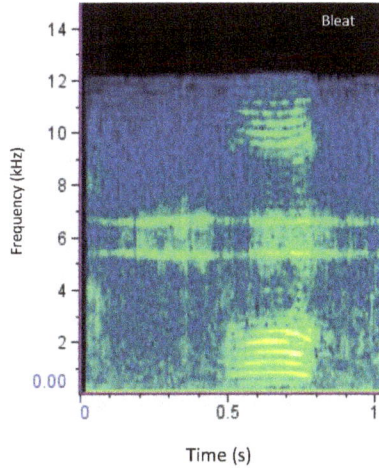

Bleat. Low-intensity contact call made by calves to females.

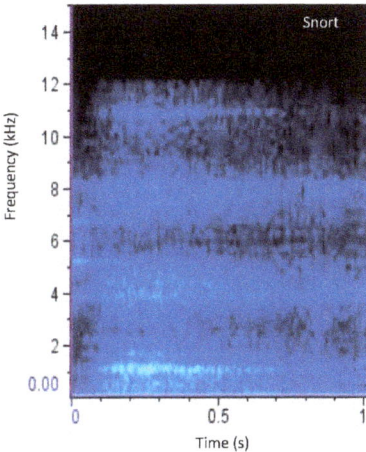

Snort. A strong exhaled loud call may infer vocal dominance from adult male or female.

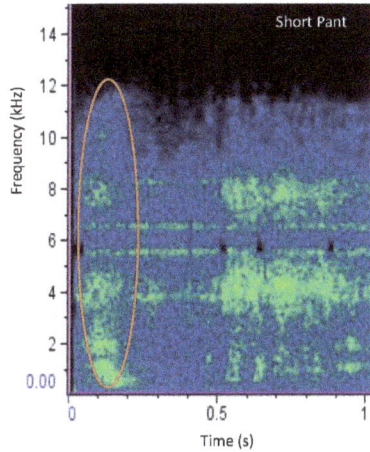

Short pant. A short, often repeated air-sounding call.

147

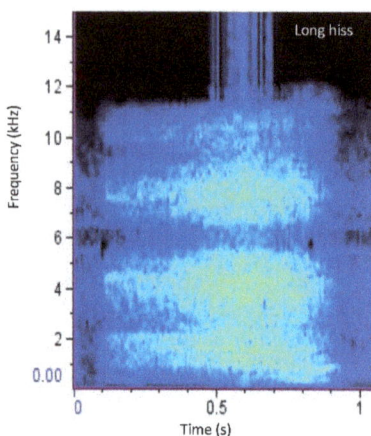

Long hiss. An extended single, strong, air-sounding, almost ear-piercing call.

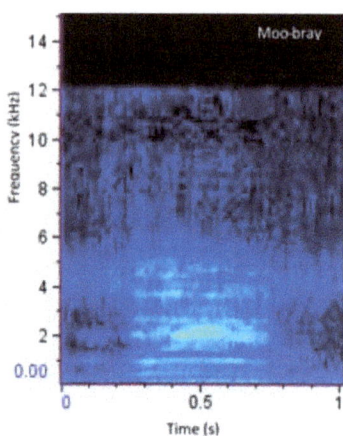

Moo-bray. A repeated single 'bleat-like' call exhibited by the female during courtship.

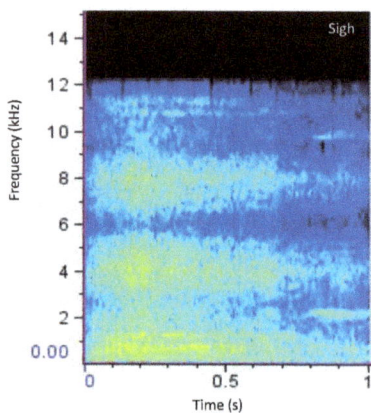

Sigh. An exhalation call, longer in duration to lip vibration, slow and softer in emphasis, comfort-like and may be used as an acknowledgement i.e., female response to calf bleat or infers comfort e.g., resting in a wallow.

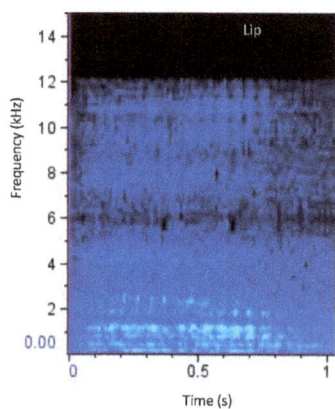

Lip vibration. Softer than snort, may be a contact response i.e., from female to calf, or indicate comfort e.g., when feeding.

148

Social behaviour of Javan rhino, what have we learnt?

Research, specifically on Javan rhino social behaviour and communication has been limited to date, due to their rarity, cryptic nature and highly protected status. There remain significant data gaps especially in understanding the reproductive repertoire of Javan rhino due mostly to lack of direct observation, the use of camera traps has improved this situation. Only limited insight was recorded during early accounts (e.g., Hoogerwerf 1970; Ammann 1985), and, the very small size, and isolation of the only extant Javan rhino population, continues to makes it a difficult species to study.

A study by Ammann (1985) considered it likely that there are dominant and subordinate Javan males, as in greater one-horned rhino, and that dominant male's occupied territories and sprayed urine to mark them significantly more than did subordinate males. The greater one-horned rhino is known to form dominance hierarchies. Adult male black, white and greater one-horned rhino are mostly solitary, with sub-adult males often clustering together to avoid pressure from dominant males. This study has shown both male and female Javan rhino to have a mostly solitary existence. Social behaviour increases at wallowing sites due to the increased chances of communicating, meeting and interacting with other rhinos given wallows are often a shared habitat resource. There was a noticeable increase in the frequency and diversity of calling at wallows compared to in forest habitat. For example, rhinos used three or more calls at wallows compared to one or more calls in forest. The most used call by rhinos in forest was the *'sniff-huff'*. This call is used by animals when investigating the environment. Females in forests kept in contact with calves using the *'bleat'* call and females responding with a *'sigh'* call. In and around wallows the *'short pant'* was the most used vocal. Adult males used the *'short pant'* to announce their presence and communicate with females. The *'lip vibration'* and *'sigh'* were also used by both sexes in wallows. Both calls appear to indicate comfort or enjoyment.

Adult males were observed to regularly visit wallows to determine female sexual receptivity. This was done either by approaching an in situ female vocally or by flehmen response. A flehmen response was also used by both sexes after drinking wallow water or when tasting or ingesting soil or mud, presumably determining the sex, reproductive and possible dominance status of other wallow users. Females with calves were noticeably more vigilant when approaching wallows, vigilance which heightened in the presence of males, often resulting in the female and calf leaving altogether. This same heightened vigilance behaviour was shown by females entering clearings, particularly with young calves, noting Javan calves follow behind the female when moving. Sumatran and black rhino calves also follow behind the female. White and greater one-horned rhino calves walk in front of the female. The calf *'bleat'* contact call and female response *'sigh'* call are not vocally loud. This may be due to the risk of loud calls attracting the attention of predators, such as Javan leopard, or the pack-hunting Javan dhole. Historically, Javan tiger (*Panthera tigris sondaica*) may have preyed on young Javan rhino.

It is worth noting Javan rhino may have lived in more social and group behaviour settings than the current low wild numbers indicate. Today's grouping behaviour is most likely marginalised relative to what it once was. This is reflected in many early accounts which speak of a more social and gregarious nature and large aggregations (e.g., Horsfield 1824; Deuve & Deuve 1962, 1964; Groves 1967; Schaller et al. 1990; Santiapillai et al. 1993a, 1993b). Historically, Javan rhino inhabited the productive lowland areas due to the availability and proximity of water and food resources, an attraction factor which would have made them easier to see and hunt. Groves (1967) suggested, at least in Java, Javan rhino may have existed in high local concentrations and was common enough in the 18th century to be actually considered a pest, and for government endorsement of its hunting. Therefore, it is reasonable to assume in quality habitat the Javan rhino may have behaved and lived a similar existence to greater one-horned rhino, and its current social behaviour is most likely an artefact of its confinement and adaptation to the conditions of Ujung Kulon.

What is the social structure of the Javan rhino?

Based on camera trap observations, adult male and females without calves are almost always solitary. Adult females with calves do not appear to form associations with other individuals regardless of sex and age. Sub-adult males may form groups of two individuals, these pairings may occupy peripheral areas of dominant male home-ranges. Presumably, sub-adult males form these groupings to increase their ability to detect and be protected from dominant males. Sub-adult greater one-horned rhino are known to form loose associations living around the edges of a dominant male's territory. The social structure of Javan rhino has similarities to other rhino species. For example, adult males of the other four rhino species are usually solitary outside of breeding events. Female white, black and greater one-horned rhino may congregate together in good habitat and foraging areas. Male greater one-horned rhino form dominance hierarchies and will defend areas where females congregate. Sumatran rhinos are mostly solitary except for females with young.

What are the intraspecific interactions that occur among Javan rhinos?

Female Javan rhinos with calves maintain the strongest social bond and social interaction. Adult male Javan rhinos regularly visit wallowing sites to monitor visiting females for sexual receptivity as well as for thermoregulatory purposes. Solitary Javan males and females would periodically drink and 'taste' soil or mud at wallows, often followed by a flehmen response. I have observed, on camera trap video, females with calves being cautious and vigilant around wallows, particularly with males present. Wallowing females are noticeably vigilant and will respond vocally to unwanted male attention. If uninterested, females would vocalise an ear-piercing *'long hiss'* warning call to males either waiting in a wallow or approaching a resting female with or without a calf.

Male rhinos are known to engage in mate guarding behaviour, following females until they come into oestrus and will tolerate close approach and physical contact with other males. For example, territorial male white rhinos are known to form attachments with females coming into oestrus approximately one to two weeks prior to mating. During this period, the male will pay close attention to the female and try and restrict her from leaving his territory. Based on this (Owen-Smith 1973) behavioural data it supports the fact that males are able to detect the onset of oestrus from dung or urine. A study by Grün (2006) on white rhino supports this, where males were recorded spending time investigating dung deposits of breeding females, suggesting the identification of female oestrus signals. It remains unproven, however, plausible that Javan males would engage in mate guarding behaviour.

Infanticide has been recorded in greater one-horned rhino. Dinerstein (2003), noted a radio-collared dominant male killed a young calf that it had not sired. The unexpected loss of a calf would stimulate the female's oestrus cycle, an opportunity that the infanticidal dominant male could benefit from. It remains unproven if Javan rhino males engage in infanticide behaviour.

Female greater one-horned rhino females in oestrus urinate frequently; and are often closely followed and monitored by males that test the female's reproductive status by tasting her urine, which is then followed by a flehmen response. I have observed on camera video male Javan rhino using flehmen response at wallow sites to determine the sexual receptivity of in-situ females. Until receptive, females may repeatedly drive males away with mock charges and other defensive behaviours. Both Laurie (1978) and Dinerstein (2003) confirmed in their studies that greater one-horned rhino engaged in aggressive combat, which is periodically fatal, to establish dominance and gain access to oestrus females. In Dinerstein's (2003) research he found breeding activity in greater one-horned rhinos is socially delayed in young adult males due to older, and stronger males excluding them from grazing areas where breeding females often reside. Both Laurie (1978) and Dinerstein (2003) observed that the sharp lower incisors, rather than the horn, inflicted injuries. Presumably, the Javan rhino who also possesses these sharp lower incisors can do similar injuries in dominance and courtship activities. I have observed on camera trap video, incisor slash injuries on the side, flanks and heads of females, presumably because of courtship chases. All three Asian rhino species use their tusks (lower outer mandibular incisors) in combat between breeding males, to control breeding females, and females use them to defend their calves from males.

What specific calls do adult male, adult female, sub-adult male, sub-adult female and calves exhibit and in what contexts?

Adult male Javan rhinos specifically use *'short pant'* calls to approach females. Males and females *'sigh'* and *'lip vibrate'* when resting, which appears to indicate comfort or pleasure. For example, rhino entering and settling into a wallow induces the *'sigh'* and *'lip vibration'* call. Interestingly, females also *'sigh'* in response to a calf's *'bleat'* call. When walking and travelling mobile adult males *'sniff-huff'* when investigating the environment. Snorting appears to be the vocal response to a disturbance; it appears to infer dominance and is used by both sexes.

The *'moo-bray'* call is used by adult females during courtship in response to an interested male's *'short pants'* and is complimented by gentle horn rubbing on the head and under the chin of the female by the male. Females with calves respond to calf *'bleats'* with a *'sigh'*. There appears to be no difference between the calls of sub-adult male and female animals and adult animals. Earlier studies by Ammann (1985) and Schenkel and Schenkel-Hulliger (1969a, 1969b) described several calls not recorded in this study, however, both authors were unclear which sex produced the call. These calls including *'neigh'*, a *'loud blowing whistle'*, and *'shriek'*, a possible response to a threat. Therefore, it is reasonable to assume the Javan rhino call vocabulary can be expanded with further research and investigation, particularly in the still understudied area of Javan rhino courtship and reproduction behaviour. Male rhinos will use the *'snort'* vocal to infer annoyance or dominance.

Comparison of Javan rhino vocalisation (call) to other rhino species

All five-rhino species are known to vocalise through a range of calls and sounds. White, black, greater one-horned and Sumatran rhinos are known to contain infrasonic properties (having frequencies below those of audible sounds i.e., < 16 Hz). All five species emit similar types of calls, for example, the *'snort'* call, which may infer annoyance, possible dominance and agonistic responses. In black rhino, the *'snort'* call may have three contexts. Firstly, the *'snort'* is used as a general call when disturbed, secondly a *'hollow snort'* is used when listening and thirdly an *'aggressive snort'* is emitted in agonistic situations. Calves of each species use similar contact calls to stay in contact with females. For example, black rhino females and calves stay connected using a *'mew'* call. Javan rhino calves emit a *'bleat'* to which the female responds with a *'sigh'*. Calves of greater one-horned rhino stay in contact by emitting a *'moo-grunt'*. Just exactly when and in what context rhino resort to emitting infrasound signals remains to be determined, including if Javan rhino use infrasonic signalling at all.

Table of vocalisation (call) comparison reported in literature for the five living rhino species.

Species	Call description	References
Black rhino *Diceros bicornis*	mew, roar, snort, aggressive snort, growl, begging call, wonk, mmwonk	Goddard (1967) Frame & Goddard (1970) Hillman-Smith & Groves (1994) Budde & Klump (2003) Dinerstein (2003, 2011)
Greater one-horned rhino *Rhinoceros unicornis*	snort, honk, bleat, squeak-pant, moo-grunt, roar	Laurie (1978, 1982) Laurie et al (1983) Hazarika & Saikia (2010) Dinerstein (2003, 2011)

Javan rhino *Rhinoceros sondaicus*	neigh, bleat, loud blowing whistle, snort, lip vibration, roar, sniff-huff, moo-bray, long hiss, sigh, short pant	Schenkel & Schenkel-Hulliger (1969a,1969b) Hoogerwerf (1970) Ammann (1985) Groves & Leslie Jr (2011) Wilson (2021)
Sumatran rhino *Dicerorhinus sumatrensis*	humming, snort, whistle-bray, squeal, squeak, grunt, blow, eep, wail, whistle-blow	Groves & Kurt (1972) Van Strien (1986) Muggenthaler et al. (2003)
White rhino *Ceratotherium simum*	squeal, grunt, snort, pant, whine, threat, puff, snarl, grouch, groan, hoarse, hic, shriek, gruff squeal	Groves (1972) Owen-Smith (1975) Van Gyseghem (1984) Dinerstein (2003, 2011) Cinková (2013) Cinková & Policht (2014)

African elephants (*Loxodonta africana*) are known to use infrasound calling to maintain group cohesion and to find a mate. The landscape in which a rhino lives may influence the use of vocalisation as a form of communication. For example, white rhinos live in open woodland and grassland habitats, are the most social rhino species and have a highly developed social system. It has been suggested by Policht et al. (2008), that white rhino may be using a repeated or pulsed contact call pant (unique to the species) for long-distance communication in open environments that is able to compensate for issues such as wind disturbance. The features of habitat (e.g., forest) and landscape (e.g., mountains) creating some form of acoustic distortion has been identified for some time.

Due to the humid rainforest environment, both Javan and Sumatran rhinos occupy wallows year-round, unlike other rhino species, and therefore, these sites are likely more important for interaction and communication for these species. Based on the examined camera trap video footage, my research has shown Javan rhino calling increases at and near wallowing sites, an often-shared habitat resource, hence the presumed need for closer vocal communication.

Future questions on the habitat soundscape of Ujung Kulon

The acoustic environment of Ujung Kulon in relation to Javan rhino communication poses several questions for future work. Are Javan rhinos calling more at wallows due to better acoustic properties at these sites? Or does calling increase because of the shared wallowing opportunity to interact, or monitor a visiting animal's reproductive or dominance status? In Ujung Kulon, wallows are often well concealed, typically have good canopy cover and the wallow itself is often situated in basin-like areas that hold and retain water. As these wallow sites are structurally different to adjacent rainforest areas, do they perform acoustically better?

Every environment has its own acoustic characteristics for sound transmission, and a consequent daily distribution of ambient noise. It has been suggested by Morton (1975) and Brown and Handford (2000) that calls are expected to be more stereotyped in closed than in open habitats, since the availability of the visual channel is restricted, and vocal delivery conditions are relatively stable in closed habitats such as rainforest.

Javan rhino social interaction and communication conservation considerations

The recorded calls highlight the importance of the knowledge gap regarding Javan rhino communication and presents fertile ground to build further understanding of Javan rhino ecology and social dynamics. Because there are very few direct observations of Javan rhinos this makes comparisons difficult. Future research in this area should focus on expanding the database of recordings and increase our understanding of the function of described calls and any calls yet to be described.

I acknowledge the importance of wallows as key habitat features and communication sites. Based on the dataset I recorded a greater individual number and increased diversity of calls at and near wallows. Wallows are important sites not only for communication but for thermoregulation also. I recorded animals utilising wallows for extended periods up to and greater than six hours per day. Any future planned translocations will need to factor in release sites that have good proximity to water and conditions that favour the maintenance of long-term wallows.

Recognition and understanding of the information that can be obtained by recordings of Javan rhino calls and videos showing a range of other behaviours is critical and is amplified when the population is so low. As demonstrated by Linklater et al. (2013) and Cinková and Policht (2016), the manipulation of chemical signals in dung and urine, and calls can be useful conservation tools. For example, translocated Javan rhinos could be stimulated to reduce stress and modify behaviour by using familiar or unfamiliar urine-impregnated water and mud at wallows, dung and playback call recordings.

A data gap remains regarding how important and what function pedal scent gland secretions present. Do females emit a scent trail when ready to mate? Do males release scent that allows females to find them? Both species of *Rhinoceros* (Javan and greater one-horned) possess pedal scent glands, how these species use pedal scent gland (cutaneous glands in their feet) secretions in their communication repertoire remains unclear. At present, our most useful guide to understanding how Javan rhinos communicate is to compare calls and communication data from its more widely studied congener, the greater one-horned rhino.

There are consequences for threatened species such as Javan rhino with long birth intervals that lower the reproductive rate (long gestation) and their recovery. The management issue of older, possibly infertile dominant males consorting with females to the detriment of younger more fertile males reducing the birth rate. For example, greater one-horned rhino produces calves at a rate of one every 2.5 years. Presumably, this is due to females needing to be a certain body weight, so they can withstand the rigours of male interest in courtship or dominance-related behaviour. Whilst unproven, I suspect Javan rhinos reproduce and calve at a similar rate. Protected and natural areas rapidly decline as human populations and the occupation of habitat landscapes expand and impact on ecological processes. This negative ecological impact trend is often seen in developing countries where urbanisation and human settlement growth occurs. Reducing human-induced adult mortality (e.g., hunting or habitat reduction) is a vital component to conservation and recovery. Due to their longevity, slow reproductive rate, many animals will suffer continued population decline if excessive hunting, poaching or other forms of impact are not brought under control.

Home-range size varies across rhino species and is dependent upon habitat quality and carrying capacity. For example, Namibian desert-dwelling black rhino may range 500 km² compared to the productive floodplains of Nepal's Royal Chitwan National Park where greater one-horned rhino ranges vary between 2.9 km² for females and 3.3 km² for males. This valuable data highlights the species' requirement for large-sized habitat areas able to cater for the needs of both male and female home-ranges and the climatic ranges within, key factors in any future proposed translocation efforts.

Wherever possible male Javan rhinos should be monitored, particularly older males who may still hold dominance, however, may be past reproductive potency e.g., low sperm count. I suspect older, larger and more experienced males may be dominating and guarding reproductive-aged females and excluding younger potentially more sexually potent males from female access. This issue has been recorded in the congeneric greater one-horned rhino. Future translocations could be trialled using older past reproductive-aged males.

There is a need for active management of Javan rhino to keep population densities lower and at more productive levels. For female rhino, the age at first reproduction can be an impediment given it takes time for a population to rebound and respond. A study by Dinerstein (2003) estimated the greater one-horned rhino female's age at first breeding in one population at 7 to 7.5 years, presumably Javan rhinos have similar age at first breeding results. With low numbers only a few Javan females may be reproductively active at any given time. Presumably, Javan rhino longevity as in other rhino species may compensate for the slower population recovery time, or at minimum reduce the disadvantage when compared to the rebounding ability of many small mammals. Under ideal conditions and in good habitat, Dinerstein (2003) suggests rhinos could produce a calf every 2.5 years. The current lack of accurate knowledge of Javan rhino age at first breeding and interbirth interval is a significant data gap and worthy of investigation. The Sumatran rhino as evergreen forest dwellers use a system of trails through their habitat, that includes access to salt and mineral deposits. My observations suggest Javan rhinos periodically use trails but often move and forage well off trail. There are no obvious salt or mineral licks in Ujung Kulon. I suspect rhinos get their salt and minerals from salt-sprayed coastal vegetation, or possible periodic ingestion of sea water, and from mineral rich vegetation. Although unproven salt and mineral rich vegetation areas may be sites of communication given there is a biological need for rhino to visit these areas.

Value of camera trapping in recording social interaction and vocalisation

Camera trapping is an emerging remote sensing tool used to study wildlife, especially for species that are endangered or difficult to observe. There are several advantages to camera trapping. Furthermore, the cameras can also run for extended periods of time in remote locations that are difficult for people to access and they provide unambiguous records of the species present and the date and time of detection. A key strength of using camera traps to study a species such as Javan rhino is it's a cost-effective and non-invasive method of sampling which eliminates observer bias. Animals are not exposed to unnecessary stress and reduces any impact on behaviours displayed. The terrain in Ujung Kulon National Park is difficult with limited opportunities for direct observation—the use of cameras is practical. Additionally, cameras also capture the movement and behaviour of other species, data which can be valuable to gain understanding of broader species ecology, behaviour and habitat use. From a translocation perspective, cameras would be valuable tool to monitor moved populations. For example, translocated animals could be checked for their movements i.e., spatial distribution, assess health and record any behaviour, identify potential predators or competitors, the activity patterns and use of key habitat features such as wallows.

The advent of camera trap technology improves individual recognition, and captures behaviour, using Griffith's (1993) identification criteria (mark-recapture), which has been verified as an effective ID criterion, and the addition of date and time capture provided by camera imagery. This technology will assist in identifying the individual animals, activity patterns (date/ time of day), visitation frequency (day/month) and behaviour in wallows and in other landscape contexts. This photo identification technique has been found to be a reliable censusing methodology.

In this study I have found that camera trap data can provide elements of the necessary information required to determine the suitability of potential translocation sites. The camera trap data highlighted coastal areas are frequently used by Javan rhino and that wallows are important sites for communication. While there has been planning to translocate Javan rhino since at least 2007, continued challenges remain in identifying a suitable translocation site, among other issues, has delayed the process. In this study I have shown that camera trap video data can be used to increase understanding of the Javan rhino ecology and behaviour which can help inform conservation management decisions. While the current camera video recordings are valuable for rhino identification and for conducting regular population censuses, the provision of more cameras at wallow sites will likely increase the number of records of behaviours and interactions that are relevant to informing conservation decisions.

Of course, in spite of all my regular exciting trips to Ujung Kulon, I still had my University of Queensland PhD obligations and regular check-ins with my supervisors. Over my journey, there were three main milestones to work through and achieve. At around the two-year mark into my studies, the first was my PhD confirmation. This essentially is to document and present on what the PhD proposal looks like, its aims, expectations, a research plan, methods, proposed timetable, budget, required skills, list of chapters and possible papers for publication and deliver an oral presentation to the faculty. This part I always enjoyed, I was already building up a significant body of photographic and research experience, and at least I thought great subject matter! Also, I've always enjoyed sharing my experiences! In most cases whenever I'd visit the University of Queensland St Lucia Campus in Brisbane, I was able to provide a good update and presentation of my progress.

Once your confirmed, the next milestone is a mid-candidature review, for me this happened at about the three-year mark, essentially documenting and presenting where you're at with your research plan, what's been completed and what's remaining to complete, plus a presentation to the faculty.

The final milestone is your thesis review, where your supervisors review a close-to-completed thesis, provide feedback and you get the opportunity to make any recommended adjustments. This occurs roughly 3 months before final submission, and again you get the chance to present to the faculty. I found this process quite rewarding and confronting, after many years of research, my work was being reviewed by experts!

Tragically, in late 2019, and early 2020, the covid beast was seriously impacting the world, and Indonesia suffered terribly, I lost many friends. National park rangers, rhino protection staff and many villagers and their extended families that I had gotten to know over my journey were lost to the virus, it was devastating. Tragically, in early April 2020, my dear friend Dr Widodo Sukohadi Ramono (04/04/1945–24/12/2020), after a long hospital fight, was taken by Covid. Widodo devoted his life to Asian rhino conservation and was pivotal to the support I needed through my PhD thesis journey. Widodo leaves a wife and two daughters, he was 75.

A year later the Asian rhino conservation community lost a very experienced advocate. In late 2021, I lost my good friend,

Mohamad '*Aphuy*' Syamsudin, senior ranger with the Ujung Kulon National Park Authority (25/10/1975–08/12/2021). Aphuy gave unwavering support to my PhD studies and actively coordinated park staff in support of my field work. I couldn't have completed my doctorate without him and will always be grateful, we were good mates. Aphuy was only 46 years old, taken by a heart attack, he leaves a wife and two daughters.

At this point it's worth acknowledging that undertaking a PhD is more than just writing a thesis. On your journey, whether you like it or not, you get exposed to people and situations you have never dealt with before. For example, I've had a lifelong struggle with mathematics, whether I liked it or not, I had to learn advanced statistics and apply it to my work, I couldn't fight it. So, I ended up sitting in front of various 'how to' presentation/YouTube videos showing me how to run, for example an ANOVA analysis, amazingly, you can teach an old dog new tricks! I had to learn spatial mapping, develop scientific writing skills, expand my knowledge from general computer to more advanced use, writing and getting peer-reviewed papers published, discovered diplomacy skills I never thought I had. I managed to catch and photograph new species of wildlife, negotiate with public servants so I could work and study in a foreign country, drop the odd 'needed' inducement, avoid saltwater crocodile, cobra, the list goes on, am I tempting you to do a PhD? You should. It will change your life!

Threats to survival, understanding the arenga palm challenge

When you spend significant time moving around Ujung Kulon, it dosent take long before you witness first hand the impact and dominance of arenga palm on the rhinos habitat. I was keen to incorporate some good understanding of arenga palm impacts and came up with Chapter 4 of my thesis *'Understanding the implications of Arenga palm (Arenga obtusifolia) dominance for the conservation and management of Javan rhino'.* This palm was taking over large sways of rainforest habitat and turning it into a monoculture, not healthy for rhino or many other species. The focal area of this study within the park was the eastern

162

Gunung Honje region of Ujung Kulon, situated at the base of the Gunung Honje massif (620 m). This area was selected due to its mix of monoculture arenga palm, healthy rainforest and access for monitoring. The landscape ecology of the eastern Gunung Honje region of the park was described by Hommel (1987) as three distinct landscapes. These include limestone plateau—arenga slopes and dissected plateaus; coastal plains—Syzigium plain; and Calcareous sandstone beach ridges and sand dunes—Dendrocinide beach ridge and sand dunes. The climate of Ujung Kulon is tropical with a seasonal mean average rainfall of 3250 mm, mean temperature range of 25–30°C and relative humidity of 65–100%. Rainfall is typically heaviest between December and January, with a drier period occurring between May and September. Rainfall and temperature patterns in Ujung Kulon are remarkably stable and even throughout the year.

Arenga palm *Arenga obtusifolia* or '*Langkap*' dominating rainforest habitat in Ujung Kulon National Park.

163

In April–May 2016, in collaboration with the Ujung Kulon National Park Authority, Indonesian Rhino Foundation (NGO) and community members we selected and manually cleared 15 one ha plots of predominantly monoculture (75–80% crown cover) arenga palms within the 5,100 ha Javan Rhino Study and Conservation Area (JRSCA), locally known as *'Jarhisca'* in the eastern section of UKNP. We also set up 15 one ha control sites with similar features.

Local community was recruited from the 19 villages living adjacent to the park to manually clear each site due to World Heritage and Ujung Kulon National Park Authority restricts using any form of herbicide such as isopropyl ammonium glyphosate, an active component of modern weed treatments (e.g., Round-Up™) in the park. So, manual control it is!

Teams of ten local community members would cut palms by chainsaw and hand saw and, in most cases, remove fallen palms from each site often at densities up to 650–750 palms/per ha. Wherever possible arenga palms with fruits were carefully removed after cutting due to risk of regrowing through seed spillage or dispersal. Where possible palm roots were also dug up and removed to prevent root regrowth.

During September 2016, five months after site clearing, I visited each site and marked out quadrats. A Garmin GPS Maps 62 sc GPS unit was used to record latitude and longitude at all sites. Maps were created using ArcMap 10.5 software (ESRI), using a World Imagery spatial layer, supported with data layers from ESRI, DigitalGlobe, GeoEye, Earthstar Geographics, USDA, USGS, AeroGRID, IGN and the GIS User Community. A member of the Arecaceae family and widely distributed across Thailand, Malaysia and the Indonesia archipelago, the arenga palm (locally known as *'Langkap'*) is an evergreen, cluster-forming species that grows rapidly up to heights of 16 metres. Arenga palms spread by subterranean root growth (root extension), constraining and outcompeting the growth of other native plants. Arenga palms also produce large quantities of seeding fruits, which enhances their dominance over other native species. Able to disperse rapidly, arenga palms establish monocultures by reducing light due to canopy dominance and reduce the growth of understorey native food plants used by Javan rhinos for feeding.

One theory that explains the arenga palm spread in the Ujung Kulon peninsula is that volcanic ash deposition following the volcano Krakatau's eruption in 1883, which increased soil fertility across Ujung Kulon and was followed by the proliferation of arenga palm in the area since. Mammalian dispersers of arenga palm seeds and fruits include the Southern palm civet (*Paradoxurus musanga javanicus* or *'Luwak'*) and long-tailed macaque who spread palm seeds through faeces or by dropped seeds during and after eating the fruit. Found right across southeast Asia, Southern palm civets are highly adaptable and can forage in both terrestrial and arboreal habitats. They feed on a diverse array of prey items including fruit (e.g., figs), small vertebrates, insects, birds, reptiles and frogs.

Civets communicate with each other visually, vocally and via olfactory means (scent/odour), usually from perineal gland secretions. In Ujung Kulon at an arenga site, I observed a Southern palm civet casually climb and move effortlessly across a large fig tree, releasing its strong 'musky' scent that lingered in the forest air for some time after disappearing. The long-tailed macaque is common across Ujung Kulon and able to utilise a broad range of habitat types. Opportunistic feeders, able to capitalise on food abundance, such as fruiting trees (e.g., *Ficus* ssp.), are also not averse to crop raiding local villages. Males are larger and heavier than females. Group size varies between 5–100 individuals. Excellent swimmers, this species will enter water for fun as well as to forage for aquatic food items such as crabs and molluscs.

Potentially, other arenga palm dispersers could include avian frugivorous birds such as hornbills (e.g., *Buceros, Anthracoceros*), rainforest pigeons (e.g., *Trevon, Ptilinopus, Ducula*) (family

Columbidae), and the diurnal squirrel group (family Sciuridae), species such as the black giant squirrel (*Ratufa bicolor* or *'Jeralang'*), and Javan red flying squirrel (*Petaurista p. petaurista or 'Bajing terbang'*).

Efforts to increase available habitat for Javan rhino appeared to be working and given the increasing amount of arenga clearing occurring investigation was needed and I started to record post-clearing plant response and rhino activity for a two-year period (April 2016 to April 2018) at the 15 x one ha 2016 cleared sites and 15 x one ha control sites. In order to test the impact of arenga palm removal on Javan rhino activity, I monitored using the following variables, including the number of native plant species, number of plant families, number of plants/stems per plot and any rhino sign including dung, spray urination sign, footprints and feeding sign (e.g., damage to food plants from browsing rhino).

Signs of rhino visitation were recorded only when there was clear evidence that a rhino had visited the site (i.e., up to 40 hours fresh dung and/or spray urination). Other signs included were, clearly defined fresh footprints, feeding signs at foraging height and evidence of rhino using their bulk to knock over small trees and saplings, and the frayed cut marks characteristic of browsing rhino. All 15 cleared arenga palm sites were visited by Javan rhinos over the two-year recording period following the arenga clearing compared with no visitation at all before clearing these sites. These findings suggest for the first time that rhino habitat manipulation and clearing of arenga palm in rainforest patches is an important management technique for increasing the remaining Javan rhino foraging habitat and for enhancing the persistence of the highly threatened Javan rhinos.

The study demonstrated the benefits of habitat manipulation, and arguably is the strongest immediate conservation action needed to actively clear monoculture/dominant arenga palm areas to increase rhino foraging.

Author in a cleared arenga palm plot, showing regrowth two years post-clearing, all good rhino food!

Ramono et al. (2009) noted, at least nine rhinos (approximately 15% of the population) periodically used the eastern Gunung Honje area, including three resident males which bodes well for future arenga palm management within the park and its positive effects on rhinos. Females with calves have been captured on camera trap videos but have not stayed in the area. Camera trap videos demonstrate how females with calves are extremely vigilant and prefer to stay and travel in areas with good cover.

Movement pathways from the western peninsula area of the park to the eastern Gunung Honje site need to be well-vegetated to assist this need. This rhino behavior has been recognised by park authorities and supplementary planting of rhino food plants is occurring along the corridor linking the peninsula to the eastern Gunung Honje area which may create the right conditions for single females to stay and ultimately breed with resident males. The positive impact and involvement of local community who are employed to manually clear arenga palms (cutting palm trunks, clearing fronds and collecting fruits) not only has an immediate effect on the landscape but it also importantly engages community into the rhino conservation effort. I monitored the impact of arenga palm removal on both native vegetation recruitment and post-clearing visitation frequency of Javan rhinos. I found that arenga palm removal led to increased richness and abundance of native Javan rhino food plants and a rapid increase in rhino visitation to cleared sites that were previously avoided by the rhinos. Within five months of clearing of the arenga palms, the experimental sites included 67 rhino food plant species belonging to 37 plant families compared with no native plants in any of the 15 control sites, only monoculture arenga palm. Furthermore, all arenga palm sites were visited by Javan rhinos over the two-year recording period following the arenga clearing compared with no visitation at all before these sites had been cleared. These findings suggest for the first time that rhino habitat manipulation and clearing of arenga palm in rainforest patches is an important management technique for increasing the remaining Javan rhino foraging habitat and enhancing the persistence of the highly threatened Javan rhino.

We know Javan rhino prefers to eat the leaves, shoots and twigs of woody species, typically at shrub level, with little to no consumption of grass or herbaceous species, however, I have observed on camera trap, an adult male stripping the leaves off giant *Dendrocalamus* bamboo. Using its mouth and strength, the male grabbed a large 5m+ thick bamboo stem, bent it over for ease of reach and proceeded to munch and strip the leaves off along its entire length. Large clumps of giant *Dendrocalamus* bamboo are found across the park, adding another valuable alternative food resource, especially if all rhinos, not just the observed male, are using bamboo as part of their diet. Its another question to explore.

Based on camera trap observations, consistently, the highest densities of Javan rhino are found in and adjacent to coastal areas. Attracted to disturbance regimes and successional habitats, their preferred habitat is open or tree-fall, storm-damaged, cleared arenga palm sites, essentially any impacted area that show signs of pioneer species rapidly appearing.

What are Javan rhinos eating?

As generalist browsers Javan rhinos feed on a broad suite of plant species. The plant species preferred by Javan rhino have been studied, with some variation among studies, ranging for example, from 150 food plant species (Hoogerwerf 1970, Schenkel & Schenkel-Hulliger 1969a, 1969b) to 190 species (Ammann 1985), 200 plant species (Putro 1997) and up to 252 species (Muntasib 2002). Generalist species tend to adapt and survive more successfully due to their occupying a broader ecological niche, food plant species can be interchangeable and there is less reliance on a few plant species. Rhinos have been recorded as preferring particular plant species including *Spondias pinnata, Amomum sp, Leea sambucina* and *Dillenia excelsa* which made up 44% of the forage of the 190 food plant species recorded. Research analysis on the nutritional quality and food digestibility of rhino food plants by (Hariyadi et al. (2016), determined through proximate analysis of dried food plant samples *Spondias pinnata* as the food plant with the highest calcium (4.70 g/100 g) and *Hibiscus tiliaceus* with the most phosphorus (0.3 g/100 g).

Identified high palatability food plant species were *Leea sambucina, Dracontomelon puberulum, Amomum megalocheilos, Spondias pinnata, Zanthoxylum rhetsa, Diospyros macrophylla* and *Ficus hispida*. Known rhino food plant species *Dracontomelon puberulum, Zanthoxylum rhetsa, Diospyros macrophylla* and *Ficus hispida* contained much higher nutritional quality, for example greater % protein, % fat and energy (kcal/kg) than many of the other high palatability species.

Highlighting the ongoing variability and availability of these plants in rhino home-ranges and the importance of having a diverse and balanced diet. Under a variety of prevailing conditions Javan rhinos can experience shortages of specific nutrients caused by periodic reductions in certain nutritionally valuable plant species. For example, *Zanthoxylum rhetsa*, is a rhino food plant species known to be high in protein (17.11%), fat (1.94%) and energy (3.667 k/cal/kg). During poor plant growth periods Javan rhino home-range size may fluctuate and change, most likely expand and potentially limit population density. As highly mobile generalist browsers, and not being restricted to certain plant species, Javan rhino have the ability to adapt, move and seek alternative food plant species during lean periods. Studies estimate Javan rhinos moved within their home-ranges between 1.4 to 3.8 km each day.

Active in situ management measures, such as supplementary planting of suitable rhino food plant which increase the availability of nutritious plant material is a practical way of ensuring rhino populations continue to thrive and get the adequate nutrition they need. It remains unclear if Javan rhino play any role in plant seed and fruit dispersal. Presumably, they may incidentally ingest seeds and fruit during their foraging behaviour. The congeneric (means from the same genus) greater one-horned rhino is a known dispersal agent of plant seeds and fruit, notably the plant species *Trewia nudiflora* (family Euphorbiaceae). I suspect at healthy densities, Javan rhino, given their mega-size and browsing behaviour, it is reasonable to expect them to have an impact on seedling and sapling recruitment of woody plants, similar to congener the greater one-horned rhino.

Experimental study design

In order to monitor plant growth within each one hectare cleared plot, four 20 m² quadrats were marked out using an eight-meter Lufkin autolock tape measure and staked out using fluorescent pink ribbon on each staked corner so the quadrat stake could be found in the future once plants grew taller than the stakes. I used Flouro string to define the quadrat boundary and record within each 20 m², smaller squares of 2, 5 and 10 m² to allow for vegetation analysis of the four stages of growth: seedling, shrub, sapling and older tree. Each of the smaller squares of 2, 5 and 10 m² within each of the four 20 m² quadrats was recorded four times.

During the five months since cutting and clearing, each site had responded with plant growth due to increased exposure to available sunlight and the elements. The rapid growth response over the five-month period since clearing enabled plant species to be identified and counted in each respective quadrat. Recorded variables included number plant species, number plant families, number plants/stems per plot and any rhino sign including dung, spray urination sign, footprints and feeding sign (e.g., damage to food plants from browsing rhino). Signs of rhino visitation were recorded only when there was clear evidence that a rhino had visited the site i.e., up to 40 hours fresh dung and/or spray urination. Other signs included were clearly defined fresh footprints and feeding sign at foraging height and evidence of rhino using their bulk to knock over small trees and saplings and the frayed cut marks characteristic of browsing rhino. Heavy rain readily degrades rhino activity signs.

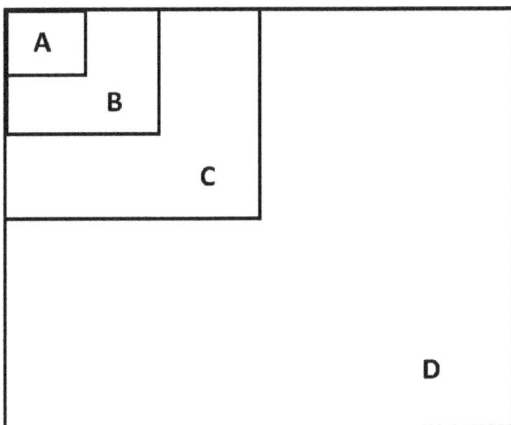

Diagram of quadrat layout for each one hectare cleared control sites. **A.** 2 m² (seedling), **B.** 5 m² (shrub), **C.** 10 m² (sapling/young tree), **D.** 20 m² (older tree) to property assess various growth stages of vegetation.

Direct observation of Javan rhinos is difficult, rhinos are shy, alert, in small numbers and avoids humans. Therefore, animals were identified based on camera trap imagery and videos following Griffith's (1993) identification criteria which compares morphological features including horn size and shape, footprint size, eye wrinkles, ear shape and distinct features such as scars, damaged skin folds or skin pigmentation. The Ujung Kulon NP Authority has been actively monitoring the rhino population across the national park since 2010, using its network of permanent video cameras and has built up a considerable database of each individual rhino and its identification characteristics.

Other large and small herbivores such as Javan Banteng, Javan wild pig, Southern red muntjac, Javan mouse deer and Javan rusa deer also utilise these cleared areas, their sign (e.g., footprints and dung) is readily distinguished from rhino. Additionally, carnivores such as Javan leopard, leopard cat (*Prionalurus bengalensis* or *'Kucing hutan'*), Javan fishing cat (*Prionailurus viverrinus rhizophoreus* or *'Kucing bakau'*), Southern palm civet and Javan *Tupaia javanica* or *'Tupai kekes'* or Horsfield's tree shrew (*T. hypochrysa*) were also recorded on camera trap as visiting cleared arenga sites. On one occasion I observed a resting Javan Sunda colugo (*Galeopterus v. variegatus* or *'Tando'* or *'Walang kopo'*) [family Cynocephalidae], high in a large 20m+ *Baccaurea* sp. tree.

Initially, Bushnell Trophy Cam HD eight-megapixel remote cameras were set up at 10 of the cleared arenga sites to record any rhino visitation, however, this was discontinued due to local community regularly interfering with cameras, presumably local wildlife poachers not wishing to be filmed. National park and rhino protection unit staff assisted with plant identification along with various rhino food plant identification sources such as Putro (1997) and Hommel (1987). A similar methodology was used by Hariyadi et al. (2012) on initial arenga palm trial sites undertaken on the Ujung Kulon peninsula and in other species determination and richness studies undertaken by Whittaker et al. (2001) and Whittaker & Heegaard (2003).

In order to compare the plant response at cleared arenga sites, I also marked out 15 individual non-cleared arenga dominated 20m^2 quadrats and recorded as per the cleared sites as control sites, following the same recording procedure of examining the number plant species/family and number plants per 20 m^2, and inside each 2, 5 and 10 m^2 square quadrat, enabling comparison of plant numbers (stems) and species composition (no species/no families) between cleared and control quadrats. These sites were established approximately two km from the cleared sites.

I used a Canon 50D digital camera to take images of plant growth response and individual rhino food plant species. Both cleared and non-cleared sites were visited at least twice annually between April 2016 and April 2018 checking for rhino visitation taking into consideration in situ field time was limited by climatic conditions i.e., monsoon period November–March, best access usually found during April–October, respecting staff limitations of Ramadan (April/May) and regular regional religious events. Plant growth (height/cm) was recorded at cleared sites in April 2018, approximately two years post-clearing.

As an ongoing management measure rhino protection staff routinely check and hand-cut any arenga regrowth and have an annual program of visiting cleared sites on their monthly routine patrol cycles to cut palm regrowth. I believe future studies should examine cleared arenga sites focusing on arenga seedbank and regrowth issues.

One-way analysis of variance (ANOVA) and t-tests were undertaken testing the statistical significance of 15 cleared arenga sites to the non-cleared control sites across the variables of plant numbers, number of plant species, number of plant families in each of the 2 x 2, 5 x 5, 10 x 10 and 20 x 20 metre quadrats. ANOVA analysis tells you if there are any statistical differences between the means of three or more independent groups. Additionally, ANOVA tests were done to compare each of the individual (recorded four) in each cleared quadrat within each 2 x 2, 5 x

5, 10 x 10 and 20 x 20 areas. For example, in site 1, 4 x (2 x 2) quadrats were each examined for plant numbers, and an ANOVA was applied comparing all four recorded 2 x 2 quadrats (e.g., A, B, C, D). The aim of this arenga palm chapter was to determine the implications for conservation and management of arenga palm on rhino, habitat and food plants, by asking the following questions and hypothesis including what are the conservation implications of arenga palm-dominated habitat for Javan rhino habitat use and distribution? Does removal of arenga palm increase the availability of rhino food plants? The time period over which rhino food plants grow, and rhino visitation occurs?

I hypothesised that habitat manipulation of arenga palm in selected forest patches is a viable management technique to increase foraging for rhinos. We discovered that arenga palm removal resulted in increased richness and abundance of native rhino food plants and rapid increase in rhino visitation to cleared sites by Javan rhinos in areas previously covered by arenga palms. In all cleared sites there was growth of native plants.

A comparison of the number of plant species and plant families across both cleared and uncleared sites showed similar results. For example, cleared sites had 67 plant species from 37 plant families compared to 71 plant species from 41 plant families at non-cleared. The average plant growth rate (height/cm), two years post-clearing (April 2016–April 2018) was highest in older tree (20 m²) sites averaging 113.48 cm, the plant family Aristolchiaceae (26%) the most recorded.

Arenga palm regrowth dominated plant growth in shrubs (5m²) and saplings (10 m²) sites, highlighting the importance of regrowth removal by rangers on regular patrols.-Post clearing the number of arenga palms to number of rhino food plants was lower at cleared sites than uncleared control sites. For example, 15 cleared 20 m x 20 m small, treed sites collectively had no arenga palm plants compared to 755 small trees (rhino food plants), a trend that presented across most cleared sites. A comparison of the average number of plant species and number of plant families across sites showed similar plant species and family diversity.

A comparison in the number of stems across cleared and uncleared sites showed higher averages of seedlings (2 m^2) 18.47 in cleared sites compared to 4.15 in uncleared and shrubs, (5m^2) 156.11 in cleared sites compared to 2.74 in uncleared. The number of stems at uncleared sites for saplings (10 m^2) and older tree (20 m^2) was higher than cleared sites. For example, uncleared sapling sites (10 m^2) averaged 14.86 stems compared to 3.86 at cleared sites.

Camera video footage and rhino tracks moving around arenga palm stands shows rhino tend to avoid these monoculture areas given there is no reliable food source within them. Prior to clearing, the sites were dominated by arenga palms. Results comparing numbers of plant species and plant families between cleared and non-cleared sites for 2 x 2 (seedlings), 5 x 5 (shrubs), 10 x 10 (saplings) and 20 x 20m (older tree). ANOVA tests compared each of the individual plants (recorded four) in each cleared quadrat within each 2 x 2, 5 x 5, 10 x 10 and 20 x 20. This same approach was also applied comparing number of species, number of families and number of arenga palms.

There was no statistically significant difference between the number of plants across respective quadrats (4 per site), each recorded similar numbers of plant numbers. These same patterns were seen when comparing plant richness, and the number of plant families at cleared and uncleared sites. Results for the average distance from known wallows in the 5,100 ha JRSCA study site to the coast was 0.64 km; SD ± 0.52; average distance from cleared sites to control sites was 2.23 km; SD ± 1.068; average distance from cleared sites to wallows was 0.98 km; SD ± 0.779; average distance from cleared sites to the coast was 1.39 km; SD ± 0.883; and, the average distance from cleared sites to the nearest waterway (often seasonal) was 0.653 km; SD ± 0.366.

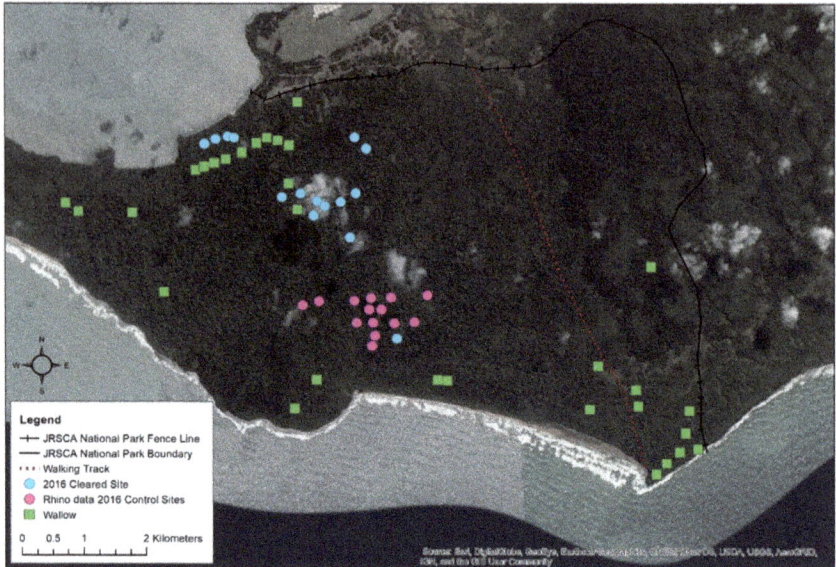

Map of eastern Gunung Honje region of Ujung Kulon National Park showing 2016 cleared (blue dots) and control (pink dots) arenga palm sites and locations of wallows (green squares), and black line (8-kilometre rhino fence). Map was created using ArcMap 10.5 software (ESRI).

Rhino visitation to cleared and non-cleared sites

Rhino visits to post-cleared sites were recorded on 32 occasions, compared to zero visits to uncleared controls sites during the September 2016–April 2018 period. Rhinos were detected visiting cleared sites and feeding on secondary growth. All of the 15 cleared sites were visited by at least three different individual rhinos based on footprint variation. At the time, there have been at least four males, and periodic incursions of females using the south-eastern Gunung Honje area. A fourth rhino known to utilise the south-eastern Gunung Honje area, *'Samson'* a 30+ year old male was found dead, presumably of natural causes on one of the park's beaches on April 23rd, 2018. Although unproven, a hole (presumably caused by a bullet) was found in his skull. If confirmed, this death will be the first rhino linked to poaching

176

in over 30 years. 1994, was the last recorded poaching record. Tragically, between 2019–2023 at least 26 animals, possibly more have been poached. Of the 32 visitation records recorded during 20/09/2016–19/09/2018, 27 were of feeding sign, two records of dung deposition, three of spray urination, three records of wallowing evidence (e.g., mud on vegetation) and 32 records of tracks and footprints. Sixteen (n=16) food plants were identified and recorded as eaten at cleared sites included: *Dillenia obovata, D. aurea, Amomum coccineum, Leea sambucina, Spondias pinnata, Ficus montana, Baccaurea javanica, Oxymitra cunneformis, Sumbaviopsis albicans, Largerstroemia flos-regime, Cladium bicolor, Vitex pubescens, Barringtonia gagantostachua, Donnax cunnaeformis, Apama tomentosa* and *Diospyros javanica.*

The 15 control sites were also sampled by our field team twice a year (April and September) to determine if rhinos had visited any of the sites. I did not record any evidence of rhino visitation at any of the control sites over the same 20/09/2016–19/09/2018 period, presumably due to the dominance and monoculture stands of arenga palms. The fact that rhinos were both spray urinating and depositing dung at cleared sites highlights the fact animals were also actively communicating via olfactory means as they would in their feeding habitat. Presumably, the spray urination and possibly the dung deposits were left by a dominant male.

The removal of arenga palm leads to increased diversity and abundance of native rhino food plants and a rapid increase in rhino visitation to cleared sites that were previously avoided by rhinos, within one month of clearing. Ujung Kulon authorities and conservation groups have used local community labor and skills in arenga palm control since 2010, clearing 400+ ha to date and now averaging up 60 ha annually across the park. This has enhanced the relationship between village communities and national park authorities in addition to making more habitat available to the rhino population. Ideally the number of hectares cleared increases annually. Prior to clearing, the sites were dominated by arenga palm. Five months after cutting and clearing of arenga palms, cleared sites were showing native plant species diversity comparable to the control sites. Rhinos have been recorded as visiting and feeding at all 15 cleared sites. From a management perspective the clearing process activated long dormant arenga palm seedbanks which can be easily cut by rhino protection staff enabling activation and competition from rhino food plants. As part of their patrolling duties rhino protection staff now routinely visit cleared sites and cut any arenga regrowth which reduces in number with every site visit. Additionally, the Ujung Kulon NP Authority has now instigated an annual arenga palm clearance program which is focussed on the western peninsula area (main rhino population lives here). I found rhinos would naturally utilise a wallow site near a foraging area, once cool would move to a feeding area, then move to a cooler coastal area which also has the added foraging value of salt-sprayed vegetation.

Implications of arenga palm-dominated habitat for Javan rhino habitat use

Over 60% (>18,000 ha) of the Ujung Kulon peninsula and an estimated >1,500 ha of the eastern Gunung Honje area is covered by monoculture stands of arenga palm. This potential rhino foraging habitat is successionally changing to a closed canopy forest with little to no plant diversity and very limited rhino forage.

Camera video footage and rhino tracks moving around arenga stands shows rhino tend to avoid these monoculture areas given there is no reliable food source within them. The study has demonstrated cleared sites respond quickly with plant diversity comparable to non-cleared sites and with large numbers of desirable food plants. Rhino visitation records showed animals were feeding on pioneer species that colonise disturbance (e.g., tree fall and storm damage) and successional habitats (e.g., *Dillenia obovata*, *Amomum coccineum*, *Leea sambucina* and *Spondias pinnata*). The clearing of arenga palm sites is relatively cost-effective at $1,000 AUD per ha given the remoteness of the site, the work undertaken is by hand and often in difficult terrain and climatic conditions. The $1,000 AUD per ha costs include labour, food and transportation for 10 people to clear one ha over a 10-day period. These costs can be further reduced to $600 AUD per ha if chainsaws are used, reducing the labour requirement to six people, and shortening the per ha clearance rate to six days. Importantly, local community can be used as a viable labour force and their contribution builds important understanding of the conservation effort.

The current World Heritage site restrictions on the use of chemicals in the park is worth trying to change given chemical trials injecting using isopropyl ammonium glyphosate into arenga palm was found similarly cost effective and you could inoculate more hectares of arenga palm than manual cutting over the same time period. Despite this treatment method having significant potential, authorities remain concerned over chemical residues in the landscape. This concern remains despite strong evidence isopropyl ammonium glyphosate is non-residual and has no long-term effect on native flora, even after a five-years of use and testing.

It is worth noting that for arenga palm clearing to be effective, other habitat components need to be available. The proximity and access to wallows is important given Javan rhinos need to wallow daily. Fortunately, the eastern Gunung Honje area supports 35 wallows which I identified and recorded during my study with the average distance from cleared arenga sites to wallows is 0.98 km. Evidence of rhinos using nearby wallows as shown by mud on saplings and vegetation at cleared arenga sites showed animals were wallowing and moving to and from to feed at the cleared sites. Javan rhino are known to urinate in wallowing sites which helps impregnate their bodies with distinctive odours; the odours are then spread throughout the habitat as mud on saplings and as the animals move through vegetation and are presumably recognised by others. Access to water sources is equally important and the average distance from cleared sites to the nearest waterway (often seasonal) is 0.653 km. Proximity to coastal areas was considered important by Setiawan et al. (2017) who found Javan rhino was found mostly in coastal areas presumably due to cooler conditions and access to salt-sprayed mineral-rich vegetation. I found the average distance from cleared arenga sites to the coast is 1.39 km.

The study showed a significant rate of plant growth and diversity at cleared sites replacing areas previously covered by mostly monoculture arenga palm. This habitat restoration approach increases habitat for foraging and space for resident and importantly visiting rhino. The focus of this research was to understand and determine the implications of the management of arenga palm on Javan rhino, and conservation benefits to habitat and food plants. The research results support the proposal that active habitat manipulation of arenga palm in selected forest patches is a viable management technique to increase foraging for rhinos when resources to clear are available.

Time period rhino food plants grow, and rhino visitation occurs

Five months after cutting and clearing of arenga palms, the native plants had grown from existing seedbanks sufficiently large enough that I was able to distinguish and identify individual plant species at each site. Two years post-clearing, many plant species were over two metres tall and the ground was barely visible due to active competition from many plant species. Rhino protection staff informed me rhino tracks were found at four cleared sites one-month post-clearing.

During September 2016, I collected evidence rhinos had visited seven different cleared sites and were feeding on various plant species (e.g., *Dillenia obovata, Amomum coccinea* and *Leea sambucina*). Dung piles and evidence of spray urination at cleared sites demonstrated the sites were now being used as habitat areas with rhinos communicating via olfactory means.

Impact of Arenga palm on Javan rhino food resources

Patterns of both natural and human disturbance in Ujung Kulon have created a mosaic of successional stages of vegetation regeneration. These early to mid-pioneer secondary stages provide valuable foraging sources of rhino food-plants, with patches of mature primary and secondary forest providing cover. Earlier studies undertaken by Supriatin (2000) identified the growing dominance of arenga palm, impacting forest successional processes through competition and consequent reductions in available rhino food plants.

Examination of vegetation cover both on ground and via remote sensing approaches suggest that these vegetation mosaics are becoming increasingly arenga palm monocultures as plant succession moves toward closed forest. As a result, it was concluded that rhino food-plant resources are declining, especially where closed forests are dominated by arenga palms. Javan rhinos are solitary and highly mobile, and dependent on food availability in their restricted habitat. With an ability to rapidly spread, arenga palm, arguably, poses the most major threat to Javan rhino habitat and animals through the loss of available food plants, forest succession moving to a closed system, with little to no light on the forest floor for secondary and understory growth processes.

Table showing comparison of plant response between number of plant species and number of plant families at cleared (15 x 1ha) and non-cleared (15 x 1ha) arenga sites after two years (2016–2018).

Cleared sites	15 x 1ha sites	Uncleared sites	15 x 1ha sites
Family (n=37)	Species (n=67)	Family (n=41)	Species (n=71)
Apocynaceae	*Anadendrum microstachyum, Alstonia sp.*	Apocynaceae	*Anadendrum microstachyum, Alstonia sp.*
Boraginaceae	*Cordia sp.*	Boraginaceae	*Cordia sp.*
Palmae	*Daemonorops melanochaetes, Caryota mitis*	Palmae	*Daemonorops melanochaetes, Caryota mitis, Calamus sp., Pinnanga coronata, Areca pumida*

Combretaceae	*Terminalia arborea*	Combretaceae	*Terminalia arborea*
Dilleniaceae	*Dillenia aurea, D. obovata, Tetracera scandens*	Dilleniaceae	*Dillenia excelsa, D. obovata, Tetracera scandens*
Aristolchiaceae	*Apama tomentosa*	Aristolchiaceae	*Apama tomentosa*
Maranthaceae	*Phrynium parviflorum, Donnax cunnaeformis*	Maranthaceae	*Phrynium parviflorum, Donnax cunnaeformis,*
Anarcardiaceae	*Dracontomelon pubarulum, D. dao, Spondias pinnata*	Anarcardiaceae	*Dracontomelon dao, Spondias pinnata*
Euphorbiaceae	*Baccaurea javanica, Glochidion sp., Alchornea ruguss, Bischofia javanica, Homolanthus populneus, Claoxylon polot, Aporoa autita, Antidesma bunius, Mallotus peltatus*	Euphorbiaceae	*Baccaurea javanica, Alchornea ruguss, Claoxylon polot, Aporoa autita, Antidesma bunius, Mallotus peltatus, Bridelia monoica*
Arecaceae	*Arenga obtusifolia, Salacca edulis*	Arecaceae	*Arenga obtusifolia, Licuala spinosa*
Myristicaceae	*Knema glauca*	Myristicaceae	*Knema glauca*
Annonaceae	*Oxymitra cunnaeformis, Uvaria littoralis, Canagium odoratum, Stelechocarpus barahol*	Annonaceae	*Oxymitra cunnaeformis, Canagium odoratum, Stelechocarpus barahol*
Vitaceae	*Leea sambucina*	Vitaceae	*Leea sambucina, L. rubra*
Costaceae	*Costus specistus*	Melastomataceae	*Mellastoma affine*
Verbenaceae	*Vitex pubescens*	Verbenaceae	*Vitex pubescens, Lantana camara*
Lauraceae	*Sumbaviopsis albicans, Litsea sp.*	Lauraceae	*Sumbaviopsis albicans, Litsea sp., Paederia scadens, Cainnanomum iners*
Moraceae	*Artocarpus elastica, Ficus callosa, F. montana, F. sagitata*	Moraceae	*Artocarpus elastica, Ficus gibbasa, F. montana*
Ranunculaceae	*Pterospermum diversifolium*	Ranunculaceae	*Pterospermum javanica*

Myrtaceae	*Eugenia polyantha, Decasperum fructicosum, Syzgium polyantha*	Myrtaceae	*Eugenia subglauca, E. polyantha, Decasperum fructicosum,*
Ebenaceae	*Diospyros pendula, D. macrophylla, Saccopetalum heterophylla*	Ebenaceae	*Diospyros macrophylla, D. frutescens, Saccopetalum heterophylla*
Rutaceae	*Zanthoxilum rhesta, Evodia latifolia*	Rutaceae	*Evodia latifolia*
Rubiaceae	*Anthocephalus chinensis*	Rubiaceae	*Anthocephalus chinensis, Uncaria sp.*
Bignoniaceae	*Radermachera gigantean*	Cyperaceae	*Tetrania sp.*
Hypoxidaceae	*Curculigo onchiodes*	Hypoxidaceae	*Curculigo onchiodes*
Musaceae	*Musa acuminata*	Schizazeae	*Lygodium circinatum*
Fabaceae	*Derris thyorsifolia*	Connaraceae	*Rourea minor*
Araceae	*Cladium bicolor*	Araceae	*Cladium bicolor*
Tilliaceae	*Microcos panniculata, Pentara polyanthra*	Tilliaceae	*Microcos panniculata, Pentara polyanthra, Microcosm comentosa*
Sterculiaceae	*Sterculia sp.*	Sterculiaceae	*Sterculia coccinea*
Violaceae	*Rinorea sp.*	Meliaceae	*Aglaia argentea*
Lythraceae	*Lagerstroemia flos-regime*	Lythraceae	*Lagerstroemia flos-regime*
Thymelaceae	*Phaleria octendre*	Thymelaceae	*Phaleria octendre*
Lechytidaceae	*Barringtonia gagantostachua, Planconia valida*	Lechytidaceae	*Barringtonia gagantostachua, Plachonia valida*
Clusiaceae	*Garcinia parvifolia*	Clusiaceae	*Garcinia parvifolia, G. diodica*
Olaceae	*Strombossia javanica*	Olaceae	*Strombossia javanica*
Myrsinaceae	*Ardisia humilis*	Myrsinaceae	*Ardisia humilis*
Zingiberaceae	*Amomum coccineum*	Kuliaceae	*Neonanchea calcina*
		Flaccurtiaceae	*Flcourtia rukem*
		Graminaeae	*Symplocus sp.*
		Sapindaceae	*Pometia pinnata*
		Piperaceae	*Piper bantamense*

Table showing comparison of arenga palm and rhino food plant numbers (stems) recorded at all (n = 15) cleared and uncleared arenga palm sites.

Quadrat (plot size)	Plant stage & type	No. of arenga palm plants across all plots (n=15)	No. of rhino food plants across all plots (n=15)
2m x 2m Cleared	seedlings	473	1297
2m x 2m Uncleared	seedlings	71	401
5m x 5m Cleared	shrubs	6349	5617
5m x 5m Uncleared	shrubs	87	145
10m x 10m Cleared	saplings	0	457
10m x 10m Uncleared	saplings	1677	1931
20m x 20m Cleared	older tree	0	755
20m x 20m Uncleared	older tree	1398	9,266

The ongoing clearance of arenga palm is enhancing rhino habitat and has value for rhino management as a tool and option to increase access and probability of connecting isolated rhinos to breeding opportunities and importantly, improving the quality of habitat in rhino home-ranges. The positive impact and involvement of local community who are employed to manually clear arenga palm has an immediate effect on the landscape. The data collected from the cleared and non-cleared sites has increased our understanding of how Javan rhino use and respond to successional habitats, both natural and manipulated.

As a proven and important management technique, habitat manipulation of arenga palm in selected forest patches increases foraging for rhinos. Removal of mostly dominant monoculture arenga palm patches also increase available space through increased habitat for rhino use. As highly mobile generalist browsers, and not being restricted to certain plant species, Javan rhinos have the ability to adapt, move and seek alternative food plant species during lean periods, which makes them an ideal species for translocation.

The genetic health of the total Javan rhino population and the kinship are unknown. The biased sex ratio and low proportion of females producing calves indicates all is not well. Given these issues, an understanding of the genetic and demographic health of the population is urgently required to develop appropriate conservation strategies for the species recovery. Javan rhino were actively poached up until the early 1990s, when active in situ rhino protection became part of park management. Today, the conservation focus of Ujung Kulon authorities' is in situ protection of Javan rhino. Despite the presence of rhino protection units patrolling Ujung Kulon, poaching remains an ever-present threat as it does for any rhino population.

Anak Krakatoa volcano, the son or successor of Krakatoa that erupted in 1883, lies only 55 km from Ujung Kulon. This active volcano grows larger each year and could erupt with little warning. An eruption would likely lead to bursts of pyroclastic water vapour (rapid current of hot gas and volcanic matter that moves along the ground at high speed and high temperature), increased risk of forest fires, rock falls and deadly, toxic gas spreading across the entire Ujung Kulon peninsula. Furthermore, an eruption is predicted to produce considerable tsunamis with wave heights estimated between 7.9–21.0 m. A tsunami as high as 10 metres, which is projected to occur within the next 100 years, could threaten 80% of the area with the highest density of Javan rhino. This would likely devastate the population and start an irreversible extinction vortex. This coupled with disease risk, for example *Haemorrhagic septicaemia* was found in 90% of domestic water buffalo in the 19 villages adjacent to the core Javan rhino area, the village population of buffalo is an estimated 6,000+ animals. Of concern is, the highly virulent Foot and Mouth disease (FMD) now listed as endemic in the Banten Province and across Indonesia (IFRC Report 2023).

One of the main threats to the remaining Javan rhino is limited suitable habitat, which is mitigated by the increasing dominance of invasive arenga palm in Ujung Kulon.

Importantly, the risk of having all Javan rhino in one population at one location with a long list of genuine threats, the establishment of a second population, with a view to expanding this option to several areas is critical. By reducing the Ujung Kulon population density, reproduction would increase and there would be less pressure on food resources, habitat would improve and recover and inbreeding depression would be reduced as well.

In early 2019, I was on patrol with four of the rhino protection staff and we were checking out some of the cleared arenga sites in the eastern Gunung Honje area of Ujung Kulon. These sites had now been cleared for over two years and the re-emergent vegetation was in some cases growing at shoulder height. It began to rain quite heavily and the boys suggested we look for cover and start a fire to brew some tea. This always made me laugh, pouring rain and they want to put the kettle on! Very early on I learnt some of the boys would often carry bamboo tubes with lids. The tube would hold hot coals, ideal to start a fire, even in the rain, however, most of the guys preferred a cigarette lighter, probably because the bamboo tubed hot coals would burn a hole in their clothing! The boys said they would rest up in the forest at the edge of the cleared arenga plot, I said I would check out the site and record any new plants and be with them in about 15 minutes. So, I kept walking and recorded the regrowth. At the far side of the plot was a beautiful big *Ficus* tree, supported by masses of aerial roots. I was checking it out and noticed a tail twitching high up in the branches, which turned out to be a Javan leopard that had recently killed a small barking deer or muntjac, which I could partially see draped over a branch. Normally I would only see leopard on camera trap footage, the Javan subspecies was listed as endangered by the IUCN Red List in 2021, and, as the saying goes these guys are as 'rare as rocking horse shit', so seeing one so close was special. I remember thinking that was awesome and turned around to head back to the boys. At the time I was standing in shoulder height vegetation and I heard a slight 'thump' sound behind me, I looked around and saw a female leopard with blood on her face in a crouched position at the base of the tree looking directly at me and growling, before I knew it the cat was bounding straight at me! I barely had time to get out of the way. I was loaded up with my backpack and camera gear, the female brushed across my shoulder as I fell over to avoid her in a tangled mess to see at my feet a pair of leopard cubs around 6–8 weeks old looking at me with a growling mother crouched beside them! Well, that explained the female's charge, unknowingly I was standing between mum and her bubs. Despite the closeness of the female, I never felt threatened, unfortunately, I was so tangled up in my backpack and camera gear, plus I kept getting leg cramps, I was unable to take what would have been an amazing photo. Front cover of National Geographic! It was not to be. Each time I tried to move, or try and get to my camera, the female would growl and lash out with her paws, fortunately never attacking or injuring me. Eventually, one of the cubs turned around and moved away, closely followed by its mate, then the female followed. Once able to get to my feet, I straightened myself up and headed back towards the boys, feeling like I'd dodged a bullet, and given there was an upset female leopard and two cubs in the vicinity I decided to make a bit of noise so the cats would move away, and after 5 minutes of loud jungle bashing, I came out near the fire started by the boys but no boys! I called out, then looked up, all four guys thought I was a rhino or banteng bull crashing through the jungle, so they all climbed a tree just in case, they were all looking down at me in amazement. When they jumped down from the tree, and I explained my '*Macan tutul*' leopard encounter, they all laughed, and said 'only Pak Steve could disturb a leopard from its kill but we are pleased you did not get hurt, so get over it!' Plenty of support from the rhino protection unit, so, I got over it!

187

In Ujung Kulon, re leopards, we see both the 'normal' spotted form, as well as the all black 'panther' melanistic form. Population numbers are unknown, as it's a difficult species to monitor. I also suspect Javan leopards, since the extinction of the larger Javan tiger in the 1980s, may have changed or expanded their range of prey species, possibly moving from hunting primates and small deer species to taking larger prey such as muntjac, Javan wild pig or even rusa deer and young banteng. Remarkably, the leopard I observed was at least 15 metres up the tree, the 'thump, I heard meant she had jumped down that distance. No wonder they are such consummate ambush hunters!

Amila

It was early October 2019, and I was just back at the homestay after a 10-day Ujung Kulon field visit and looking forward to some rest, a day before Dewo was due to pick me up and get me to Jakarta for my flight home. On the 12th October, around 7.30am, I was relaxing having breakfast outside at the homestay, I was expecting Aphuy to call in and say goodbye as he was heading back to Bogor to see his family after the 10-day stint in the jungle with me. I remember it was a pleasant, sunny day and I noticed a young woman, not dressed in the typical local Muslim attire, walking through the coconut palms towards me. She had short cropped hair, and was carrying a netting bag that looked like it was holding some form of tin canisters. I estimated she was 15 years old; it turned out she was 14. The girl's English was about as good as my Bahasa but she said in very broken English, the local villagers had told her Pak Steve was a good person and could possibly help her.

This had me intrigued, and the conversation happened just as Aphuy rode in on his motorbike, perfect timing! I badly needed him to help translate. After introductions Aphuy discovered the girl's name was Amila, and she was from a local Buddhist family. What transpired was on the 22nd of December 2018, the girl's family, all fishing people, who lived just south of Tanjung Lesung beach were killed by the subsequent tsunami caused by the Anak Krakatoa volcano eruption, which struck large portions of the western Java coastline up towards Ujung Kulon. The day before the eruption, Amila had walked up into the hills from her coastal village to a farming family, to babysit their young kids for the day. When she returned to her village home the following morning, she found it all a wasteland, totally destroyed and tragically, had lost her mum, dad, two younger sisters and her only surviving grandmother to the tsunami.

What a sad and tragic story, I clearly remember both Aphuy and I being rattled and upset upon hearing it. Eventually, Amila was able to find, connect and live with some distant relatives in Labuan, and had only recently received the five cremated remains of her family. So, now we know what's in the tin canisters she was carrying in the netting bag! As we were speaking, many of the local villages adjacent to Ujung Kulon had also been struck again in May 2019, by a tsunami that again did significant damage to coastal communities, damaging fishing boats, jetties and structures all along the Ujung Kulon coast. By October 2019, these communities were still in recovery mode. Amila informed us that it was always her families' wish for their ashes to be scattered at sea, and would I be willing to help her do this. Aphuy also noted Amila had mentioned before coming back to her village and looking to find and see me, a Buddhist monk had blessed the five family members cremated remains and gave Amila permission to scatter the ashes at sea.

Cremation for Buddhist beliefs is normal, the burial at sea is not a common practice, hence the monk's permission and blessing. By comparison Muslim burials are always in the earth, definitely no cremation and definitely no sea burials. I remember at the time thinking with Aphuy's help, we could potentially sort something. And, I was already considering what we needed to do to assist, i.e., organise a boat, possibly two? A growing challenge was on the day the authorities had let local communities know about an impending coastal storm, and a storm warning was given out, as

Minggu, the homestay manager told me at breakfast, and he was already actively tying down gear around the homestay in readiness.

Dewo had called Minggu by phone to say he was worried about the weather as well, and was coming earlier, in case the roads deteriorated. It was pretty clear it was all happening! I said to Aphuy, 'what do you think?' Aphuy replied, 'let's go down to the old jetty and see who has a boat available.' Amila nodded in agreement. Aphuy rode his bike and I walked with Amila. After a 10-minute walk, we arrived at what was left of the jetty in Taman Jaya, and despite the poor physical state of the jetty due to tsunami damage, there was a couple of long timber dugout fishing boats with pontoons on either side, with single masts tied up.

At this point I remember thanking my lucky stars and was so grateful to have Aphuy, despite really needing to be on the road home, he stayed at least long enough to find two local fishermen squatting on a rock having a smoke, both a bit disgruntled as the weather was poor and it was too risky to go fishing. It always impressed me how locals could squat for hours without any discomfort; I couldn't squat for five minutes to save myself! Aphuy negotiated and asked them if we could hire them and their boats to scatter the ashes for the young girl, they agreed and we hoped and suggested the exercise wouldn't take too long. I would eventually pay them 100,000 rupia or around $10.00 Australian each for their help. Aphuy was happy with the result, he shook my hand, said 'goodbye and be careful.' Looking at the growing storm clouds, he then bowed to Amila and wished her 'very good luck with your family's ashes,' and jumped on his bike, hoping to get as far away from the coming storm as quickly as possible, as the coastal roads get quite treacherous in heavy rain.

At this point as I looked out to sea, in the far distance I could see the darkening clouds, the odd flash of lightning and regular thunderclaps, a potential boating nightmare and risk central! Amila and I both agreed we would not go out too far, we ended up taking both boats, we really only needed one but both boats were not what I would call super seaworthy, you could only dream of having a life jacket each! Having two boats operating together was good insurance, if one capsized or fell apart we could use the other one, my thinking anyway! So, we worked out I would paddle up front on one boat, with Amila sitting behind me in the middle of the boat, with her netting bag and five canisters, with one of the fishermen paddling at the back. The second boat had one fisherman up front, who was able to coerce his teenage son to help paddle from the back, I can clearly remember the dad and son arguing, I think the son had better things to do, fortunately he assisted the cause. Remember, all this activity was organised in about one hour after Amila had met Aphuy and I!

So, we start paddling out, and in no time, we have two large saltwater crocs or *'Buaya muara'* following us, the fishermen were clearly toey about this, apparently the crocs would regularly annoy them, hoping to get some free fish or steal from their lines and nets. One croc came in quite close; I gave it a wack on the nose with my paddle and it backed off, unfortunately in its response and recoil reaction caused it to break one of the bamboo supports to one of pontoons! My two-boat idea was gaining substance. My back of the boat paddling fisherman quickly jumped over Amila and myself, moving about the boat in his bare feet like a gymnast, he quickly tied up the damaged support strut and we continued on. He shrugged his shoulders and said *'Buaya muara'* which I interpreted as 'bloody crocs!'

Fortunately, it didn't take us long to get out there, we had paddled out about 400 metres from shore, the storm was definitely getting closer, heavy, side angled showers of heavy rain began to hit us and the sea was getting increasingly choppy. I clearly remember thinking let's get this job done and not tempt fate any further. I nodded to Amila if she thought we were out far enough, she nodded back that she was, then amazingly, the sky opened up, the storm seemed to shift away and around us, and we had a burst of sunshine! Sensing the break in the storm and the ray of sunshine, Amila quietly began scattering the contents of each canister, chanting words each time

191

she dispensed them, it was quite an unusual and unique experience. Even the crocs behaved, hovering on the surface about 100 metres away from the boats. We eventually finished scattering the ashes after around 10 minutes, then turned the boats around and we slowly paddled back to shore. Once back, I paid both fisherman; they walked back to their rock for a chat and smoke as if nothing had happened, the son walked off in a huff and was chatting loudly on his mobile. All of us were ringing wet, despite this I felt quite elated and privileged to be part of something so special. Amila, came to me and said very clearly, '*Pak Steve Terima kasih banyak,*' which translates to thank you very much in Bahasa, then in broken English said, 'I knew you were a good person and would help me,' she bowed with her hands together and gave me a gentle hug. Then she quietly walked off, with her string bag and now empty canisters. I never saw her again.

I walked back to the homestay thinking what the hell just happened, or was it some things are meant to happen! The timing was amazing, especially Aphuy turning up at just at the right time to help translate, if Amila had come the next day, Dewo and I would be heading back to Jakarta, it was perfect karma, it was meant to happen. I remember reflecting on what a mature person Amila was, so responsible for one so young, she did her family proud and upheld their wishes, crocs and all! I've often wondered why Amila asked me for help, it felt like she had no other options, certainly Amila had no local family members to help, her community was devastated by the tsunami. I suspect there was sensitivities with the predominantly local Muslim community being involved in a Buddhist activity. Also, Indonesia is a patriarchal society, men rule, so it looks like I was it, with some great and timely assistance from Aphuy and local fisherman. Whatever the reason Amila came to see me, I was grateful and privileged to help, an experience I won't forget. I was devastated when we lost Aphuy in December 2021, he was such a great mate and help to me on my rhino work and the many other issues you have to confront being a foreigner, undertaking research and operating in another country. I miss you, my friend, you were taken way too soon.

The local community never cease to amaze and impress me, they are incredibly resilient, they endure regular tsunami strikes and bad storm events, they lose family members to all sorts of disasters but they plough on with grace and dignity. Little did I know when I arrived back in Australia two days later, it would be my turn to manage and face a human tragedy.

Stewie

I had just arrived back from Java, when mum called me late afternoon on October 14th, 2019 and told me we had lost my younger brother Stewart in a motorbike accident. I was devastated and in shock, walking around the back lawn at home, I vomited in response to the news but immediately sorted my work commitments at the time and booked a plane to Cairns, arriving late the next day. Again, my partner Tracy was a pillar of strength, so supportive, driving me to the airport and wanting to help. I know she wanted to come and help but work commitments and taking care of our family Labrador 'Juno' were important.

Stewie's mate Casper, appropriately all snow-white hair and beard, picked me up that night from the Cairns airport and dropped me off at Stew's place at Kuranda. On the drive up the Kuranda Range, Casper was going out of his way to run over Cane toads (*Rhinella marinus*). Casper said 'sorry for the swerving but I just fucking hate those shitty toads, any chance I get to squish the little bastards I'll do it!'

Walking into Stew's place I could feel his presence everywhere; it was quite disarming. My plan was, as the first family member on the scene, in spite of coming to terms with his loss, I needed to start working through what needed to happen. I needed to be useful; it kept me focused and my mind off Stewie's loss as best I could. I coordinated with the coroner, worked through all the administrative processes, getting him handed over from the state, getting Stew moved from Mareeba to Cairns, sorting his funeral arrangements, getting everyone together and importantly, keeping the family informed, and dealing with the growing challenge of dealing with the grieving as I called them 'the hairy men', all of Stewie's close bikey and defence force mates.

After a couple of days, I felt things were reasonably sorted, I said to the family now's a good time to come up from Melbourne and be together at Stewie's place in Butler Drive, Kuranda. It's important to acknowledge my sister Peta's work and support down in Melbourne, whilst I was sorting things in Kuranda. We worked well together and no mean feat getting the clan sorted and also getting paperwork together from our parent's Jude and Bill Pinder re Stewie's estate.

In early 2019, my father Bill had been diagnosed with Parkinson's and dementia, and as at the time, an 89-year-old man not in the best mental and physical shape to be jumping on planes and come up to the coordinated madness of sorting Stewie's funeral and farewell, he needed to be carefully managed. Both Peta and mum did a great job of keeping Bill calm. I know mum was feeling it but felt Bill staying home was the right thing to do. Mum's good friend and neighbour Ngaire, despite being in her late nineties, helped by checking in on Bill regularly, also mum and I called him often to keep him updated on what was happening, which was pretty tough. I remember speaking to Bill and he asked me if I'd seen Stewy, I said I had and told him how we were going to send him off, he cried, and so did I. It was one of the most difficult but necessary conversations I'd ever had with him.

I found keeping everyone in the loop that couldn't be there helped me get through it. I regularly spoke to my uncle Rob Whitehill, close friends the Fudge family, and my extended family, it helped keep me going. Once everyone was there, the family clan, mum, Peta, Lorry, Jenny, Cathy and Jenna and Jamie, everyone was supportive, and we all helped get things done as well as interacting with all of Stewie's mates who now were occupying whatever space they could grab. There were swags and tents and

Harley's parked all over the place. Despite this, some funny things occurred. Stew's next-door neighbour Mary was very helpful, she ran a B&B and homestay and offered us a couple of rooms for mum, and sisters Cathy and Jenny to stay. Also Mary provided us with a car, which was really handy, given I had to go up and down the Kuranda range regularly organising things. By this time, the boys were calling me the General, as I was Commander in Chief and giving everyone jobs. I'd give someone $150 and say 'can you go and pick up as many sausages and veges for tonight's barby as you can, or we need more stubbies.' Yes General! The boys also noticed the very single Mary was quite taken with me, regularly saying in military jargon, 'look out Mary's on patrol, quick boys, we better set up a perimeter around the General!' All light-hearted fun, which probably helped lighten the load for us all.

The growing connection between all Stewie's mates and the family was special. I was pleased but saddened to meet and get to know Stew's new partner Lindy. They were such a good fit and she a lovely person who slotted in seamlessly with the family. Everyone could see they were a good match. Meeting and connecting strongly with Stew's close friends Frank and Janne Clark from Mackay was terrific. Frank, a carpenter and Stew were planning to build a deck at one end of Stew's place. Sadly, Frank lost his battle to cancer soon after Stew, I was devastated as we really hit it off, I felt his loss even though I'd only known him for such a short time. The joy of meeting all the bikey boys, the 'hairy men', close friends Ash and Rusty, mates Casper and Neil. Catching up with Stew's kids, Jack and Taylor Pinder in person for the first time, and great nephew little George, Stew's grandson, and seeing Stew's ex-Jenny Pinder (Jenny Birt) now a qualified geologist, again after many years. It was amazing to be a part of this coming together.

Stewy and I had spoken on the phone a few weeks earlier, and we were planning on getting together to go fishing, which we loved to do whenever we could. He was in a good space, his place at Kuranda was going well, he'd met Lindy a few months earlier, they clicked, he was off the smokes, stopped the grog, was making plans. Bottom line is Stew's final days were good, and, as an ex-serviceman who'd been in combat, he'd seen some bad shit and had baggage. Like many veterans Stew only rarely shared stuff with me but at this point in his life he was positive, and I felt it, I was rapt.

How mum survived us kids growing up is a modern-day miracle. We all got up to mischief, especially Stewie and I. With Stewie being six years younger than me I found him very useful when out and about exploring. He could get into places because he was small. For example, one weekend it was hard rubbish time, we found a long canvas fire hose which we grabbed and took to a mine shaft I had found in bushland near Park Orchards. I suspected the mine was a good place to find micro-bats. My plan was to tie the newly found canvas hose to a tree, then around Stewie's waist and lower him down into the mine, this was okay, except for a few tiger snakes (*Notechis scutatus*) that had fallen in and were all climbing over each other in the corner at the base of the mine! As I lowered him down, Stewie could see them moving, he was pretty toey, I told him 'Not to panic, you'll be fine, when you reach the bottom just keep away from them and do not get bitten, as mum would kill us'. Fortunately, Stewie avoided being bitten and found me a nice colony of micro-bats living happily in the recessed shadows of the mine.

I was happy my plan had worked and later after extracting Stew I used the same hose to slide down and check the bats out for myself. On our way home, I discovered a freshly dug common wombat (*Vombatus ursinus*) hole in the side of a hill. A perfect opportunity to send little brother in with a torch to see if anyone was home. Well, there was, Stewie disappeared down the hole, he didn't have to go in far I could see the soles of his runners. The wombat was growling and soon Stew extracting himself totally covered in dirt and was a bit flustered. I remember him saying 'there was one in there and it wasn't happy,' saying 'it kept grinding its teeth and rammed his head and face with its bum,' taking a bit of bark off his face, which by the way is how wombats protect themselves from five-year-old intruders! We rode our bikes home, going straight to the fridge to re-fuel after a hard day's exploring. Mum walked in and asked 'why Stewie was so grubby and had like a gravel rash on his face?' Mum looked at me sternly then put her finger on my forehead and said 'do not move, do not breathe,' the interrogation had begun! Mum then looked at Stewie and said 'speak.' Straight away Stewie coughed up what had happened. Stew sold me out to the judge, all in monotone. Telling mum, 'Steve tied a hose around my waist and lowered me into the mine, there were tiger snakes at the bottom, and Steve said 'don't get bitten, or mum would kill us, so I didn't.'

Mum replied, 'how thoughtful, so you're dangling your little brother in a hole with a pit full of snakes.'

I replied, 'we were looking for bats mum.' Exasperated, mum says 'I don't give a shit about your bloody bats, why can't you two go and kick a football like normal kids.' Mum then looks at Stewie and says 'what else happened.' Stewie replies 'on the way home Steve gave me a torch and sent me down a wombat hole, there was a wombat in there, and it wasn't happy.' Mum jokingly said 'of course, why didn't I think of that!' After Stew's re-telling, I remember mum saying, 'well at least you're both alive! Now, can you please pick your bikes up off the driveway before your father gets home or there will be hell to pay, and you,' pointing at me said, 'get Stew into the shower and cleaned up before tea, your grounded for life, and put some Dettol on his bloody wombat rash,' and, tapping me on the chest said 'please, please stop using your little brother for wildlife target practice, you know he'll do anything you ask him to.' 'Yes mum!' Moral of the story is when entering a wombat hole always wear a helmet, and, Dettol is good for wombat rash!

In his later teenage years and early twenties, Stew went through an extended bad patch where he wrote off several cars and was drinking heavily, unhappy at the time, exacerbated by a troubled relationship with his father. In many ways its remarkable he survived this period unscathed, although he almost didn't. On one occasion, while using the backyard room I lived in before leaving home, Stew came home in the middle of the night drunk, fell asleep with a cigarette and set his mattress on fire, all while passed out, mum sensing something wasn't right, woke up to find smoke billowing out of the room, she managed to grab Stewie by the head and pulled it through a window so he could breath, then a groggy Stew, despite the heavy smoke managed to get out, a lucky escape due only to a mother's uncanny intuition.

To this day I still struggle with his loss; I reckon I'll always have some form of PTSD; he was my little brother and mate and were connected by that bond. I still see him lying there in his bikie gear, it's an image that never leaves me, a vision I'll have until my time is up.

Soon after I arrived in Cairns, Stew's bikey mates Mick Dowling and Angela Piper, who were with him at the end, came to see me. They wanted to share what had happened. It was heart-wrenching and emotional for all of us, for them re-living the experience, and me hearing intimate details about the accident. What transpired was the three guys were riding in formation on their way to Dimbulah, when Stewie, who was the middle rider on a corner, left the road, went over a bank and crashed. Angela got to him first, he was unconscious and struggling to breath, in spite of CPR they couldn't revive him, the medics pronounced him dead around 1.00 pm. Stewie died from traumatic chest injuries, and this was confirmed in the coroner's report. It was a tough and emotional conversation, especially for Mick and Angela who re-lived the accident in detail, just so I would know what had happened. I'll be eternally grateful to them for sharing, they were very respectful. My sense was it helped them both, it certainly did for me.

The funeral home I chose to cater for Stew was based in Smithfield, Trinity Community Funerals. The business was run by a couple of switched-on young guys, and I found them user-friendly, and they understood what we needed. As the news of Stew's loss grew, more and more of his mates wanted to see him physically, pay their respects and say goodbye. The funeral home had a nice chapel, which would have sat around 50 people at best. What we organised was for Stewie to be laid out with no coffin wearing his favourite Hawaiian shirt and his bikey jacket and club colours, with his bikey boots on the floor beside him. On the day of his viewing, my niece Jenna had coordinated and collected images of Stew and sorted a continuously running picture show. So, those that wanted to could sit in the chapel, see Stew, or watch the picture show, it was great, and Jenna did a great job pulling it together.

On the day of the viewing, I took mum in first and let her spend some time alone with him, then his twin sister Cathy, then the immediate family followed and then his mates. Some people felt they couldn't see him and preferred to wait outside and just talk and catch up, there was no pressure, people could do whatever they felt they needed too. Mum and I recently reflected on Stewie's service, mum said she was pleased I'd made the decision not to present Stew to family and friends in a coffin, we both agreed seeing him laying peacefully was better than seeing him cramped in a box, it's a small detail, however, the result made everyone feel better regarding a lasting memory.

Stewie's service was simple, and it worked. We were able to have around two hours for the viewing, after which we all met up for a counter meal at a local pub, then in the evening went back to Stew's place for a big barby. It was a great gathering for everyone and special to be involved in. After Stew's viewing, the boys organised a larger bikie farewell on the Kuranda Range at Charlie's, one of Stew's mates' places. The plan was all the boys and bikes would meet and leave from the Bunnings carpark at Smithfield at the base of the Kuranda Range. Stew's coffin was placed on a bike side car carriage and ridden up to Charlie's place in convoy for a final farewell barby and beers, where late on the same day, the funeral home guys would pick him up for cremation. I remember out of courtesy going to see the Smithfield Bunning's store manager to let him know that for just for a short period, his car park could have 100+ Harley's and assorted bikes ready to follow my brother's final ride up the range. The manager said 'no way, it's not happening.'

I said 'that's fine, I'm just letting you know out of courtesy what is happening!' I left the meeting saying, 'I'll let you argue with the 100+ grieving bikers, best of luck!' By this time after five days of sorting things I was emotionally fried and said to mum and the girls I needed to head home. Mum felt the same, she said it's time for Stew to be with the boys, so Mum, myself, Peta, Lorry, Jenna and Jamie said goodbye and we headed home. My sisters Jenny and Cathy wanted to stay longer, and they joined the bikey crew for Stew's last ride which was awesome. Eventually Stew's ashes were scattered at his crash site, where his last ride ended, with his mates, it's what he would have wanted. A fitting gesture to a great guy, never to be forgotten. Despite all the suffering from Stewie's loss, the family and friends coming together was really special and something I'll never forget being a part off. RIP Stew.

Bikie mate convoy in Cairns, heading towards the Kuranda Range for Stewie's final farewell.

Barby and beers for Stewie and friends at mate Charlie's place
on the Kuranda Range.

It would be remiss of me, not to share Stew's active service life. Stewie, 'Seaweed' to his mates, was the president of the North Queensland Chapter of the Veteran's Motorcycle Club of Australia. Stewie had served in the Army from 20/02/1991 to 23/02/2002, achieving the rank of Corporal. Stew then moved to the Navy, serving from 24/02/2002 to 01/05/2012, achieving the rank of Leading Seaman. Stew served in Cambodia, East Timor, Hawaii, Bougainville, Solomon Islands and Iraq. Stewie was also a member of the Active Reserve Force from 01/05/2012 to 01/05/2015.

Stewie was the kind of guy you wanted in your corner; he was a great mate and always had you're back. This was proven in 2004, when Executive Officer, Warrant Officer Ian Chill 'Chilly' of the HMAS *Tarakan* fell into a crevasse on the Solomon Islands suffering serious spinal injuries. Stewie was the was the first one down the hole. He'd shimmied down on his own shirt! Stewie held Chilly steady because his ribs were broken, and he couldn't breathe. For

201

hours Stew held his head and neck, until the medics arrived. Stew was awarded a Deputy Chief of Operations Commendation for his action in the rescue, and his mate Aaron 'Smouch' Smith received a Maritime Commander Commendation. This rescue all happened at night, was a medical recovery/extraction nightmare and they had no end of trouble extracting Chilly from and through the hole he fell in. For hours Stew held Chilly's head in a position so he could breathe. At the time I felt the Navy hadn't really appropriately recognised Stew's role in saving Chilly. I felt a commendation was pretty weak, so I wrote a letter to the Navy voicing my thoughts. I told Stew I was going to write something, he was flattered but had no expectations anything would occur.

Well, it did. Unexpectedly Stew was called before the Commandant of the Navy in Townsville. I remember Stew telling me what transpired. Stewy is standing at attention opposite the Commandant, who is telling Stew he has received a letter from a Steve Wilson, who is not happy with the recognition he received regarding the Solomon's rescue. 'Who the fuck is Steve Wilson?'

Stew replied, 'it's my older brother Sir, we have the same mother but different fathers.' 'Well, did you put him up to this?' 'No, believe me sir, my brother doesn't get put up to anything unless he feels the need to.'

Well Seaman Pinder, he writes a good letter, you clearly understand what he is aggrieved of. 'Yes sir that's my brother!' Despite the Navy theatrics, unfortunately, I wasn't able to change the Navy's thoughts on the matter. I think Stewy was pretty chuffed I had a crack; I reckon that's what older brothers should do. At the time Bill and mum were pleased I went in to bat for Stew, even Bill thought my letter was good. Mum has Stew's original Navy commendation now nicely framed in pride of place on her wall at her Ocean Grove home, a fitting reminder of Stew's efforts to help an injured mate. Chilly, now in a wheelchair but doing okay post-accident, came to see and say goodbye to Stew, and pass on his respects to the family.

Chilly was adamant, telling us all that he wouldn't be here without Stew's rescue efforts. 'I couldn't breathe without his help.' Chilly was devastated at Stewie's passing, they were good mates. Believe me, after Stewie's loss it wasn't easy to get back in the PhD game but I did, knowing Stew was excited and amazed at what I was doing, so I kept ploughing on!

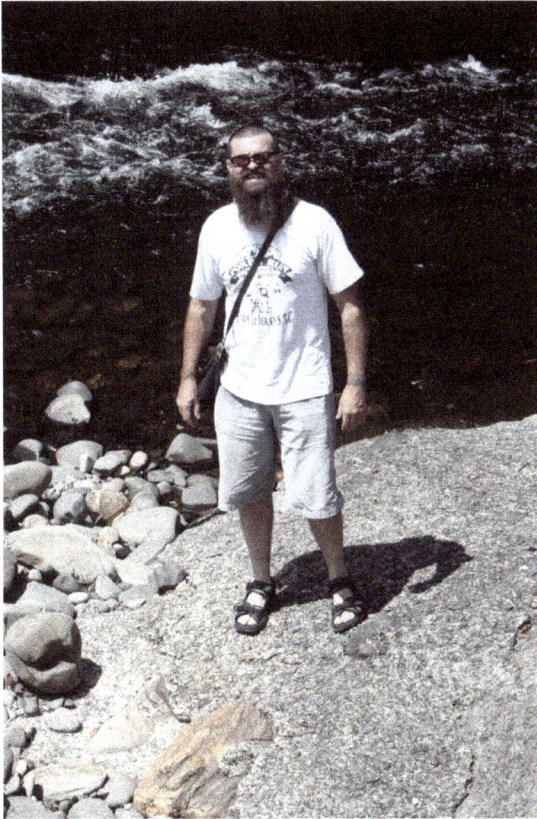

My late brother Stewie

The future, where to from here?

Given the Javan rhino persists only in one small stronghold in Java, one of the most populated islands on the planet, its survival depends on our understanding of its ecology, behaviour, factors impacting and shaping its future, conservation management, the ongoing efforts of Ujung Kulon NP rangers and rhino protection units and the impacts both positive and negative from the growing local community living in villages surrounding the park.

The instigation over the past 85 plus years of conservation action in Ujung Kulon is undoubtedly the reason why the species remains extant today and must be viewed as a major conservation success. However, the suite of real threats still remains. The protection and management efforts in Ujung Kulon National Park require intensification and the rhino's need to be actively managed for population and genetic recovery.

In summary

- My research identified the local community maintained only a basic awareness of Ujung Kulon National Park's boundaries, rules and regulations, and held only limited understanding of the rhino conservation efforts and management actions. Noting this study is the first to examine community attitudes and approaches to rhino management across all 19 villages surrounding Ujung Kulon National Park.

- All village communities agreed regular communication from the authorities will be important to Ujung Kulon and the rhinos moving forward.

- Frontline staff acknowledged the inception of rhino protection units and working partnership with the Ujung Kulon NP Authority, is meeting the needs of rhino protection at present. Staff attributed this success to regular patrol cycles and some awareness of such in local communities. Despite this success, staff noted challenges remain, notably natural resource competition. They did acknowledge if for example, poaching increases, then more resources i.e., field staff and surveillance will be needed. Staff however, given recent events, would acknowledge increased park patrolling and rhino protection is needed.

- Anthropogenic (human-induced) pressure driven mainly by poverty (encroachment and need for more agricultural land) is impacting negatively on Javan rhino and their habitat.

- Frontline staff acknowledged the biggest threat to Javan rhino was disease risk to rhino from domestic stock. An estimated 6,000+ domestic buffalo, and significant numbers of domestic goat, pig and cattle are held in the 19 villages around Ujung Kulon, so the potential for disease transfer is high and a genuine threat. Staff however, would, given recent poaching events, change their biggest threat to poaching.

- Arenga palms have vastly expanded in the region since the explosion of the Krakatoa (Krakatau) volcano in 1883, and now dominate the rainforest canopy in many areas of the park, substantially limiting the growth of native rhino food plants and for available rhino foraging, threatening Javan rhino persistence.

- To examine the impact of arenga palms on rhino habitat and foraging, arenga palms were manually cleared across 15 x one ha experimental sites by local community members and I monitored these sites over two years (2016–2018), including 15 x one ha control plots, for the impact of palm control, plant response and post-clearing visitation frequency of rhino. Palm control resulted in increased diversity and abundance of rhino food plants, and rapid visitation to cleared sites by rhinos replacing areas initially covered by monoculture palm. The findings suggest that rhino habitat manipulation and clearing of arenga palm in selected forest patches is a viable management technique to increase foraging for rhinos. The fact that rhinos were both spray urinating and depositing dung at cleared sites highlights the fact animals were also actively communicating via olfactory means as they would in their feeding habitat.

- Javan rhino utilise wallows not only for thermoregulatory function, they are also critically important in their habitat, interaction and behavioural repertoires. Any future planned translocations will need to factor in release sites that have a viable proximity to water and conditions that supports the maintenance of long-term wallows.

- In this study, we identified, spatially mapped and studied the characteristics of 35 wallows in eastern area of the park, where rhinos were active. We identified and categorised eight behavioural patterns observed at and near wallows related to rhino daily activities and found that wallows have several key features for the Javan rhinos, e.g., Javan rhinos who construct wallows themselves, choose sites with 75% shade cover and often at an elevation.

- Our knowledge of Javan rhino vocalisation has improved through camera trap recordings. Fifty-five video recordings comprising 196 individual calls, identifying eight individual call descriptors with accompanying sonograms (a first for the species), were developed after reviewing 392 camera trap videos (2011–2016). 137 from the peninsula area, taken during and 255 from the eastern Gunung Honje section of the park. The identified eight call descriptors taken from the audio-video data were categorised in a manner consistent with terms used by previous researchers (e.g., Schenkel & Schenkel-Hulliger 1969a, 1969b; Ammann 1985). This is an extremely understudied aspect of Javan rhino ecology.

- The recorded vocalisations (calls) highlight the importance of filling the knowledge gap regarding Javan rhino communication and presents fertile ground to build further understanding of Javan rhino ecology and social dynamics. Because there are so very few direct observations of Javan rhinos this makes comparisons difficult. As demonstrated by Linklater et al. (2013) and Cinková and Policht (2016), the manipulation of chemical signals in dung and urine, and calls can be useful conservation tools. For example, translocated Javan rhino could be stimulated to reduce stress and modify behaviour by using urine-impregnated water and mud at wallows, and playback call recordings. Future research in this area should focus on expanding the database of recordings and increase our understanding of the function of described vocals and any vocals yet to be described.

- We now know the Javan rhino vocal frequency band width range varies between 100 Hz–12 kHz, and have good baseline of data regarding the characteristics of the eight described vocal descriptors, and the communication purpose of vocalisations used in both forest and wallow interactions. For example, camera trap video showed adult males approaching females in wallows in situ, where they would vocalise a repeated '*short pant*' call as they approached females, and when close enough would use flehmen to determine the reproductive status of the female. Females with calves and non-receptive females would respond to males with an agonistically vocalised '*long hiss*'. Males would then subdue their attention and share the wallow in harmony. Females with calves approaching wallows with males in situ, would often demonstrate vigilance behaviour and often leave the wallow entirely without interaction.

- Historically, the eastern Gunung Honje area only had periodic visitation by rhino. Today the area only gets occasional visits, noting females with calves have been captured on camera trap videos but have not stayed in the area. The challenge moving forward is the eastern Gunung Honje site is still prone to illegal grazing of domestic stock, notably buffalo (who often carry noisy bells so villagers can find them), this disturbance does nothing to entice rhinos from staying in the area.

- In the little-known area of Javan rhino social interaction and behaviour I have increased our knowledge by identifying and categorising 11 behavioural patterns, and these were related to their daily activities. Additionally, within each behavioural pattern, 11 sub-categories of behaviour were identified.

- Whilst yet to be confirmed, it appears Javan rhino breed throughout the year so the use of wallows as scent-posts to communicate oestrus may be occurring. Solitary females would regularly drink wallow water, often followed by flehmen, and on two occasions were observed eating mud (geophagy), followed by a flehmen response. Presumably, the drinking, geophagy and flehmen response is determining the presence, and possible dominance status of males.

- On multiple occasions calling was recorded at a wallow site, several which could represent the rhino 'announcing' its presence to any rhino that might be in the vicinity. Investigating the environment, through sniffing at the ground, and vigilance behaviour were frequently recorded in and around wallow sites, suggesting the rhinos are receiving information about previous visitors and are possibly wary about whether another rhino is in the area. As rhinos have poor eyesight, they rely on calling, urine, dung deposits and scent to communicate with conspecifics.

- My observations showed there is little variation in the frequency of wallow use between male and female Javan rhino. Early research by Yahya (2002) supports this suggestion. Camera trap recordings, showed rhinos of both sexes periodically shaking their heads allowing water and mud to infiltrate the skin folds, no doubt a cooling behaviour.

- Although data gaps remain, for example, understanding rhino reproductive ecology and behaviour, we have increased understanding of rhino interaction and communication.

The data captured from this study will help inform national park, conservation planners and government policy makers of local community awareness and understanding of current conservation activity and assist in identifying future risks. This study also helped reveal what community attitudes exist towards conservation activities, protected areas and threatened species management, which may serve as a useful model to better explain community behaviour in other areas (e.g., Lepp and Holland, 2006; Triguero-Mas et al. 2010; Moreto et al. 2017).

This concern over natural resource competition and use is also documented at a higher strategic level by rhino range countries. For example, the Strategy and Action Plan for the Conservation of Rhino in Indonesia (Rhino Century Program 2007–2017), is the Indonesian Government's official conservation policy for the country's rhino populations. The issue of balancing such objectives and the needs of local community is challenging. Frontline staff residing in local villages can inform and educate local community through their presence. There are consequences for threatened species such as Javan rhino with long birth intervals that lower the reproductive rate (long gestation) and their recovery.

Protected and remaining natural areas rapidly decline as human populations occupy habitat landscapes and impact on ecological processes. This negative ecological impact trend is often seen in developing countries where urbanisation and human settlement growth occurs (e.g., Langpap & Wu 2008; Acharya et al. 2016; Allendorf & Gunung 2016; Pálinkás 2018). Reducing human-induced adult mortality (e.g., hunting or habitat reduction) is a critical component to conservation and recovery. Indonesia is a rapidly developing country, it's inevitable the human population will expand, along with needed supporting infrastructure such as roads and access. This will significantly increase pressure on remaining natural landscapes, like Ujung Kulon National Park.

Recommendations moving forward

- To reduce and mitigate against the ongoing risk of disease spread from domestic stock to rhino, authorities could respond by undertaking regular domestic stock vaccinations to reduce disease transfer to rhinos. Supporting this action, undertake regular soil and faecal analyses to identify the presence, location and type of pathogenic agents both within local villages and Ujung Kulon, and develop an emergency action plan in the event of a disease outbreak. Supporting this, an education and awareness program needs to be instigated to highlight the risks and benefits to both domestic animals and local wildlife of such an initiative.

- As stated earlier, I believe, as a biosecurity measure, a suitable stock fence be built with gates across the narrow isthmus area (1.5 km wide) separating the peninsula from the eastern Gunung Honje area of the park which can be closed off in the event of a disease outbreak. This 'when needed' second line of defence barrier fence would at least contain any disease outbreak from infiltrating the main peninsula rhino population. Outside of a disease outbreak the fence would remain open to allow natural movement of wildlife.

- The recent (2019–2023) rhino losses (26) due to poaching in Ujung Kulon have highlighted the need to increase in situ patrol efforts and intelligence. South African authorities have begun to translocate large numbers of southern white rhino into the Greater Kruger National Park and adjacent game reserves after active surveillance and anti-poaching measures have significantly eliminated the poaching threat. Antipoaching methods include using drones with thermal imaging to survey animals, increasing poaching threat intelligence activity, including regular polygraphs for protection staff, satellite and AI tracking technology, smart fences, dehorning and 24-hour monitoring. Elements of this broad-based technology could be readily adapted to the remaining Javan rhino population, for example, the drone-based thermal imaging could accurately monitor population numbers, which has been problematic in recent times.

- On a positive note, since the recent poaching events, the UKNP Authority has increased its park surveillance and anti-poaching activities. Coordinating with local law enforcement, 7 poachers were apprehended, each receiving 12-year sentences. Two buyers were also apprehended, one receiving a 4.5-year sentence, the other one year. Additionally, 5 bird poachers were also captured in the law enforcement net, each received 2 years jail. To date, a community awareness program has seen 345 illegal firearms handed in. Physical barriers have been placed in estuaries to prevent sea-based poaching incursions. Increased patrolling of land-based movement has increased also.

- Given that interviewed staff live in the local communities surrounding the park, understanding local community impacts and insight may reveal opportunities to improve relationships and develop conservation-based programmes with local community input. The community development program initiated by the World Wildlife Fund between 1996–2017 activated many excellent programs to enhance local villages skills in many areas, for example the establishment of an ecological agricultural field school. I would love to see these practical initiatives expanded even further to include working with local community to find viable 'alternatives' across a number of key impact areas to reduce the need for national park resources. For example, solar power (e.g., solar panels with storage batteries) to reduce firewood collection and charcoal fires, or explore other low emission-energy sources such as wind or wave power.

- Across all local villages, effective recycling of local waste is an issue, from green to plastic waste; however, it is also an opportunity to help the village environment and generate income. Local community clean up teams could remove the abundance of plastic waste that litters all the beaches around Ujung Kulon. Noting green turtles (*Chelonia mydas* or *'penyu'*) use these beaches as nesting sites, any clean up would benefit them. The illegal logging of rainforest timber is an ongoing challenge, and with education, the use of timber alternatives i.e., recycled timber or the use of long-lasting composite products can be introduced.

- Opportunities exist for community to expand into community forestry, carbon sequestration plantings, rhino food plant plantations, bee keeping (for pollination enhancement and for (profit/commodity) and options that allow rhino entry, including creating wetlands (possible tourism opportunity). Running in parallel is an education program that teaches the benefits of rainforest habitat not only to biodiversity, also benefits crop pollination, carbon sequestration and flood mitigation.

- An untapped local resource is the community occupying the 19 villages surrounding the park. A potential workforce of over 75,000+ people. Ecotourism as an alternative livelihood should be encouraged particularly if buffer zones are created. Eco-lodges could be set up in these areas with strict controls on access to the park, including using local guides. There are many good examples of where local communities have benefited economically from ecotourism in buffer zone areas, creating greater awareness and respect for the core areas of national parks (e.g., Chitwan National Park, Nepal) (Dinerstein 2003; Aryal et al 2017). Supporting this approach would be an ongoing education and awareness program in local communities and to visitors of Javan rhino ecology and the broader conservation issues that affect its ongoing existence. Worth noting there is small scale guided bird and wildlife watching tours happening. The local community needs to recognise rhinos are more valuable alive than dead.

- Carefully managed local tourism is an obvious opportunity, visitors could learn and be exposed to Sundanese village life, their culture and cuisine. I'm not suggesting a Bali resort, just visitor exposure to the 'real' village experience. Any economic development opportunities that reduce encroachment of land and moves people out of poverty would be welcome. Potentially, satellite work teams across the 19 villages could support the suggested initiatives, assisting the consequent reductions in natural resource take from the national park. Many development organisations could help in the economic, new technological and modern science integration space. For example, The Organisation for Economic Co-operation and Development (OECD); Asian Development Bank (ADB); International Fund for Agriculture Development (IFAD); and the Asian Infrastructure and Investment Board (AIIB) are just a few in a long list.

- An escalation of arenga palm clearing using local community labour particularly in the core Ujung Kulon peninsula habitat area would benefit rhinos through increased available habitat and foraging opportunity. For example, an annual arenga clearance target of 250 ha would rapidly return significant rhino habitat and increase food resources. Additionally, research into arenga palm control methods, regrowth and existing seed banks is essential, and should occur as a parallel activity along with active control. Investigation into arenga seed dispersal agents is warranted, which may involve a larger cohort of dispersers than is currently known, and will need to be factored into control operations. Recently, to aide rhino movement, corridors have been created in dense patches of palm.

- A data gap remains regarding how important and what function pedal scent gland secretions present. Both species of *Rhinoceros* (Javan and greater one-horned) possess pedal scent glands, just how these species use pedal scent

213

gland (cutaneous glands) secretions in their communication repertoire remains unclear.

- Wherever possible male Javan rhinos should be monitored, particularly older males who may still hold dominance, however, may be past reproductive potency (e.g., low sperm count). I suspect older, larger and more experienced males may be dominating and guarding reproductive-age females and excluding younger potentially more sexually potent males from female access. Male guarding has been recorded in the congeneric greater one-horned rhino. Future translocations could be trialled using older, past their reproductive prime males.

Marine pollution on beach. Despite its remoteness, Ujung Kulon National Park is not immune from marine pollution. Many of its beaches are covered in plastic waste, a global scourge that degrades marine and coastal ecosystems.

- The current lack of accurate knowledge of female age at first breeding and interbirth interval is a significant data gap worthy of investigation. The age at first reproduction can be an impediment given it takes time for a population to rebound and respond. For example, it is estimated the congeneric greater one-horned rhino female's age at first breeding is 7 to 7.5 years, presumably Javan's have similar age at first breeding results. With low numbers only a few Javan females may be reproductively active at any given time. I suspect, Javan rhino longevity, as in other rhino species, may compensate for the slower population recovery time, or at minimum reduce the disadvantage when compared to the rebounding ability of many small mammals.

- The carrying capacity of Ujung Kulon was demonstrated to be a significant constraint to population growth by a Population and Habitat Viability Analysis (PHVA). Any decrease in carrying capacity would restrict population growth leading to a population reduction over time but a negligible likelihood of extinction. The distribution of the Javan rhino population is largely constrained to the peninsula connecting to the mainland by narrow isthmus (1.5 km wide). This situation limits expansion of the species' area of occupancy, meaning that to increase the population, the density on the peninsula needs to increase, animals need to move through the isthmus onto the mainland, or animals need to be translocated out of the peninsula. Rhino reproduction is density-dependent, with lowered reproduction rates at higher densities. Given the need for optimal reproduction rates for such a critically endangered species, decreasing the density of rhinos on the peninsula is therefore important.

- Importantly, the need for a second population of Javan rhino remains a critical requirement and the current population would benefit from active biological management to keep the population at a lower level, maximise growth, reduce the constraints of environmental factors and high densities. Translocation of a small group of Javan rhino to a safe and suitable site remains a concern. The eastern JRSCA site is an ideal location to set up a pre-translocation facility. Although not without risk, I believe Sumatra's Way Kambas and Bukit

Barisan Selatan National Parks are prime sites for translocated animals, especially given rhino protection units are already in place and active in these areas to monitor and protect, and it's within the species former range.

- Training the Javan conservation authorities' staff in the darting, chemical immobilisation, wild capture, radio tagging and translocation of Javan rhino is a critical skill set, and the Nepalese and Indian authorities have this skill set in spades, having worked with and translocated greater one-horned rhino successfully for many years. This is a resource to be tapped into. The opportunity to radio-collar translocated animals is enticing given this has never been done before on this species.

- The experience of national park staff (av. 21.9 years), and rhino protection staff (RPU) (av. 5.4 years) is a skill set to be tapped into. Training of conservation and field staff from tropical and sub-tropical countries who could learn and pass on valuable skills in tracking, effective use and management of camera traps, wildlife observation, navigation and surveying; operating in rough conditions, bush craft and, they are excellent bush cooks!

- A data gap is our lack of understanding regarding resource competition between Javan rhino and banteng. This needs to be resolved. A solid research project should sort this issue out once and for all, and could be useful information for any future Java to Sumatra rhino translocations given Sumatra has healthy banteng populations as well.

- Understanding the current Javan rhino population is critical as there remains many gaps. Yes, the authorities have a good understanding of the age class and sex of animals which is not without worry. For example, the population has a skewed sex ratio with more males than females, the population is aging with few animals under seven years of age, the most likely age at which breeding begins for the Javan rhino is three, at least eleven females are known not to have produced a calf in the last four years resulting in only ten known females currently successfully breeding, and camera-trap images suggest there are increasing signs of physical deformities, possibly from in-breeding. The current 2025 post-recent poaching event population status needs to be understood, including sex ratio and age class. Recent increased monitoring and surveillance has identified several new calves and previously unidentified adults, to date 58 individuals have been identified.

- Deeper understanding is needed of kinship relationships between all individuals and analysis on the breeding success of each female is urgently required for effective population management strategies to be designed and acted on. The age at first reproduction for female rhino is an important metric when investigating population management. With such a small population only a few females may be reproductively active at any given time. Understanding if this issue affects Javan rhino is important, identified older males could be translocated to increase viable breeding returns.

- Ujung Kulon and its wildlife (e.g., endangered dhole, Javan leopard, Javan gibbon and Grizzled leaf langur), including rhino presents fertile ground for research across a number of disciplines. For example, undertake a comprehensive fauna survey across the park; examine the mechanisms behind mammal, bird and others regarding seed dispersal; plant and tree surveys; current and future climate change impacts and options for mitigation; mangrove studies; feasibility studies on the benefits and risks of an increase in ecotourism; exploring the economic and local community livelihood needs vs biodiversity needs. How long is a piece of string? The research topics are endless, and ideal for universities to establish themselves as centres of rainforest and conservation learning.

- The need for a real time 2025 onward, well-resourced, all risks identified recovery plan is long overdue. Such a plan must include clear decision-making protocols to activate mitigation actions for identified risks such as tsunami/volcanic impact i.e., setting up a second population, disease outbreaks, arenga palm control and poaching.

The integration of landscape approaches to broaden the area and scope of Ujung Kulon through practical village planning to establish buffer zones, and where appropriate, begin identifying habitat corridors where rhino can move or be attracted to. Core habitat areas remain critical and may need additional protection as roads, infrastructure and access to the Ujung Kulon peninsula becomes easier, and the human population grows along with associated risks, let alone the ticking time bomb of disease risk from domestic stock. The isolation of the only extant Javan rhino population makes it a difficult species to study. Camera trapping is an emerging remote sensing tool used to study wildlife, especially for species that are endangered or difficult to observe. The advent of camera trap technology improves individual recognition, and captures behaviour, using Griffith's (1993) identification criteria (mark-recapture), which has been verified as an effective ID criterion, and the addition of date and time capture provided by camera imagery. This technology will assist in identifying the individual animals, activity patterns (date/time of day), visitation frequency (day/month) and behaviour in wallows and in other landscape contexts. This photo identification technique has been found to be a reliable census methodology (e.g., Hiby & Lovell 1993; Haryono et al. 2015). The composite risks of natural disasters, human population growth, land encroachment, illegal poaching and lack of or reductions in the amount and quality of habitat remain some of many challenges both conservation managers and endangered wildlife face.

For example, the impact of any poaching on the population would be severe. A poaching rate of 1% per year would lead to negative growth rates and a 6.3% chance of extinction in the next one hundred years. The Javan rhino, despite significant conservation effort and intervention over the past 50 years, remains one of the world's rarest and most critically endangered species.

For many years, discussions have been held to increase the current Javan rhino population outside of Ujung Kulon. The establishment of a captive breeding program and in situ facility may be helpful to the survival and recovery of the Javan rhino and at minimum could be used as a temporary pre-translocation facility, however, apologies for sounding like a broken record, the establishment of a second wild population in suitable habitat would likely provide the biggest conservation impact and produce results more quickly.

The idea of establishing a second wild population of Javan rhinos within Indonesia but outside Ujung Kulon, was first proposed by Schenkel and Schenkel (1982) as a response to the death of five rhinos to disease. The idea is widely accepted and was an activity in the Strategy and Action Plan for the Conservation of Rhinos in Indonesia (2007–2017), and the vision produced from the multi-stakeholder PHVA consultation process which states 'secure the habitat and develop three well-managed sites for in situ populations to ensure an increase to at least 150 Javan rhinos by 2040'.

The first study to look at possible sites to establish a second population was in 2013, when the government of Indonesia and conservation organisations assessed seven candidate locations based on several assessment parameters: the physical geography (slope, elevation, road network, water source availability and mineral salt content), habitat (food availability, vegetation and canopy cover), mammal community (mammal and predator existence) and social constraints and opportunities (human disturbance, local community perception and public support).

At the time, all sites assessed were on Java because it was deemed poaching rates across Sumatra were too high and there was a lack of local government support for translocations outside Java. The

Javan sites were ranked by Rahmat (2013) for their their suitability, they were: 1. Cikepuh Wildlife Reserve in Sukabumi; 2. Leuweung Sancang Natural Reserve in Garut; 3. Cikeusik Forest Management Unit in Pandeglang; and 4. Rawa Danau Natural Reserve in Serang. The three other sites Gunung Halimun Salak National Park, Hutan Tutupan Baduy (Baduy Forest) and Malingping Forest Management Unit in Lebak were not deemed suitable because they have steep slopes above 25% on average and gentle slopes were deemed necessary for suitable Javan rhino habitat.

Needless to say, no progress has been made in this space, despite some good investigation for options in Java. When looking at the survival of a newly created second population it was shown that a founder population of 5 females and 3 males performed best all round, showing a lower extinction risk, higher average population size over the longer term and lower inbreeding accumulation at 100 years. The carrying capacity of any new site needs to be at least 50 individuals to allow for population growth; below this, the risk of extinction was deemed unacceptably high. Not surprisingly, no newly established second population could withstand any loss to poaching or disease. Also, we know it is also more economical to protect and recover rhino populations in the wild. Wild-to-wild translocations of the closely related greater one-horned rhino have proved very successful at increasing breeding rates, establishing new populations and generally increasing the total size of the species' meta-population (e.g., Singh et al. 2012; Thapa et al. 2013).

A recent study by Granger (2021), based on pre-population collapse occurrence records from across Asia shows that Javan rhino can inhabit a much broader range of habitats than is suggested by the ecology of their remnant extant population. In fact, Granger (2021) found both altitude and slope contributed 0% to the habitat suitability models when looking at historical distribution data. This data increases the range of options for suitable locations to establish a second wild population of Javan rhinos in both Java and southern Sumatra. So, we really are at a pivotal point of setting up a second population which now, with new data, has more scope.

Are we keeping up with modern poaching trends? Current and future expected climate change impacts? The human population growth wave we know is coming? These are just some identified research gaps that need to be investigated, and with mitigation plans put in place. Management authorities need to have clear pathways to deal with threats and impacts as they arise, and importantly the resources to react quickly. The lack of ability to move and react with resources to solve a problem i.e., increased poaching protection and need for increased habitat vs economic development, despite significant effort, ultimately led to the demise post the 1988 discovery of the last population of the Indochinese Javan rhino subspecies *R. s. annamiticus* in Vietnam. Tragically, this population wasn't protected effectively and was declared extinct due to poaching in 2011 (Brook et al. 2014). In spite of the above suggested recommendations, I do acknowledge the long-term conservation work and current efforts in the establishment, management and protection of Ujung Kulon National Park by the Indonesian Government's Ministry of Environment and Forestry, and the rhino protection mechanisms put in place; initially those supported by WWF and later those of the Rhino Protection Units managed by Ujung Kulon National Park Authority and the Rhino Foundation of Indonesia supported by the International Rhino Foundation.

In most cases the challenges of Javan rhino conservation and recovery have been clearly identified and solutions exist. Our ability to control arenga palm has been successfully piloted, endemic diseases in the livestock surrounding Ujung Kulon have been identified and solutions to the small population constraints articulated. Currently, a coalition of conservation organisations and academic institutions are working closely together under an aligned set of priorities for the species is present. Given the demographic and genetic risks facing the species, the threat of tsunami, volcanic eruption, poaching and disease, each has the possibility of destroying decades of conservation efforts in a very

221

short space of time. Lack of funds, conflicting local and national interests, a too narrow definition of suitable habitat for the species, competing land uses, the perceived high risk and political risk of authorizing this action have all hampered a second population from being established. Decisive action needs to be taken to identify, protect and populate a second site for the species, before it's too late. Ralls et al. (2018) noted the lack of action due to conflicting national and local priorities, and the risk aversion of governments to support comprehensive conservation actions, facilitated by a lack of data, is in itself a decision, and has been a repeated failure for Javan rhino conservation over the past decades.

In closing and to summarise, today there remains two main conservation issues to address for the Javan rhino. Firstly the surviving, single population is highly vulnerable to inbreeding and demographic effects that are slowing the breeding rate of the species, these include close kinship, possibility of male guarding, skewed sex ratio and a high-density population. Secondly, the ongoing threats of poaching and disease risk facing the population in Ujung Kulon need to be addressed at much higher intensity than is currently occurring. This search for a second relocation site needs to recognise the habitat requirements of the Javan rhino based on its historical distribution, not the conditions found today in Ujung Kulon, which are most likely an artefact of former habitat, given impacts on Ujung Kulon from past tsunamis and recent arenga palm infestations.

Globally, outside of the conservation industry, few people are aware of Javan rhino's existence and its challenges. A public education and awareness campaign, sharing the species' ecology and natural history background is warranted. It's a remarkable story of species survival against the odds. I believe the Sundanese (Javan) people living in and around Ujung Kulon are supportive of their rhino, and want to see it persist. It's part of their identity, and in spite of low incomes and often seasonal work, will adapt and be open to using other opportunities, and reduce their reliance on Ujung Kulon resources.

I'm very grateful to the humanity shown by the local people, in spite of cultural and language differences, we could always find a way to 'non-verbally' communicate and work together. I was interested in them and they me, it was a privilege and one I won't forget. Covid devastated their families, but they were always up for a cuppa and a chat.

In 2023, NGO Auriga Nusacantara undertook a comprehensive 32-page review and investigation of the current state of Javan rhino and the conservation efforts behind it. The review identified a number of concerns including, increased poaching presence and consequent illegal removal of camera traps, discrepancies in rhino population monitoring and lack of investigation into rhino deaths since 2011. This review was timely given the recent poaching events, the population is under more threat than ever. The review provided the following key recommendations: increased protection of Javan rhino and Ujung Kulon NP, monitoring of the rhino population should be in accordance with academic standards, encourage research and importantly implement a second population or second habitat program in earnest. I'm encouraged this report has occurred; it's a real-time update. I see its value as applying positive feedback. The Indonesian Ministry of Environment and Forestry and Ujung Kulon National Park Authority is well aware the global conservation community is watching, and has been for some time, since the mid 1980s, particularly around the importance of setting up a second population as a risk mitigation measure. I acknowledge the Indonesian Ministry of Environment and Forestry and Ujung Kulon National Park Authority current rhino management regime has protected the albeit often slow and incremental rise of the rhino population, it continues to monitor the population via its camera trap network, and undertake habitat enhancement activities, such arenga palm control and food plant regeneration.

The ever-active frontline teams continue to keep rhino safe from poaching harm. However, there is always room for positive change. Constructive criticism of existing management processes is valuable and can be a powerful motivator, and if proposed professionally can really benefit the situation moving forward. If the report's recommendations are implemented, it will only help Javan rhino and its management moving forward. Way back in time, Hoogerwerf (1938); Schenkel and Schenkel–Hulliger (1960b) and Talbot (1960) all held long-term conservation concerns about Javan rhino, noting 85 years ago the population during Hoogerwerf's (1938) work may have been as low as 15–20 animals. The ongoing challenges Javan rhino face will require ongoing political will and active support at the highest levels of government, along with united alliances between local authorities and philanthropic organisations.

I fully appreciate and understand the Indonesian Ministry of Environment and Forestry and Ujung Kulon National Park Authority's reticence to change the current state of play, it has worked so far, however, all the risk factors still remain and have intensified. As stated earlier, the UKNP Authority has responded positively to the poaching events, and should be commended for their ongoing efforts to improve the protection and management of Javan rhino. In a positive step moving forward, two fenced paddocks, 40 and 25 – ha in size have been erected in the eastern JRSCA area, with an aim to capture and translocate two rhinos, hopefully a pair? This exercise will build valuable skills in translocation, wild capture and semi-captive management. Three pitfall traps have been installed in readiness. The Strategy and Action Plan for the Conservation of Rhinos in Indonesia (2007–2017) plan has been in place for some time, it just needs activation and updating. As an eternal optimist, I believe this is achievable, given significant conservation actions have already been happening, and certainly it goes without saying, I'm happy to help the cause in any way I can!

On a positive note, in late 2021, after six years, I completed my thesis: 78,000 words, 280 pages and seven chapters. To gain the title of doctor, you need to be independently examined. A week prior to catching up, both my assigned independent examiners were sent copies of my thesis to review. Then a date is set and essentially, over a two-hour period the assigned independent examiners will ask and test your knowledge on your PhD topic. In my case, the Chair of Examiners at the University of Queensland was Associate Professor Diana Fischer who attends the examination as adjudicator. My two independent examiners were Associate Professor Dr Amal Bhattacharya from Raiganj University, India, and Dr Bibhab Kumar Talukdar, who heads up the IUCN Asian Rhino Specialist Group. We all hooked up online and the academic torture began!

Fortunately, I answered everything satisfactorily, to be brutally honest, I found it quite an enjoyable experience, I genuinely wanted to be tested on my knowledge and work, and if I didn't have my shit together by then I deserved to fail! After close to two hours of questioning and discussion, they asked me to go offline for 30 minutes, suggested I grab a cuppa and something to eat, then when I hooked up again, they both happily said, 'well done Dr Wilson!' Importantly, they were very happy with my work, I didn't have to do any revisions, which is unusual but I was very grateful for!

At the time due to covid I wasn't able to attend the University of Queensland's official cap and gown awards ceremony, I was slightly disappointed but got over it pretty quickly, plus I've never felt comfortable wearing a suit, I'm a short's and covered in mud man! I was very pleased in February 2023 to be accepted and join the IUCN's SSC Asian Rhino Specialist Group 2021–2025. This will give me the opportunity to apply what I've learned and hopefully influence future conservation measures at the highest level for not only the Javan rhino but Sumatran and the greater one-horned rhino as well. It's for a five-year term. Over my six-year journey I undertook many trips to Java, Indonesia, spending on average 1–3 weeks per trip roughing it in the jungles of Ujung Kulon National Park. An ongoing challenge was that I'd get distracted by something I'd observed, an unusual lizard or snake, feeding primates, nesting birds, something I hadn't seen before except in a book, so many individual wildlife experiences. I would regularly remind myself, stay focused you're here to PhD!

The whole experience was amazing, I had a few doubters, many smarter people than me said it was impossible and too difficult. Somehow, I found a way. I would like to acknowledge the efforts of past and present rhinologists, scientists, field staff, non-government and government officials for their ongoing work to protect and save this species, and the other four species as well, it's a continuing collective effort, that just can't stop. I hope you enjoyed reading this book and learning about rhinos and my memoir journey as much as I did. Remember, rhinos rock!

A nice end to a good time chasing rhinos, sunset over Taman Jaya.

Part III—Bibliography

Pálinkás 2018; Grün 2006; Cinková & Bičík 2013; Hoogerwerf 1938, 1970; Amman 1985; Schenkel & Schenkel-Hulliger 1969a, 1969b; Owen-Smith 1973, 1988, 2004; Dinerstein 1991b, 2003, 2011; Seidensticker 1987; IUCN Red List 2023; Hazarika & Saikia 2010; Talukdar 2002; Ministry of Forestry 1995; Fernando et al. 2006; Rookmaaker 1998, 1980, 2005, 2011, 2018, 2019; Jones 1979; Reynolds 1960, 1961, Groves & Leslie Jr 2011; Sody 1959; Brook et al.2014; Horsfield 1824; Van Strien et al. 2008; Nardelli 2013, 2016;

Hommel 1987; Indonesian Ministry of Forestry 2007; Isler & van Schaik 2009; Clutton-Brock 2009; Ricklerfs 2010; Muntasub 2002; Putro 1997; Hariyadi et al. 2012, 2013, 2016; Budiansky 1997; van der Made & Grub 2010; Setiawan et al.2017; Groves 1967, 1982; Venter & Hanekon 2010; Wood et al. 2005; Bhattacharya & Chakraborty 2016; Linklater et al. 2013; Charpentier et al. 2008; Cavaliers & Colwell 1995; De Poncins 1935; Burton 1961; Dutta et al. 2015; Shannon et al. 2003; Pinter-Wollman 2009; Archya et al. 2016; Allengorf & Gunug 2016; Hazwinkel 1933; Muggenthaler et al. 1993, 2003; Budde & Klum 2003; Olicht et al. 2008, Hart 1983; Raychlow et al. 1988; Kretzschmar et al. 2001; Marneweck et al. 2018; Griffith 1993; Stevenson & Poole 1976; Hockings 2016; Deuve & deuve 1962; Schaller et al. 1990; Santiapillai et al. 1993a, 1993b; Van Strien 1986; Laurie 1978; Policht et al. 2008; Morton 1975; Brown & Handford 2000; Aryal et al. 2017; Lepp & Holland 2006; Triguero et al. 2010; Moreto et al. 2017; Langpap & Wu 2008; Rahmat 2013; Talbot 1960; Yahya 2002; Hiby & Lovell 1993; Supriatin 2000; IFRC Report 2023; Auriga Nusacantra 2023; Whittaker et al. 2001; Whittaker & Heegaard 2003; Ralls et al. 2018; Brook et al. 2014; Ramono et al. 2009; Singh et al. 2009; Thapa et al. 2013; Cave 1961; Granger 2021; Beden & Guérin 1973; Griffith, Hamilton-Smith & Pigeon 1827; Geoffroy-Saint-Hilaire & Curvier 1824; Jardine 1836; Cuvier 1829; Falconer & Cautley 1847; Gray 1868; von Martens 1876; Lydekker 1886; Dubois 1908; von Koenigswald 1933; Deriniyagala 1938, 1946; Barnard 1932; Heissig 1972; Wilson & Mittermeier (eds.) 2009; Nelson et al. 2016; Haryono et al. 2016; Nardelli & Robovský 2022.

Glossary

ADB Asian Development Bank

AIIB Asian Infrastructure and Investment Board

AREAS WWF's Asian Rhino and Elephant Action Strategy

ARP Asian Rhino Project

ASPG Australian Self-Publishing Group Pty Ltd

AsRSG Asian Rhinos Specialist Group (under IUNC-SSC)

AfRSG African Rhinos Specialist Group (under IUNC-SSC)

AUD Australian dollar

BBSNP Bukit Barisan Selatan National Park

CBD Convention on Biological Diversity

CBNRM Community-based natural resource management

CEPF Critical Ecosystem Partnership Fund

CITES Convention on Trade in Endangered Species of Fauna and Flora

CTNP Cat Tien National Park

DNPWLM Department of National Parks and Wildlife Management

EU European Union

FFI Fauna and Flora International

GBCMA Goulburn Broken Catchment Management Authority

GLNP Gunung Leuser National Park

JRSCA Javan Rhino Study and Conservation Area

LIF Leuser International Foundation

MPB Global Management and Propagation Board (Sumatran rhinos)

IFAD International Fund for Agriculture Development

IDR Indonesian Rupiah

IPB Institut Pertanian Bogor

IPZs Intensive Protection Zones

IRIS Indonesian Rhino Information System

IRF International Rhino Foundation

IRV Indian Rhino Vision

IUCN-SSC International Union for Conservation of Nature (The World Conservation Union)-Species Survival Commission

JRSCA Javan Rhino Conservation Study Area

KSNP Kerinci Seblat National Park

KTP Kgalagadi Transfrontier Park

LIPI Lembaga Ilmu Pengetahuan Indonesia

NGO Non-Governmental Organization

NRS National Rhino Sanctuary

NP National Park (e.g., Bukit Barisan Selatan)

NTFP Non-Timber Forest Products

MOEF Indonesian Ministry of Environment and Forestry

MoU Memorandum of Understanding

MPU Marine Protection Unit

PHKA Perlindungan Hutan dan Konservasi Alam (Directorate General of Forest Protection and Nature Conservation of the Ministry of Forestry)

PKBI Program Konservasi Badak Indonesia (Indonesian Rhino Conservation Program)

KZN KwaZulu-Natal

OECD The Organisation for Economic Co-operation and Development

PKBA Perlindungan Hutan dan Konservasi Alam (Directorate General of Forest Protection and Nature Conservation of the Ministry of Forestry)

PKBI Program Konservasi Badak Indonesia (Indonesia Rhino Conservation program)

RCO Rhino Conservation Officer

RPU Rhino Protection Unit

RTF Rhino Task Force

SADC Southern African Development Community

SBN Suaka Badak Nasional

SDIs Spatial Development Initiatives

STCP Sumatran Tiger Conservation Program

SPU Sea Protection Unit

SVC Savé Valley Conservancy

TBNRM Transboundary natural resource management

TFCA's Transfrontier Conservation Areas

UKNP Ujung Kulon National Park

UNEP United Nations Environmental Program

UNESCO United Nations Educational Scientific Cultural Organisation

UNICEF United Nations International Children's Emergency Fund

USD United States Dollar

USFWS-RTCF US Fish and Wildlife Service's Rhino and Tiger Conservation Fund

WCS Wildlife Conservation Society

WI Wetland International

WKNP Way Kambas National Park

WTTC World Travel and Tourism Council

WWF Worldwide Fund for Nature

YABI Rhino Foundation of Indonesia

YMR Yayasan Mitra Rhino (Indonesian Rhino Foundation)

Bibliography

Acharya, K.P. (2016). An assessment of zero poaching of *Rhinoceros unicornis* in Nepal. Ministry of Forest and Soil Conservation, Kathmandu.

Acharya, K.P., Paudel, P.K., Neupane, P.R. & Köhl, M. (2016). Human-Wildlife Conflicts in Nepal: Patterns of Human Fatalities and Injuries Caused by Large Mammals. *PloS ONE*, 11(9): E0161717. doi: 10.1371/journal.pone.0161717

Acharya, K.P. (2018). Conservation conflict in Nepal: An examination of the patterns of ecological dimension of human-wildlife conflict and wildlife conservation. PhD dissertation, Faculty of Mathematics, Informatics and Natural Sciences, University of Hamburg, Germany.

AfRSG (2012). A report from the IUCN Species Survival Commission (IUCN/SSC) African and Asian Rhino Specialist Groups and TRAFFIC to CITES Secretariat pursuant to solution Conf. 9.14 (Rev.CoP14) and Decision 14.89. IUCN, Gland, Switzerland.

AfRSG (2012). Update on African Rhino Status and Poaching Trends from IUCN SSC African Rhino Specialist Group (AfRSG). IUCN, Gland, Switzerland.

AfRSG & AsRSG. (2016). African and Asian Rhinoceroses - Status, Conservation and Trade. A report from the IUCN Species Survival Commission (IUCN/SSC) African and Asian Rhino Specialist Groups and TRAFFIC to the CITES Secretariat pursuant to Resolution Conf. 9.14 (Rev. CoP17) African and Asian Rhino Specialist Group (AfRSG and AsRSG). IUCN, Gland, Switzerland.

Alamgir, M., Sloan, S., Campbell, M.J., Engert, J., Kiele, R. & Porolag, G. (2019). Infrastructure expansion challenges sustainable development in Papua New Guinea. PLoS ONE, 14(7), e0219408. https://doi.org/10.1371/journal.pone.0219408

Allendorf, T.D. & Gurung, B. (2016). Balancing conservation and development in Nepal's protected area buffer zones. PARKS, Vol. 22.2, 69-82.

232

Alliance for Zero Extinction (2016). AZE Overview. Alliance for Zero Extinction.

Ammann, H. (1980). Final Report WWF Project 1958. Annexe II, Home, and movement pattern of the Javan rhinoceros. Basel, Switzerland. Unpublished.

Ammann, H. (1985). Contributions to the ecology and sociology of the Javan Rhinoceros (*Rhinoceros sondaicus* Desm.). Inaugural Dissertation. Zur Erlangung der Wurde eines Doktors der Philosophie vorgelegt der Philosophisch-Naturwissenschaftlichen Fakaltat der universitat Basel. Economy-druck AG, Basel.

Agil, M., Supriatna, L., Purwantara, B. & Candra, D. (2008). Assessment of fertility status in the male Sumatran rhino in the Sumatran Rhino Sanctuary, Way Kambas National Park, Lampung. Hayati: *Journal of Biosciences,* 2008 (March), 39-44.

Ahmad, A.H., Payne, J. & Zainuddin, Z.Z. (2014). Preventing the extinction of the Sumatran rhinoceros. *Journal of Indonesian Natural History*, Vol. 1, No. 2, 11-22.

Andrade, G.S.M. & Rhodes, J.R. (2012). Protected areas and local communities: An inevitable partnership toward successful conservation strategies? *Ecology & Society,* 17, 14.

Angelicic, F.M. (2015). Problematic wildlife: a cross-disciplinary approach. Springer.

Angelsen, A. & Kaimowitz, D. (1999). Rethinking the Causes of Deforestation: Lessons from Economic Models. *The World Bank Research Observer,* 14(1), 73-98.

Anonymous (2018). World's last northern white rhino dies. Newsletter of the East African Wildlife Society, April: 1-2.

Anthony, B. (2007). The dual nature of parks: attitudes of neighbouring communities towards Kruger National Park, South Africa. *Environmental Conservation,* 34(3), 236-245.

Aryal, A., Acharya, K. P., Shrestha, U. B., Dhakal, M., Raubenhiemer, D. & Wright, W. (2017). Global lessons from successful rhinoceros' conservation in Nepal. *Conservation Biology,* 31(6), 1494-1497.

AsRSG (1995). Ujung Kulon National Park. Javan Rhino - Current Status, Protection, and Conservation Management, IUCN SSC Asian Rhino Specialist Group Report, November 22, 1995, 1-32. IUCN/SSC Conservation Breeding Specialist Group, Apple Valley, MN, USA.

AsRSG (2012). A report from the IUCN Species Survival Commission (IUCN/SSC) African and Asian Rhino Specialist Groups and TRAFFIC to CITES Secretariat pursuant to resolution Conf. 9.14 (Rev.CoP14) and Decision 14.89. IUCN, Gland, Switzerland.

Aucoin, C. & Deetlefs, S. (2018). Tackling supply and demand in the rhino horn trade. ENACT Policy Brief, Issue 2, 1-12.

Auriga Nusantara. (2023). Javan Rhino in Jeopardy: Conservation Setbacks in Ujung Kulon National Park. Jakarta, Indonesia, Report, 1-32.

Ayling, J. (2012). What sustains wildlife crime? Rhino horn trading and the resilience of criminal networks. Transnational Environmental Crime project. Working Paper 2/2012, 1-18.

Balmford, A., Green, R. & Phalan, B. (2012). What conservationists need to know about farming. Proceedings Royal Society Biology. *Biological Sciences,* 279 (1739), 2714-2724.

Barnard, B.F.H. (1932). The one-horned rhinoceros. Malayan Forester 1:183-185.

Barnosky, A.D., Matzke, N., Tomiya, S., Wogan, G.O.U., Swartz, B., Quental, T.B., Marshall, C., McGuire. J.L., Lindsey, E.L., Maguire, K.C., Mersey, B. & Ferrer, E.A. (2011). Has the Earth's sixth mass extinction already arrived? *Nature*, Vol. 471, 51-57.

Barret, C.B. (2010). Measuring food security. *Science,* 327(5967), 825-828.

Beden, M., & Guerin, C. (1973). Le gisement de vertebres du Phnom Loang (Province de Kampot, Cambodge). Faune Pleistocene moyen terminal (Loangien). Travaux et Documents de l'Office de la Rechereche Scientifique et Technique d'Outre-Mer (Paris) 75:6-97.

Bernard, H. R. (2002). *Research methods in anthropology. Qualitative and quantitative approaches.* Third Edition. Altamira Press, Lanham, Maryland, USA.

Bernard, H., Ahmad, A. H., Brodie, J., Giordano, A. J., Lakim, M., Amat, R., Hue, S. K. P., Khee, L. S., Tuuga, A., Malim, P. T., Lim-Hasegawa, D., Wai, Y. S. & Sinun, W. (2013). Camera-trapping survey of mammals in and around Imbak canyon conservation area in Sabah, Malaysian Borneo. *Raffles Bulletin of Zoology*, 61, 861-870.

Bhattacharya, A. & Chakraborty, K. (2016). Defecation Behaviour of Great One Horned Rhinoceros (*Rhinoceros unicornis,* Linn.). *International Journal of Science and Research,* Vol 5, Issue 7, 923-928.

Biggs, D., Courchamp, F., Martin, R. & Possingham, H.P. (2013). Legal trade of Africa's rhino horns. *Science,* 339, 1038-1039.

Blake, S., Strindberg, S. & Boudjan, P. (2007). Forest elephant crisis in the Congo Basin. *PloS Biology,* 5, e111.

Blyth, E. (1862). A memoir on the living Asiatic species of Rhinoceros. *Journal of the Asiatic Society of Bengal,* 31(2), 151-175, pls. 1-4.

Bodmer, R.E., Eisenberg, J.F. & Redford, K.H. (1997). Hunting and the likelihood of extinction of Amazonian mammals. *Conservation Biology,* 11, 460-466.

Bolle, J. (2000). L'Afrique est-elle hors course? *Revue des Questions Humanitaires,* 11, 56-62.

Bradbury, J.W. & Vehrencamp, S.L. (1998). *Principles of Animal Communication.* Sinauer Associates Sunderland, MA.

Brasheres, J.S., Abrahms, B., Fiorella, K.J., Golden, C.D., Hojnowski, C.E., Marsh, R.A., McCauley, D.J., Nunez, T.A., Seto, K. & Withey, L. (2014). Wildlife declines and social conflict. *Science,* 345, 376-378.

Brook, B.W., Sodhi, N.S. & Bradshaw, C.J.A. (2008). Synergies among extinction drivers under global change. *Trends in Ecology & Evolution,* 23, No. 8, 453-460.

Brook, S. M., Dudley, N., Mahood, S. P., Polet, G., Williams, A.C., Duckworth, J.W., Ngoc, T.V. & Long, B. (2014). Lessons learned from the loss of a flagship: The extinction of the Javan rhinoceros (*Rhinoceros sondaicus annamiticus*) from Vietnam. *Biological Conservation,* 174, 21-29.

Brown, T.J. & Handford, P. (2000). Sound design for vocalisations: quality in the woods, consistency in the fields. *Condor,* 102, 81-92.

Budde, C. & Klump, G.M. (2003). Vocal repertoire of the black rhino *Diceros bicornis* ssp. and possibilities of individual identification. *Mammalian Biology,* 68, 42-47.

Budhathoki, P. (2004). Linking communities with conservation in developing countries: Buffer zone management initiatives in Nepal. *Oryx,* 38, 334-341.

Budiansky, S. (1997). *The Nature of Horses. Exploring Equine Evolution, Intelligence and Behaviour.* Free Press. https://books.google.com/books?

Butchart, S. H. M., Scharlemann, J. P. W., Evans, M. I., Quader, S., Aricò, S., Arinaitwe, J., Balman, M., Bennun, L. A. , Bertzky, B., Besançon, C., Boucher, T. M., Brooks, T. M., Burfield, I. J., Burgess, N. D., Chan, S., Clay, R. P., Crosby, M. J., Davidson, N. C., de Silva, N., Devenish, C., Dutson, G. C. L., Fernández, D. F. D., Fishpool, L. D.

C., Fitzgerald, C., Foster, M., Heath, M. F., Hockings, M., Hoffmann, M., Knox, D., Larsen, F. W., Lamoreux, J. F., Loucks, C., May, I., Millett, J., Molloy, D., Morling, P., Parr, M., Ricketts, T. H., Seddon, N., Skolnik, B., Stuart, S. N., Upgren, A. & Woodley, S. (2012). Protecting important sites for biodiversity contributes to meeting global conservation targets. *PLoS ONE*, 7, 1-8.

Cantu-Salazar, L. & Gaston, K.J. (2010). Very large protected areas and their contribution to terrestrial biological conservation. *Bioscience*, 60, 808-818.

Carlson, A.M. & Gorchov, D.L. (2004). Effects of herbicide on the invasive biennial *Alliara petiolata* (garlic mustard) and initial responses of native plants in a south-western Ohio Forest. *Restoration Ecology*, 12(4), 559-567.

Carmignani, K. (2015). The Crash of the Northern White Rhino. *ZOONOOZ* (San Diego), May 8-10.

Caro, T.M., Pelkey, N., Borner, M., Severre, E.L., Campbell, K.L., Huish, S.A., Ole Kuwai, J., Farm, J.P & Woodworth, J.L. (1998). The impact of tourist hunting on large mammals in Tanzania: an initial assessment. *J. Anim. Eco*, 36, 321-346.

Carter, N.H., Shrestha, B.K., Karki, J.B., Man, N., Pradhan, B. & Lui, J. (2012). Coexistence between wildlife and humans at fine spatial scales. *Proceedings Royal Society London. Biological Science,* 109, 15360-15365.

Cave, A.J.E. (1961). The pedal scent gland in *Rhinoceros. Proceedings Zoological Society of London*, 139, 685-690.

Ceballos, G. & Ehrlich, P.R. (2002). Mammalian population losses and the extinction crisis. *Science*, 296, 904-907.

Ceballos, G. & Ehlrich, P.R. (2009). Discovery of new mammal species and their implications for conservation and ecosystem services. *Proceedings of the National Academy of Sciences*, 106, 3841-3846.

Ceballos, G., Ehrlich, P.R., Barnosky, A.D., Garcia, A., Pringle, R.M. & Palmer, T.M. (2015). Accelerated modern human-induced species losses: Entering the sixth mass extinction. *Science Advances*, 1(5), e1400253-e1400253. http://doi.org/10.1126/sciady.1400253

Ceballos, G., Ehrlich, P.R., & Dirzo, R. (2017). Biological annihilation via the ongoing sixth mass extinction signalled by vertebrate population losses and declines. *Proceedings of the National Academy of Sciences USA*, 114, E6089-E6096. https://doi.org/10.1073/pnas.1704949114

Chandradewi, (2011). *Perilaku berkubang dan tipologi kubangan badak jawa* (*Rhinoceros sondaicus*) di Taman Nasional Ujung Kulon (thesis). Bogor: Graduate School, Bogor Agricultural University.

Charlton, B.D., Keating, J.L., Rengui, L., Huang, Y. & Swaisgood, R.R. (2010). Female giant panda (*Ailuropoda melanoleuca*) chirps advertise the caller's fertile phase. *Proceedings Royal Society B*, 277, 1101-1106.

Charpentier, M.J., Boulet, M. & Drea, C.M. (2008). Smelling right: the scent of male lemurs advertises genetic quality and relatedness. *Molecular Ecology*, 17, 3225-3233.

Cinková, I. & Bičík, V. (2013). Social and reproductive behaviour of critically endangered northern white rhinoceros in a zoological garden. *Mammalian Biology* - Zeitschrift für Säugetierkunde, 78, 50-54.

Cinková, I. (2013). Vocal and olfactory communication of the white rhinoceros. PhD dissertation, progress report 2, Department of Zoology and Lab of ornithology, Palacky University in Olomouc, Czech Republic.

Cinková, I. & Policht, R. (2014). Contact calls of the Northern and Southern White Rhinoceros allow for individual and species identification. *PLoS ONE*, 9(6), e98475. Doi: 10.1371/journal.pone.009847

Cinková, I. & Policht, R. (2015). Discrimination of familiarity and sex from chemical cues in dung by wild southern white rhinoceros. *Animal Cognition*, 18, 385-392.

Cinková, I. & Policht, R. (2016). Sex and species recognition by wild male southern white rhinoceros using contact pant calls. *Animal Cognition*, 19(2), 375-386.

Climate Data (2018). https://en.climate-data.org/location/573872/ (Accessed 1 May 2018).

Clutton-Brock, T.H. (2009). Structure and function in mammalian societies. *Philosophical Transactions of the Royal Society B*, 364, 3229-3242.

Colles, A., Liow, L.H. & Prinzing, A. (2009). Are specialists at risk under environmental change? Neoecological, paleoecological and phylogenetic approaches. *Ecology Letters*, 12, 849-863.

Collette, B.B. & Parin, N.V. in Paxton, J.R. & Eschmeyer, W.N. (Eds) (1994). Encyclopaedia of Fishes. Sydney: New South Wales Press, San Diego: Academic Press (1995). Pp. 240.

Conde, D.A., Colchero, F., Güneralp, B., Gusset, M., Skolnik, B., Parr, M., Byers, O., Johnson, K., Young, G., Flesness, N., Possingham, H. & Fa, J.E. (2015). Opportunities and costs for preventing vertebrate extinctions. *Current Biology,* 25, R219-R221.

Cross, H.B., Zedrosser, A., Nevin, O. & Rosell, F. (2014). Sex discrimination via anal gland secretion in a territorial monogamous mammal. *Ethology,* 120, 1044-1052.

Cotta-Larson, R. (2010). 'Yemen no longer destination for illegal rhino horn', savingrhinos.org/rhino_horn_yemen.html (accessed 24 November 2014).

Courchamp, F., Angulo, E., Rivalan, P., Hal, R.J., Signoret, L., Bull, L. & Meinard, Y. (2006). Rarity value and species extinction: the anthropogenic Allee effect. *Public library of science,* 4, 2408-2410.

Cousins, J.A., Sadler, J.P. & Evans, J. (2008). Exploring the role of private ranching as a conservation tool in South Africa: stakeholder perspectives. *Ecology & Society,* 13(2), 43.

Cozzuol, M.A., Clozato, C.L, Holanda, E.C., Rodrigues, Flávio. H.G., Nienow, S., de Thoisy, B., Redondo, R.A.F. & Santos, F.R. (2013). A new species of tapir from the Amazon, *Journal of Mammology,* 94(6), 1331-1345.

Craigie, I.D., Baillie, J.E.M., Balmford, A., Carbone, C., Collen, B., Green, R.E. & Hutton, J.M. (2010). Large mammal declines in Africa's protected areas. *Biological Conservation,* 143, 2221-2228.

Cumming, D.H.M., Du Toit, R.F. & Stuart, S.N. (1990). *African Elephants and Rhinos: Status Survey and Conservation Action Plan,* Gland, IUCN, iv, 72 pp.

Czaja, R. & Blair, J. (2005). Designing surveys: a guide to decisions and procedures. Sage, Thousand Oaks, California, USA.

Daily, G. (Ed.) (1997). Nature's services: societal dependence on natural ecosystems. Island Press, Washington, DC.

Dar, N.I., Minhas, R.A., Zaman, Q. & Linkie, M. (2009). Predicting patterns, perceptions and causes of human-carnivore conflict in and around Machiara National Park, Pakistan. *Biological Conservation,* 142, 2076-2082.

Date, E.M. & Lemon, R.E. (1993). Sound transmission: a basis for dialects in birdsong? *Behaviour,* 124, 291-312.

Daly, M. (1937). *Big Game Hunting and Adventure:1897-1936.* London: Macmillan.

Dean, C. (2018). State of the rhino. The Horn (Save the Rhino International), 4-5.

DeFries, R., Hansen, H., Turner, B. L., Reid, R. & Liu, J. (2007). Land use change around protected areas: management to balance human needs and ecological function. *Ecological Applications,* 70, 974-988.

DeFries, R., Karanth, K.K. & Pareeth, S. (2010). Interactions between protected areas and their surroundings in human-dominated tropical landscapes. *Biological Conservation,* 143, 2870-2880.

Deng T., Lu, X., Wang, S., Flynn, L.J., Sun, D., He, W., Chen, S. (2021). An Oligocene giant rhino provides insights into Paraceratherium evolution. Commun Biol. 4:639–648. doi:10.1038/s42003-021-02170-6.

Department of National Parks and Wildlife Conservation (DNPWC) (2015). National Rhino Count 2015 Press Release. Kathmandu, Nepal: DNPWC.

http://www.dnpwc.gov.np/downloads/press_release (Accessed December 27 2017).

Deraniyagala, P.E.P. (1938). Some fossils from Ceylon. Part II. Journal of the Ceylon Branch of the Royal Asiatic Society of Great Britain and Ireland 34:231-239.

Deraniyagala, P.E.P. (1946). Some mammals of the extinct Ratnapura fauna of Ceylon. Spoila Zeylanica 24:161-167.

Deuve, J. & Deuve, M. (1962). Note sur les Rhinocerotidae du Laos. *Bull. Soc. R. Sci. Nat.* Laos, 3, 99-105.

Deuve, J. & Deuve, M. (1964). Contribution a la connaissance des mammiferes du Laos (troisieme partie). *Bull. Soc. R. Sci. Nat.* Laos, 10, 25-35.

Dickman, A.J., Macdonald, E.A. & Macdonald, D.W. (2011). A review of financial instruments to pay for predator conservation and encourage human-carnivore coexistence. *Proceedings National Academy Science* USA, 108, 13937-13944.

Dinerstein, E., Shrestha, S. & Mishra, H. (1990). Capture, chemical immobilisation, and radio-collar life for greater one-horned rhinoceros. *Wildlife Society Bulletin,* New York, 18, 36-41, Table 1.

Dinerstein, E. (1991b). Seed dispersal by greater one-horned rhinoceros (*Rhinoceros unicornis*) and the flora of *Rhinoceros* latrines. *Mammalia,* 55, 355-362.

Dinerstein, E. (2003). *The Return of the Unicorns.* The Natural History and Conservation of the Greater One-Horned Rhinoceros, Columbia University Press, New York.

Dinerstein, E. (2011). Family Rhinocerotidae. Pp. 144-181 in *Handbook of the Mammals of the World*. Vol. 2. Hoofed mammals (D.E. Wilson and R.A. Mittermeier, Eds.). Lynx Edicions, Barcelona, Spain.

Distefano, E. (2015). Human-wildlife conflict worldwide: collection of case studies, analysis of management strategies and good practices. Rome, Italy: Food and Agricultural Organisation of the United Nations (FAO), Sustainable Agriculture and Rural Development Initiative (SARDI).

Dobson, A., Borner, M. & Sinclair, T. (2010). Road will ruin Serengeti. *Nature,* 467, 272-273.

Dubois, B. & Laurent, G. (1998). The new age of luxury living. *Financial Times Mastering Management Review,* 437, 32-35.

Dubois, E. (1908). Das Geologishe Alter de Kendeng oder Trinil-Fauna. Tijdschrift van de Koninklijle Veren voor Neder-landse Aardrijikskunde, Series 2 25:1235-1270.

Duffy, R.V., Emslie, R.H. & Knight, M.H. (2013). Rhino poaching: How do we respond? *The Journal of Peasant Studies,* 39, 479-502.

Duffy, R.V. (2014). Waging a War to War to Save Biodiversity: The Rise of Militarized Conservation. *International Affairs,* 90(4), 819-834.

Duffy, R.V. (2016). War, by conservation. *Geoforum,* 69, 238-248.

Dutta, D., Kumar, D. D. & Rita. M. (2015). A study on the behavior and colonization of translocated Greater One-horned Rhinos *Rhinoceros unicornis* (Mammalia: Perissodactyla: Rhinocerotidae) during 90 days from their release at Manas National Park, Assam India. *Journal of Threatened Taxa,* 7, 6864-6877.

Edwards, D.P., Sloan, S., Weng, L., Dirks, P., Sayer, J. & Laurance, W.F. (2014). Mining and the African Environment. *Conservation Letters,* 7(3), 302-311.

Ellis, S. (2010). *Enhancing the Survival of the Javan Rhino*, Endangered Species Bulletin, Spring, 40-41.

Emslie, R.H. & Brooks, M. (1999). African rhino: status survey and conservation action plan. IUCN/SSC African Rhino Specialist Group. IUCN, Gland, Switzerland and Cambridge, UK, 1-92.

Emslie, R.H., Milliken, T., Talukdar, B., Burgess, G., Adcock, K., Balfour, D. & Knight, M.H. (2019). *African and Asian Rhinoceroses - Status, Conservation and Trade*. A report from the IUCN Species Survival Commission (IUCN SSC) African and Asian Rhino Specialist Groups and Traffic to the CITES Secretariat pursuant to Resolution Conf.9.14 (Rev.CoP17), Report to CITES 17th meeting

(Columbo, June 2019, CoP 18 Doc.83.1 annex 3: 1-38. IUCN, Gland, Switzerland.

Emslie, R.H. (2020). Northern White Rhino, *IUCN Red List of Threatened Species, 2020*. (Retrieved 8 May 2020).

Estes, R.D. (1991). The behaviour guide to African mammals. Berkerley, CA: University of California Press.

Estes, J.A., Terborgh, J., Brashares, J.S., Power, M.E., Berger, J., Bond, W.J. & Wardle, D.A. (2011). Trophic Downgrading of Planet Earth. *Science,* 333(6040), 301-306.

Estrada, A., Garber, P.A., Rylands, A.B., Roos, C., Fernandez-Duque, E., Di Fiore, A., Anne-Isola Nekaris, A., Nijman, V., Heymann, E.W., Lambert, J. E., Rovero, F., Barelli, C., Setchell, J. M., Gillespie, T.R., Mittermeier, R. A., Arregoitia, L.V., de Guinea, M., Gouveia, S., Dobrovolski, R., Shanee, S., Shanee, N., Boyle, S.A., Fuentes, A., Mackinnon, K.C., Amato, K.R., Meyer, A.L.S., Wich, S., Sussman, R.W., Pan, R., Kone, I. & Li, B. (2017). Impending extinction crisis of the world's primates: Why primates matter. *Science Advances,* 3, e1600946

Ey, E. & Fischer, J. (2009). The "acoustic adaptation hypothesis" - A review of evidence from birds, anurans, and mammals. *Bioacoustics*, 19 (1-2), 21- 48.

Falconer, H., and Cautley, P.T. (1847). Fauna Antiqua sivalensis. Part VIII. Suidae and Rhinocerotidae. Smith Elder, London, United Kingdom.

Fernando, P., Polet, G., Foead, N., Ng, L.S., Pastorini, J. & Melnick, D.J. (2006). Genetic diversity, phylogeny, and conservation of the Javan rhinoceros (*Rhinoceros sondaicus*). *Conservation Genetics,* 7, 439-448.

Fisher, D.O. (2011). Trajectories from extinction: where are missing mammals rediscovered? *Global Ecology and Biogeography,* 20, 415-425.

Fitzgerald, S. (1989). International wildlife trade: whose business, is it? World Wildlife Fund, USA, Washington, D.C.

Fowlds, G, & Spence, G. (2019). Saving the Last Rhinos. Johnathon Ball Publishers, Johannesburg & Cape Town, 336p.

Foose, T.J., Molur, S. & Walker, S. (1993). Briefing material on population and habitat viability analysis workshop for Indian/ Nepali Rhinoceros. Asian Rhino Specialist Group, Zoo outreach organisation, CBSG India; 307p.

Foose, T.J. & van Strien, N. J. eds. (1997). *Asian Rhinos. Status Survey and Conservation Action Plan.* IUCN/SSC Asian Rhino Specialist Group, IUCN, Gland, Switzerland.

Foose, T.J. & van Strien, N. J. (1998). Conservation Programmes for Sumatran and Javan rhinos in Indonesia and Malaysia. Pachyderm, 26, 100-115.

Forestry Statistics of Indonesia (2007). (http://www.dephut.go.id/files/Stat_2007.pdf) (Accessed 20 May 2015).

Frame, G.W. & Goddard, J. (1970). Black rhinoceros vocalisations. *East African Wildlife Journal,* 8, p. 207.

Geoffroy Saint-Hillaire, E & Cuvier, F (1824). Unnumbered page associated with pl. 309, vol. vi, liver.45 in Historie naturelle des mammiferes, avec figures originales, coloriees, dessinees d'apres des animax vivants; publiee sous l'autorite de I'Administration du Museum d'Historie Naturelle. Tome cinquieme. Chez A. Belin, Libarairie-Edituer, Paris, France.

Ghosh, D. (1991). Studies on the Eco-status of the Indian Rhinoceros (*Rhinoceros unicornis*) with special reference to its altered habitat due to human interference in Jaldapara Sanctuary, West Bengal. PhD Thesis, University of Ranchi, India.

Global Invasive Species Database (GISD) (2011). *Arenga obtusifolia* palm. http://www.issg.org/database/species/ecology.asp?si=1834&fr=1&sts&sts=&lang=EN. (Accessed 17 February 2017).

Goddard, J. (1967). Home range, behaviour, and recruitment rates of two black rhino population. *E. Afr. Wildl. J.,* Vol. 5, 133-150.

Godfray, H.C., Beddington, J.R., Crute, I.R., Haddad, L., Lawrence, D., Muir, J.F., Pretty, J., Robinson, S., Thomas, S.M. & Toulmin, C. (2010). Food security: The challenge of feeding 9 billion people. *Science*, 327(5967), 812-818.

Gokkon, B. (2018). Javan rhino population holds steady amid ever-present peril. Mongabay Series: Asian Rhinos. https://news.mongabay.com/2018/03/javan-rhino-population-holds-steady-amid-ever-present-peril Viewed 05/03/2018

Gokkon, B. (2018). Two newborn Javan rhinos spotted on camera in Indonesian park. Mongabay Series: Asian Rhinos. https://news.mongabay.com/2018/04/two-newborn-javan-rhinos-spotted-on-camera-in-indonesian-park (Accessed 4 May 2018).

Gokkon, B. (2019). Newly spotted calves boost Javan rhino population to 72. Mongabay Series: Asian Rhinos. https://news.mongabay.com/2019/12/javan-rhino-calves-population-72-ujung-kulon-indonesia/

Gokkon, B. (2020). Two new Javan rhino calves are spotted in the species' last holdout. Mongabay Series: Asian Rhinos. https://news. mongabay.com/2020/09/two-new-javan-rhino-calves-are-spotted-in-the-species-last-holdout/

Granger, M. (2021). Using insights from the past to plan the future: Rethinking the ecological preferences of the critically endangered Javan and Sumatran Rhino (MSc thesis). Imperial College London. London, United Kingdom.

Gray, J. E. (1868). Observations on the preserved specimens and skeletons of the Rhinocerotidae in the collection of the British Museum and Royal College of Surgeons, including in descriptions of three new species. Proceedings of Zoological Society of London 1867:1003-1032. (Dated 1867 but published April 1868 according to Duncan 1937).

Griffith, E., Hamiliton-Smith, C. & Pigeon, E. (eds). (1827). The animal kingdom, arranged in conformity with its organisation, by the Baron Cuvier, with additional descriptions of all the species hitherto named, and many not before noticed. Vol. V. Synopsis of the species of the class Mammalia, as arranged with reference to their organisation. G.B. Whittaker, London, United Kingdom.

Griffith, M. (1993). The Javan rhino of Ujung Kulon an investigation of its population and ecology through camera trapping. Joint project of the PHPA and WWF Bogor. Pp. 1-92.

Groenendijk, L. (2003). *Planning and Management Tools.* International Institute for Geo-Information Science and Earth Observation (ITC), Enschede, the Netherlands. ISBN 90-6164-219-1.

Groves, C. P. (1967). On the rhinoceroses of Southeast Asia. *Saügetierkundliche Mitteilungen*, 15, 221-237.

Groves, C. P. & Kurt, F. (1972). *Dicerorhinus sumatrensis. Mammalian Species*, 21, 1- 6.

Groves, C. P. (1972). *Ceratotherium simum. Mammalian Species*, 8, 1-6.

Groves, C.P., Fernando, P. & Robovsky, J. (2010). The sixth rhino: a taxonomic re- assessment of the critically endangered Northern White Rhinoceros. PLoS ONE, 5(4): e9703.

Groves, C.P. & Leslie, Jr. D.M. (2011). *Rhinoceros sondaicus* (Perissodactyla: Rhinocerotidae), *Mammalian Species,* 43 (887), 190-208.

Groves, C.P. & Grubb, P. (2011). *Ungulate taxonomy*. Baltimore: Johns Hopkins University Press.

Grubb, P. (2005). Artiodactyla. In: D.E. Wilson and D.M. Reeder (eds.) *Mammal Species of the World. A Taxonomic and Geographic Reference (3rd ed.)*, 637-722. Johns Hopkins University Press, Baltimore, USA.

Grün, V. (2006). The influence of faecal scent marks on the behaviour of the white rhinoceros (*Ceratotherium simum simum*). MSc Thesis, University of Canterbury.

Gunawan, H., Ramono, W.S., Gillison, A. & Isnan, W. (2012). Kajan social ekonomi dan persepsi masyarakat lokal terhadap (assessment of socioeconomics and perceptions of local community on reintroduction of Javan rhinos). *Journal Penelitian Hutan dan Konservasi Alam,* 9(4), 395-407.

Guriev, S. & Rachinsky, A. (2009). The Evolution of personal wealth in the former Soviet Union and Central and Eastern Europe. In *personal wealth from a global perspective*: 134-149. Press, O.U. (Ed.). Helsinki: UNU-WIDER research paper.

Gurung, B., Smith, J.L.D., McDougal, C., Karki, J.B. & Barlow, A. (2008). Factors associated with human-killing tigers in Chitwan National Park, Nepal. *Biological Conservation,* 141, 3069-3078.

Hackel, J. D. (1998). Community Conservation and the Future of Africa's Wildlife. *Conservation Biology*, 13, No. 4, 726-734.

Hall-Martin, A.J. & Knight, M.H. (1994). Conservation and Management of Black Rhinoceros in South African National Parks. Proceedings of a Symposium "Rhinos as Game Ranch Animals", Onderstepoort, 9-10th September 11-19.

Harris, R.B., Cooney, R. & Leader-Williams, N. (2013). Application of the Anthropogenic Allee Effect Model to Trophy Hunting as a Conservation Tool. *Conservation Biology,* 27, No. 5, 945-951.

Harada, K. (2003). Attitudes of local people towards conservation and Gunung Halimun National Park in West Java, Indonesia. *Journal Forestry Research*, 271-282.

Hariyadi, A.R.S. (2009). Javan Rhinos Share Wallow Holes: Impact of Climate Change? *The Rhino Print*, November 2009. Asian Rhino Project. Pp.14.

Hariyadi, A.R.S., Setiawan, R., Daryan, D., Yayus, A. & Purnama, H. (2010). Preliminary behaviour observations of the Javan rhinoceros (*Rhinoceros sondaicus*) based on video trap surveys in Ujung Kulon National Park. *Pachyderm*, 47, 93-99.

Hariyadi, A.R.S., Priambudi, A., Setiawan, R., Daryan, D., Yayus, A. & Purnama, H. (2011). Estimating the population structure of Javan rhinos (*Rhinoceros sondaicus*) in Ujung Kulon National

Park using mark-recapture method based on video and camera trap identification. *Pachyderm,* 49, 90-99.

Hariyadi, A.R.S., Priambudi, A., Setiawan, R., Daryan, D., Purnama, H. & Yayus, A. (2012). Optimizing the habitat of the Javan rhinoceros (*Rhinoceros sondaicus)* in Ujung Kulon National Park by reducing the invasive palm *Arenga obtusifolia. Pachyderm,* 52, 49-54.

Hariyadi, A.R.S., Sajuthi, D., Astuti, D.A., Alikoda, H.S. & Maheshwari, H. (2016). Analysis of nutritional quality and food digestibility in male Javan rhinoceros (*Rhinoceros sondaicus*) in Ujung Kulon National Park. *Pachyderm,* 57, 86-96.

Harjanto, E. (2017). On a territorial competition between *Rhinoceros sondaicus* and *Bos javanicus* at Ujung Kulon National Park. *Bio Mathematical Society*, Vol. 1, No.1, 46-53.

Harper, F. (1945). Extinct and vanishing mammals of the Old World. Special Publication No 12. American Committee for International Wildlife Protection, New York Zoological Park, New York.

Hart, B.L. (1983). Flehmen Behaviour and Vomeronasal Organ Function. In: Müller-Schwarze D., Silverstein R.M. (eds) Chemical Signals in Vertebrates 3. Springer, Boston, MA. 87-103.

Haryono, M. (1996). *Analisis kesesuaian kawasan Gunung Honje sebagai habitat badak jawa* (*Rhinoceros sondaicus* Desmarest). (Javan Rhinoceros Habitat Suitability Analysis of the Honje Mountains). Master of Science Programme of the Agricultural Institute of Bogor (IPB).

Haryono, M., Rahmat, U.M., Daryan, M., Raharja, A.S., Muhtarom, A., Firdaus, A.Y., Rohaeti, A., Subchiyatin, I., Nugraheni, A., Khairani, K.O. & Kartina, I.R. (2015). Monitoring of the Javan rhino population in Ujung Kulon National Park, Java. *Pachyderm,* 56, 1-5.

Haryono, M., Miller, P.S., Lees, C., Ramono, W., Purnomo, A., Long, B., Sectionov, M, Isnan, Aji, B.D., Talukdar, B. & Ellis, S. (Eds.) (2016). Population and Habitat Viability Assessment for the Javan rhino. Workshop Report, 1-64.

Hazarika, B.C. & Saikia, P.K. (2010). A study on the behaviour of Great Indian One-horned Rhino (*Rhinoceros unicornis* Linn.) in the Rajiv Gandhi Orang National Park, Assam, India. *NeBIO*, 1(2), 62-74.

Hazewinkel, J.C. (1933). *Rhinoceros sondaicus* in Zuid Sumatra. *Tropische Natuur,* 22, 101-109.

Hermes, R., Hildebrandt, T.B., Walcer, C., Goeritz, F., Patton, M.L., Silinski, S., Anderson, M.J., Reid, C.E., Wibbelt, G., Tomasova, K.

& Schwarzenberger, F. (2006). The effect of long non-reproductive periods on the genital heath in captive female white rhinoceros (*Ceratotherium. s. simum* and *C. s. cottoni*). *Theriogenology,* 65, 1492-1515.

Hiby, A. & Lovell, P. (1993). Specially commissioned study by Conservation Research Ltd, Cambridge, England (11 p). In: Griffiths M. 1993. The Javan Rhino of Ujung Kulon: an investigation of its population and ecology through camera trapping. Jakarta, Directorate General of Forest Protection and Nature Conservation and the World Wildlife Fund Indonesia Program, 92 p.

Heissig, K. (1972). Palaontologische und geologische Untersuchhungen im Tertiar von Pakistan. 5. Rhinocerotidae (Mamm) aus den unteren und mitteren Siwalik-Schichten. Abhandlungen der Bayerische Akademie der Wissenschaften, Mathematisch-Naturwissenschaftliche Klasse, Nue Folge 152:1-112.

Hillman-Smith, A.K.K. & Groves, C.P. (1994). *Diceros bicornis. Mammalian Species,* 455, 1-8.

Hochstedler, WW., Slaughter, B.S., Gorchov, D.L., Saunder, L.P. & Stevens, M.H.H. (2007). Forest floor plant community response to experimental control of the invasive biennial *Alliara petiolata* (garlic mustard). *Journal of the Torrey Botanical Society,* 134(2), 155-165.

Hockings, G. (2016). Using camera traps to investigate the behaviour and ecology of the Javan rhino (*Rhinoceros sondaicus*) to inform future conservation actions. Honours Thesis, University of Queensland, Brisbane.

Hoffmann, M., Belant, J.L., Chanson, J.S., Cox, N.A., Lamoreux, J., Rodrigues, A.S.L., Schipper, J. & Stuart, S.N. (2011). The changing fates of the world's mammals. *Philosophical Transactions Royal Society B,* 366, 2598-2610.

Hommel, P.W.F.M. (1987). *Landscape ecology of Ujung Kulon (West Java, Indonesia).* Private published. Soil Survey Institute. Wageningen, The Netherlands.

Hoogerwerf, A. (1938). Among rhino and Javanese wild ox (banteng) in the Oedjoeng Koelon Game Reserve. *Nature Protection in the Netherlands Indies,* 1938, 1-8.

Hoogerwerf, A. (1970). *Ujung Kulon, Land of the Last Javan Rhinoceros.* E. J. Brill, Leiden, The Netherlands.

Horsfield, T. (1824). *Zoological researches in Java, and neighbouring islands.* Kingsbury, Parbury, & Allen, London, United Kingdom.

Horspool, N., Pranantyo, I. & Griffin, J. (2014). A probabilistic tsunami hazard assessment for Indonesia. *National Hazards & Earth System Sciences,* 14, 3105-3122.

Hubback, T. (1939). The Asiatic two-horned rhinoceros. *Journal Mammalogy,* 20, 1-20.

Hutchins, M. & Kreger, M.D. (2006). Rhinoceros behaviour: implications for captive management and conservation. *International Zoo Yearbook,* 40, 150-173.

Indonesian Ministry of Forestry (2007). Strategy and Action Plan for the Conservation of Rhinos in Indonesia 2007-2017. Jakarta, Indonesia, 1-68.

Indonesian Ministry of Forestry (2010). Ujung Kulon Indonesia's National Park Handbook. Revised Edition, 1-72.

IFRC Report (2023). DREF Operation Final Report 2023. 1-20pp.

International Rhino Foundation (2011). Javan Rhino update June 2011. *Journal of the Rhino Print (Newsletter of the Asian Rhino Project),* Vol. 2011, 2-4.

International Rhino Foundation (2015). Black rhinoceros. http://www.rhinos.org/rhinos/black-rhino (Accessed 7 December 2015).

International Rhino Foundation (2016). Javan, Sumatran, Greater one-horned, Black and White Rhino distribution maps. International Rhino Foundation (http://www.irf.org) (Accessed 15 April 2016).

International Rhino Foundation (2024). State of the Rhino Report 2024. International Rhino Foundation (http://www.irf.org) (Accessed 6 December 2024).

Isler, K. & van Schaik, C.P. (2009). Why are there so few smart mammals (but so many smart birds)? *Biological Letters,* 5, 125-129.

IUCN 2024. The IUCN Red List of Threatened Species. Version 2024-2. http://www.iucnredlist.org (Accessed December 2024).

Jardine, W. (1836). The naturalist's library. Vol. XXIII. Mammalia. Thick-skinned quadrupeds. Henry G Bohn, London, United Kingdom.

Jablonski, D. (1994). Extinctions in the fossil record. *Philosophical Transactions of the Royal Society London B,* 344, 11-17.

Janečka, J.E. & Janečka, M.J. (2018). Family Cynocephalidae (Colugos). Pp. 272-285 in: Wilson, D.E. and Mittermeier, R.A. eds. (2018). *Handbook of the Mammals of the World.* Vol. 8. Insectivores, Sloths and Colugos. Lynx Edicions, Barcelona.

Johnson, C.N., Balmford, A. & Brook, B.W. (2017). Biodiversity losses and conservation responses in the Anthropocene. *Science* 356, 270-274.

Jooste, J. & Ferreira, S.M. (2018). An Appraisal of Green Militarization to Protect Rhinoceroses in Kruger National Park. *African Studies Quarterly*, Volume 18, Issue 1, September 2018.

Joubert, E. & Ellof, F.C. (1971). Notes on the ecology and behaviour of the black rhinoceros Diceros bicornis Linn, 1758 in South West Africa Madoqua Series 1, No.3, 5-53.

Kappeler, P.M., Barrett, L., Blumstein, D.T. & Clutton-Brock, T. (2013). Constraints and flexibility in mammalian social behaviour: introduction and synthesis. *Philosophical Transactions of the Royal Society,* 368, 20120337.

Karanth, K.K. & Nepal, S.K. (2012). Local residents perception of benefits and losses from protected areas in India and Nepal. *Environmental Management*, 49, 372-386.

Karma, N. & Toikka, A. (2012). Cultural map of Finland 2007: analysing cultural differences using multiple correspondence analysis. *Cultural Trends,* 21, 113-131.

Karthikeyan, K., Muniasamy, S., Sankar Ganesh, D., Achiraman, S. & Archuman, G. (2013). Faecal chemical cues in water buffalo that facilitate estrus detection. *Animal Reproductive Science,* 138, 163-167.

Kavaliers, M. & Colwell, D.D. (1995). Discrimination by female mice between the odours of parasitised and non-parasitised males. *Proceedings of the Royal Society B: Biological Sciences,* 261, 31-35.

Keltner, D. & Lerner, J.S. (2010). Emotion. In *Handbook of Social Psychology*: pp. 317-352. Gilbert, D.T., Fiske, S.T. & Lindzey, G. (Eds.) New York: Wiley.

Kerley, G.I.H., Levi, T., Lindsey, P. A., Macdonald, D. W., Malhi, Y., Painter, L. E., Sandom, C. J., Terborgh, J. & Van Valkenburgh, B. (2015). Collapse of the world's largest herbivores. *Science Advances,* 1, 1-12.

Khairani, K.O., Nydam, D.M., Felippe, J., McDonough, P., Barry, J., Mahmud, R., Haryono, M. & Radcliffe, R.W. (2018). Surveillance for haemorrhagic septicaemia in buffalo (*Bubalus bubalus*) as an aid to range expansion of the Javan rhinoceros (*Rhinoceros sondaicus*) in Ujung Kulon National Park, Indonesia. *Journal of Wildlife Diseases*, 54, 14-25.

Khan, M. (1989). Asian Rhinos: and action plan for their conservation. Gland, IUCN, 1-23.

Khan, M., Foose, T.J. & van Strien, N.J. (1997). Chairman's report: Asian Rhino Specialist Group. *Pachyderm*, 24, 7-8.

Kideghesho, J.R., Røskaft, E. & Katterborn, B.P. (2007). Factors influencing conservation attitudes of local people in Western Serengeti, Tanzania. *Biodiversity Conservation,* 16, 2213-2230.

Kimura, R. (2001). Volatile substances in feces, urine and urine-marked feces of feral horses. *Canadian Journal of Animal Science,* 81, 411-420.

Kiwia, H.Y.D. (1989). Ranging patterns of the black rhinoceros (*Diceros bicornis* L.) in Ngorongoro Crater, Tanzania. *African Journal of Ecology,* 27, 305-312.

Kleiman, D.G. & Peters, G. (1990). Auditory communication in the giant panda: motivation and function. In: Second international symposium on the giant panda (Eds. S. Asakura & S. Nakagawa), pp. 107-122. Tokyo, Japan: Tokyo Zoological Park Society.

Knapp, E.J., Peace, N. & Bechtel, L. (2017). Poachers and poverty: Assessing objective and subjective measures of poverty amongst illegal hunters outside Ruaha National Park, Tanzania. *Conservation and Society,* 15, 1, 24-32.

Knight, M. (2018). The rhino challenge: a continental perspective. The Horn (Save the Rhino International), 29.

Kolar, D., Kretzschmar, P. & Ganslosser, U. (2002). Do urinary scent marks influence behaviour of male and female white rhinoceros (*Ceratotherium simum simum*)? In: Dehnhard, M and Hoffer, H. (eds.) *4ᵗʰ International Symposium on Physiology and Ethology of Wild and Zoo Animals.* Berlin, Germany: Blackwell Verlag.

Kondo, N. & Watanabe, S. (2009). Contact calls: Information and social function. *Japanese Psychological Research*, 3, 197-208.

Kretzschmar, P., Ganslosser, U., Goldschmid, A. & Aberham, A. (2001). Stimulation of territorial and mating behaviour by faecal samples. A comparative study on behaviour of captive and free-living white rhinoceros. In: Schwammer, H. (ed.) *International Elephant and Rhino Research Symposium.* Vienna, Austria: Schüling Verlag.

Kretzschmar, P., Sipangkui, R. & Schaffer, N.E. (2009). Eye disorders in captive Sumatran rhinoceros (*Dicerorhinus sumatrensis harrissoni*) in Sabah, Malaysia. *Proceedings of the International Conference on Diseases of Zoo and Wild Animals* 2009, 236-242.

Laiolo, P. (2010). The emerging significance of bioacoustics in animal species conservation. *Biological Conservation,* 143, 1635-1645.

Langpap, C. & Wu, J. (2008). Predicting the Effect of Land-Use Policies on Wildlife Habitat Abundance. *Canadian Journal of Agricultural Economics,* 56, 195-217.

Laurance, W.F., Goosem, M. & Laurance, S.G. (2009). Impacts of roads and linear clearings on tropical forests. *Trends in Ecology & Evolution,* 24, 659-669.

Laurance, W.F., Sayer, J. & Gassman, K.G. (2014). Agricultural expansion and its impacts on tropical nature. *Trends in Ecology & Evolution,* 29, 107-116.

Laurance, W.F., Clements, G.R., Sloan, S., O'Connell, C.S., Mueller, N.D., Goosem, M., Venter, O., Edwards, D.P., Phalan, B., Balmford, A., Van Der Ree, R., & Arrea, I.B. (2014). A global strategy for road building. *Nature,* 513, 229-232.

Laurie, W.A. (1978). The Ecology and Behaviour of the Greater One-Horned Rhinoceros (*Rhinoceros unicornis*). PhD. Dissertation, University of Cambridge, UK.

Laurie, W.A. (1982). Behavioural ecology of the Greater one-horned rhinoceros (*Rhinoceros unicornis*). *Journal Zoology,* 196, 307-341.

Laurie, W.A., Lang, E.M. & Groves, C.P. (1983). *Rhinoceros unicornis. Mammalian Species*, 211, 1-6.

Leader-Williams, N. (1992). *World Trade in Rhino Horn: A Review.* TRAFFIC International, Cambridge, UK.

Leader-Williams, N., Milledge, S., Adcock, K., Brooks, M., Conway, A., Knight, M., Mainka, S., Martin, E.B. & Teferi, T. (2005). Trophy hunting of Black Rhinos *Diceros bicornis*: proposals to ensure its future sustainability. *Journal International Wildlife Law Policy,* 8, 1-11.

Leader-Williams, N. (2009). Conservation and hunting: friends or foes? In: *recreational hunting, conservation, and rural livelihoods,* 9-24. Dickson, B., Hutton, J. & Adams, W.M. (Eds.). London: Wiley-Blackwell.

Leader-Williams, N. (2013). Fat riding on their horns - and genes? Fauna & Flora International, *Oryx,* 47(3), 311-312.

Leakey, R. & Lewin, R. (1992). *The Sixth Extinction: Patterns of Life and the Future of Humankind*, Doubleday Publishers.

Lessee, J. (1994). Ujung Kulon Park shelters World's last 47 Javan rhinos. *Really Rhinos*, 8, 3.

Lepp, A. & Holland, S. (2006). A comparison of attitudes toward state-led conservation and community-based conservation in the village of Bigodi, Uganda. *Society and Natural Resources,* 19, 609-623.

Lewis, D.M. & Alpert, P. (1997). Trophy hunting and wildlife conservation in Zambia. *Conservation Biology,* 11, 59-68.

Ling, S., Kümpel, N. & Albrechtsen, L. (2002). No new recipes for bush meat. *Oryx,* 36, 330-330.

Linklater, W.L., Mayer, K. & Swaisgood, R.R. (2013). Chemical signals of age, sex, and identity in black rhinoceros. *Animal Behaviour*, 85, 671-677.

Lindsey, P.A., Romanach, S.S. & Davies-Mostert, H.T. (2009). The importance of conservancies for enhancing the value of game ranch land for large mammal conservation in southern Africa. *Journal Zoology (Lond.),* 277, 99-105.

Lindsey, P.A., Balme, G., Becker, M., Begg, C., Bento, C., Bocchino, C., Dickman, A., Diggle, R.W., Eves, H., Henschel, P., Lewis, D., Marnewick, K., Mattheus, J., McNutt, J.W., McRobb, R., Midlane, N., Milanzi, J., Morley, R., Murphee, M., Opyene, V., Phadima, J., Purchase, G., Rentsch, D., Roche, C., Shaw, J., van der Westhuizen, H. & Van Vliet, N. (2013). The bushmeat trade in African savannas: Impacts, drivers, and possible solutions. *Biological Conservation,* 160, 80-96.

Linskens, H.F., Martens, M.J.M., Hendriksen, H.J.G.M., Roestenbergs-Sinnage, A.M., Brouwers, W.A.J.M., van der Staak, A.L.H.C. & Strik-Jansen, A.M.J. (1976). The acoustic climate of plant communities. *Oecologia*, 23, 165-177.

Loch, C.W. (1937). *Rhinoceros sondaicus*. The Javan or Lesser one-horned rhinoceros and its geographical distribution. *Journal Malayan Branch Royal Asiatic Society,* 15, 130-149.

Loh, J & Loh, K (1994). *TRAFFIC Bulletin,* 14, 55.

Le Saout, S., Hoffman, M., Shi, Y., Hughes, A., Bernard, C., Brooks, T.M., Bertzky, B., Butchart, S.H.M., Stuart, S.N., Badman, T.& Rodrigues, A.S.L. (2013). Protected Areas and Effective Biodiversity Conservation. Science, 342, 803-805.

Løvholt, F., Glimsdal, S. & Harbitz, C.B. (2014). Global tsunami hazard and exposure due to large co-seismic slip. International Journal of Disaster Risk Reduction, 10, 406-418.

Lucas, P.W. & Corlett, R.T. (1992). Notes on the treatment of palm fruits by long-tailed macaques (*Macaca fascicularis*). *Principles,* 36(1), 45-48.

Lucas, S.G., and J. Sobus. (1989). The systematics of Indricotheres. In D.R. Prothero and R.M. Schoch, eds., *The Evolution of Perissodactyl*, 341-55. New York: Oxford University Press.

Lydekker, R. (1886b). Preliminary note on Mammalia of the Karnal Caves. Records of the Geological Survey of India 19:120-122.

Malhi, Y., Gardener, T. A., Goldsmith, G. R., Silman, M. R. & Zelazowski, P. (2014). Tropical forests in the Anthropocene. *Annual Review Environment & Resources,* 39, 125-159.

Malpas, R. (1981). Elephant losses in Uganda, and some gains. *Oryx,* 16, 41-44.

Marneweck, C. (2013). Silent signals: identifying dung odour profiles that indicate age, sex, and status in white rhino olfactory communication. Master's dissertation, School of Life Sciences, University of KwaZulu-Natal, South Africa. 1-64.

Marneweck, C., Jürgens, A. & Shrader, A.M. (2017a). Dung odours signal sex, age, territorial and oestrous state in white rhinos. *Proceedings of the Royal Society B,* 284, 20162376.

Marneweck, C. Jürgens, A. & Shrader, A.M. (2018). The role of middens in white rhino communication. *Animal Behaviour,* 140, 7-18.

Marshall, L. (2012). *Newswatch,* 11 December; http://newswatch. nationalgeographic.com/2012/12/11/record-618-south-african-rhinos-poached-for-their-horns-in-2012-so-far.

Martin, E. & Martin, C. (1982). *Run Rhino Run.* Chatto & Windus, London, pp.136.

Martin, E. & Vigne, L. (2012.) Successful rhino conservation continues in West Bengal, India. *Pachyderm,* 51, 27-37.

Mattioli, S. (2011). Family Cervidae (Deer). Pp. 350-444 in: *Handbook of the Mammals of the World.* Vol. 2. Hoofed mammals (D.E. Wilson and R.A. Mittermeier, Eds.). Lynx Edicions, Barcelona, Spain.

May, R.M., Lawton, J.H. & Stork, N.E. (1995). In Extinction Rates (Eds. Lawton J.H. & May, R.M.), Ch.1, 1-24. Oxford University Press.

McGregor, P.K. & Peake, T.M. (2000). Communication networks: social environments for receiving and signalling behaviour. *Acta ethologica,* 2, 71-81.

Meijaard, E., Garcia-Ulloa, J., Sheil, D., Wich, S.A., Carlson, K.M., Juffe-Bignoli, D. & Brooks, T.M. (eds.) (2018). Oil palm and biodiversity. A situation analysis by the IUCN Oil Palm Task Force. IUCN Oil Palm Task Force Gland, Switzerland: IUCN. xiii + 116pp.

Melliti, M, Talukdar, B. & Balfour (eds.,) (2025). Rhinos of the World, Springer Nature Switzerland AG, 423pp, https://doi.org/10.1007/978-3-031-67169.2

Milliken, T. & Shaw, J. (2012). *The South Africa - Vietnam Rhino Horn Trade Nexus: A Deadly Combination of Institutional Lapses, Corrupt Wildlife Industry Professionals and Asian Crime Syndicates* (Johannesburg: TRAFFIC).

Milner-Gulland, E.J. & Bennett, E.L. (2003). Wild meat: the bigger picture. *Trends Ecological Evolution,* 18, 351-357.

Milner-Gulland, E.J. & Bennett, E.L. (2003). The SCB 2002 Annual Meeting Wild Meat Group, Wild Meat: The bigger picture. *Trends Ecological Evolution,* 18, 351-357.

Ministry of Forestry (1995). Ujung Kulon Indonesia's National Park Handbook. 1-72.

Ministry of Forestry, Indonesia. (2007). Rhino Century Program. Jakarta. http://www.rhinoresourcecenter.com/index.

Ministry of Forestry (2010). Ujung Kulon Indonesia's National Park Handbook. Pp. 1-72.

Mitro, S., Gordon, A.R., Olsson, M.J. & Lundström, J.N. (2012). The smell of age: perception and discrimination of body odours of different ages. *PLoS One,* 7, 1-7.

Mohd-Azlan, J. & Engkamat. L. (2013). Camera trapping and conservation in Lanjak Entimau wildlife sanctuary, Sarawak, Borneo. *Raffles Bulletin of Zoology*, 61, 397- 405.

Mohamed, A., Vellayan, S., Radcliffe, R.W., Lowenstine, L.J., Epstein, J., Reid. S.A., Paglia, D.E., Radcliffe, R.M., Roth, T.L. & Foose, T.J. (2004). Trypanosomiasis (surra) in the captive Sumatran rhinoceros (*Dicerorhinus sumatrensis sumatrensis*) in Peninsula Malaysia. In: Proceedings of joint conference, American Association of Zoo Veterinarians, and the Wildlife Diseases Association, Health and conservation of captive and free-ranging wildlife, 28 August - 3 September 2004, San Diego, California.

Moneron, S., Okes, N. & Rademeyer, J. (2017). Pendants, Powder, and Pathways: A rapid assessment of smuggling routes and techniques used in the illicit trade in African rhino horn. Pretoria: TRAFFIC, 3.

Morrison, J.C., Sechrest, W., Dinerstein, E., Wilcove, D.S. & Lamoreux, J.F. (2007). Persistence of large mammal faunas as indicators of global human impacts. *Journal Mammology,* 88, 1363-1380.

Moreto, W.D., Gau, J.M., Paoline III, E.A., Singh, R., Belecky, M. & Long, B. (2017). Occupational motivation and intergenerational linkages of rangers in Asia. *Oryx,* 10, 1-10.

Moreto, W.D. & Gau, J.M. (2017). Deterrence, Legitimacy and Wildlife Crime in Protected Areas. *Conservation Criminology,* 45-58.

Morton, E.S. (1975). Ecological sources of selection on avian sounds. *American Naturalist,* 109, 17-34.

Muggenthaler, E.K. von, Stoughton, J.W. & Daniel Jr, J.C. (1993). Infrasound from the Rhinocerotidae, pp. 136-140. In: Ryder, O.A. (1993). *Rhinoceros Biology and Conservation: Proceedings of an International Conference.* San Diego, U.S.A, San Diego Zoological Society, i-v, 386 pp.

Muggenthaler, E.K. von, Reinhart, P., Lympany, B. & Craft, R.B. (2003). Songlike vocalisations from the Sumatran Rhinoceros (*Dicerorhinus sumatrensis*). *Acoustic Research Letters* Online, 4(3), 83-88. https://doi.org/10.1121/1.1588271

Munson, L., Koehler, J.W., Wilkinson, J.E. & Miller, R.E. (1998). 'Vesicular and Ulcerative Dermatopathy resembling Superficial Necrotic Dermatitis in Captive Black Rhinoceroses (*Diceros bicornis*)'. *Veterinary Pathology,* 35, 31-42.

Muntasib, E.K.S.H. (2000). The changes of feeding pattern of Banteng (*Bos javanicus*) and its effect on Javan rhino (*Rhinoceros sondaicus*) in Ujung Kulon National Park, West Java. *Media Konservasi,* 7, 71-74.

Muntasib, E.K.S.H. (2002). *Penggunaan ruang habitat oleh badak jawa (Rhinoceros sondaicus Demarest, 1822) di Taman Nasional Ujung Kulon* (dissertation). Bogor Graduate School, Bogor Agricultural University.

Myers, N. (1990). Mass extinctions: what can the past tell us about the present and future? Palaeogeography, Paleoclimatology, Palaeoecology, 82, 175-185.

Nardelli, F. (1987). Project to conserve the Javan rhinoceros (The Lesser one-horned Asiatic Rhinoceros *sondaicus* Desm.). Project rationale and outline from Asian Rhino Action Plan meeting held in Kuala Lumpur, October 1987.

Nardelli, F. (2013). The mega-folivorous mammals of the rainforest: feeding ecology in nature and in a controlled environment: A contribution to their conservation. *International Zoo News,* Vol. 60, No. 5, 323-339.

Nardelli, F. (2014). The last chance for the Sumatran rhinoceros? *Pachyderm,* 55, 43-53.

Nardelli, F. (2016). Current status and conservation prospects for the Javan rhinoceros *Rhinoceros sondaicus* Desmarest 1822. *International Zoo News*, Vol. 63. No. 3, 180-201.

Nardelli, F. & Robovský, J. (2022). New data on the ecology and conservation of the Javan rhinoceros *Rhinoceros sondaicus* Desmarest, 1822 (Perissodactyla, Rhinocerotidae). GAZELLA 49, 2022, Zoo Praha, pp. 183-205.

Nelson, J.S, Grande, T.C & Wilson, M.V.H (2016). Classification of fishes, from Fishes of the World, 5th Edition.

Ng, J., Zainal-Zahari, S.C. & Nordin, A. (2001). Wallows and wallow utilisation of the Sumatran rhinoceros (*Dicerorhinus sumatrensis*) in a natural enclosure in Sungai Dusun Wildlife Reserve, Selangor, Malaysia. *Journal of Wildlife and Parks,* 19, 7-12.

Norman, J.E. & Ashley, M.V. (2000). Phylogenetics of Perissodactyla and tests of the molecular clock. *Journal of Molecular Evolution,* 50(1), 11-21.

Nowak, R.M. & Paradiso, J.L. (1983). *Walker's Mammals of the World.* 4th Edition, Vol. ll, Johns Hopkins University Press, Baltimore, USA and London, UK, 1155-172.

Nowak, R.M. (ed.) (1991). *Walker's Mammals of the World.* 5th Edition, Vol. II, Johns Hopkins University Press, Baltimore, USA.

Nowell, K., Wei-Len, C. & Chia-Jai, P. (1992). The horns of a dilemma: The market for rhino horn in Taiwan. *Traffic International*, Cambridge, England.

Nowell, K. & Jackson, P., eds. (1996). *Wild Cats: Status Survey and Conservation Action Plan.* Gland, Switzerland, IUCN.

Nowell, K. (2012a). Species trade and conservation - Rhinoceroses. Assessment of rhino horn as a traditional medicine. Report prepared for the CITES Secretariat on behalf of TRAFFIC, SC62 Doc. 47.2, Annex, pp. 1-42.

Ntiati, P. (2002). Group ranch subdivision study in Loitokitok Division of Kajiado District, Kenya. Lucid Working Paper Series No. 7, LUCID Project, International Livestock Research Institute, Nairobi.

O'Brien, T. G. & Kinnaird, M. F. (2011). Estimation of species richness of large vertebrates using camera traps: An example from an Indonesian rainforest. Pages 233-252 Camera Traps in Animal Ecology: Methods and Analyses. Springer.

Owen-Smith, N. (1973) The behavioural ecology of the white rhinoceros. University of Wisconsin Madison.

Owen-Smith, N. (1975) The social ethology of the white rhinoceros *Ceratotherium simum* (Burchell, 1817). *Zeitschrift fur Tierpsychologie,* 38, 337-384.

Owen-Smith, N. (1988) *Megaherbivores: The Influence of Very Large Body Size on Ecology.* Cambridge Studies in Ecology. Cambridge: Cambridge University Press.

Owen-Smith, N. (1992). Megaherbivores: the influence of very large body size on ecology. Cambridge University Press.

Owen-Smith, N. (2004). Rhinoceroses. In *Grizimek's animal life encyclopedia* (2nd edn), 15. *Mammals IV*: 249-262. Hutchins, M., Kleiman, D.G., Geist, V. and McDade, M. (Eds). Framington Hills, MI: Gale Group.

Packer, C., Brink, H., Kissui, B.M., Maliti, H., Kushnir, H. & Caro, T. (2011). Effects of trophy hunting on lion and leopard populations in Tanzania. *Conservation Biology,* 25, 142-153.

Packer, C., Loveridge, A., Canney, S., Caro, T., Garnett, S.T., Pfeifer, M., Zander, K.K., Swanson, Macnulty, D., Balme, G., Bauer, H., Begg, C.M., Bhalla, S., Bissett, C., Bodasing, T., Brink, H., Burger, A., Burton, A.C., Clegg, B., Dell, S., Delsink, A., Dickerson, T., Dioniak, S.M., Druce, D., Funston, P., Gichohi, N., Groom, R., Hanekom, C., Heath, B., Hunter, L., Deiongh, H.H., Joubert, C.J., Kasiki, S.M., Kissui, B., Knocker, W., Leathem, B., Lindsey, P.A., Maclennan, S.D., McNutt, J.W., Miller, S.M., Naylor, S., Nel, P., Ng'weno, C., Nicholls, K., Ogutu, O., Okot-Omoya, E., Patterson, B.D., Plumptre, A., Salemo, J., Skinner, K., Slotow, R., Sogbohossou, E.A., Stratford, K.J., Winterbach, C., Winterbach, H. & Polasky, S. (2013). Conserving large carnivores: dollars and fence. *Ecological Letters,* 16, 635-641.

Pálinkás, M. (2018). Characteristics of Collapsing Ecosystems and Main Factors of Collapses. In *Ecosystem Services and Global Ecology.* IntechOpen.

Panksepp, J. (2009). Emotional causes and consequences of sicial-affective vocalization. In *Handbook of mammalian vocalisation - an integrative neuroscience approach:* pp. 201-208. Brudzynski, S.M. (Ed.). London: Academic.

Paudel, P.K., Bhattarai, B.P. & Kindlmann, P. (2012). An overview of the biodiversity in Nepal, In: Kindlmann, P. (Ed.), Himalayan Biodiversity in the changing world. Springer, Dordrecht, 1-40.

Payne, J. & Yoganand, K. (2017). Critically Endangered Sumatran Rhinoceros. Inputs for Recovery Strategy and Emergency Actions 2017 - 2027, 1-95.

Penny, M. (1987). Rhinos: an endangered species. Christopher Helm Publishers Limited, Kent.

Peterson, M.N., Birckhead, J.L., Leong, K., Peterson, M.J. & Peterson, T.R. (2010). Rearticulating the myth of human-wildlife conflict. *Conservation Letters,* 3, 74-82.

Piennar, D.J. (1994). Habitat preference of the white rhino in Kruger National Park. *Proceedings of a symposium on "Rhinos as Game Ranch Animals"* Onderstepoort, South Africa, 9-10th September 1994, 59-64.

Plein, M., Bode, M., Moir, M. L. & Vesk, P. A. (2016). Translocation strategies for multiple species depend on interspecific interaction type. *Ecological Applications,* 26, 1186-1197.

Policht, R., Tomášova, K., Holečková, D. & Frynta, D. (2008). The vocal repertoire in northern white rhinoceros (*Ceratotherium simum cottoni*) as recorded in the last surviving herd. *Bioacoustics,* 18, 83-88. Doi:10.1121/1.1588271

Poole, C.M. & Duckworth, J.W. (2005). A documented 20th century record of Javan rhinoceros (*Rhinoceros sondaicus*) from Cambodia. *Mammalia*, 69, 443-444.

Poole, J.H., Payne, K. & Langbauer Jr, W.R. (1998). The social contexts of some very low frequency calls of African elephants. *Behavioural Ecology and Sociobiology,* 22, 385-392.

Prothero, D.R., Manning, E, and Hansen, C.B. (1986). The phylogeny of the Rhinocerotidae (Mammalia, Perissodactyla). Zoological Journal of the Linnean Society 87:341-366.

Prothero, D.R., C. Guerin, and E. Manning. (1989). In D.R. Prothero and R.M. Schoch, eds., *The Evolution of Perissodactyls*, 341-55. New York: Oxford University Press.

Prothero, D.R. (1993). Fifty million years of rhinoceros evolution. Pp.82-81 in Proceedings of an international conference: rhinoceros biology and conservation (O.A. Ryder, ed.). Zoological Society of San Diego, Sandiego, California.

Putro, H.R. (1997). Heterogenitas habitat badak Jawa (*Rhinoceros sondaicus* Desm. 1822) di Taman Nasional Ujung Kulon. *Media Konservasi* edisi khusus, 17-40.

Qiu, Z., & Wang, B. (2007). Paracerathere fossils of China. Palaeontologia Sinica, New Series C. 29:1–396.

Rabinowitz, A. (1995). 'Helping a Species Go Extinct: The Sumatran Rhino in Borneo', *Conservation Biology,* 9(3), 482-488.

Rachmat, A.R.S., Handayani, Priambudi, A. & Ridwan, S. (2011). Investigation of the death of Javan rhinoceros (*Rhinoceros sondaicus*) in Ujung Kulon National Park. In: Joint proceedings of the 5th congress of the Asian society of veterinary pathology, 24th November 32-34.

Rachlow, J.L., Berkeley, E.V. & Berger, J. (1998). Correlates of male mating strategies in white rhinos (*Ceratotherium simim*). *Journal of Mammology,* 79, 1317-1324.

Rahmat, U.M. (2007). Analisis tipologi habitat preferensial badak jawa (*Rhinoceros sondaicus* Demarest 1822) di Taman Nasional Ujung Kulon (thesis). Bogor: Graduate School, Bogor Agricultural University.

Ramono, W. S., Santiapillai, C. & Mackinnon, K. (1993). Conservation and management of Javan rhino (*Rhinoceros sondaicus*) in Indonesia. Pp. 265-273 in Rhinoceros biology and conservation: proceedings of an international conference (O.A. Ryder, Ed.). San Diego, Zoological Society, San Diego, California.

Ramono, W. S., Isnan, M. W., Sadjudin, H.R., Gunawan, H., Dahlan, E.N., Sectionov, Pairah, Hariyadi, A.R., Syamsudin, M., Talukdar, B.K. & Gillison, A.N. (2009). Report on a Second Habitat Assessment for the Javan Rhinoceros (*Rhinoceros sondaicus sondaicus*) within the Island of Java. International Rhino Foundation, Yulee, FL, USA.

Rangarjan, M. (2001). India's Wildlife History: An Introduction. Permanent Black, New Delhi, India.

Ranjan, R. (2018). Shooting at the poachers while the rhinos drown: Managing short and long-term threats to endangered wildlife in conservation reserves. Natural Resource Modelling. DOI:10.1111/NRM.12188

Raup, D.M. & Sepkoski, J.J. (1982). Mass extinctions in the marine fossil record. *Science,* 215, 1501-1503.

Reading, R.P. & Kellert, S.R. (1993). Attitudes toward a Proposed Reintroduction of Black-Footed Ferrets (*Mustela nigripes*). *Conservation Biology,* 7, No. 3, 569-580.

Redpath, S.M., Young, J., Evely, A., Adams, W.M., Sutherland, W.J., Whitehouse, A., Amar, A., Lambert, R.A., Linnell, J.D.C., Watt, A.

& Gutiérrez, R.J. (2013). Understanding and managing conservation conflicts. *Trends in Ecology and Evolution,* 28, No.2, 100-109.

Ricklefs, R.E. (2010). Life-history connections to rates of aging in terrestrial vertebrates. *Proceedings of the National Academy Science, USA* 107, 10314-10319. (doi:10.1073/pnas.1005862107).

Ripple, W.J., Newsome, T.M., Wolf, C., Dirzo, R., Everatt, K.T., Galetti, M., Hayward, M.W., Kerley, G.I.H., Levi, T., Lindsey, P.A., Macdonald, D.W., Malhi, Y., Painter, L.E., Sandom, C.J., Terborgh, J. & Valkenburgh, B.V. (2015). Collapse of the world's largest herbivores. *Scientific Advisor,* 1, e1400103

Ripple, W.J., Chapron, G., López-Bao, J.V., Durant, S.M., Macdonald, D.W., Lindsey, P.A., Bennett, E.L., Beschta, R.L., Bruskotter, J.T., Campos-Arceiz, A., Corlett, R.T., Darimont, C.T., Dickman, A.J., Dirzo, R., Dublin, H.T., Estes, J.A., Everatt, K.T., Galetti, M., Goswami, V.R., Hayward, M.W., Hedges, S., Hoffmann, M., Hunter, L.T.B., Kerley, G.I.H., Letnic, M., Levi, T., Maisels, F., Morrison, J.C., Nelson, M.P., Newsome, T.M., Painter, L., Pringle, R.M., Sandom, C.J., Terborgh, J., Treves, A., Valkenburgh, B. Van., Vucetich, J.A., Wirsing, A.J., Wallach, A.D., Wolf, C., Woodroffe, R., Young, H. & Zhang, L. (2016). Saving the World's Terrestrial Megafauna. *BioScience,* 66(10), 807-812.

Rissman, A.R., Lozier, L., Comedant, T., Karieva, P., Joseph, M., Shaw., M.R. & Merenlender, A.M. (2007). Conservation Easements: Biodiversity Protection and Private Use. *Conservation Biology,* 21, 709-718.

Roberts, S.C. & Lowen, C. (1997). Optimal patterns of scent marking in klipspringer (*Oreotragus oreotragus*) territories. *Journal of Zoology,* 243, 565-578.

Robertson, H. A., Karika, I. & Saul, E. K. (2006). Translocation of Rarotonga monarchs *Pomarea dimidiata* within the southern Cook Islands. *Bird Conservation International*, 16, 197-215.

Rodrigues, A.S.L., Akcakaya, H.R., Handelman, S.J., Bakarr, M.I., Boitani, L., Brooks, T.M., Chanson, J.S., Fishpool, L.D.C., Da Fonseca, G.A.B., Gaston, K.J., Hoffman, M., Marquet, P.A., Pilgrim, J.D., Pressey, R.L., Schipper, J., Sechrest, W., Stuart, S.N., Underhill, L.G., Waller, R.W., Watts, M.E.J. & Yan, X. (2004). Global Gap Analysis: Priority Regions for Expanding the Global-Protected Area Network. Bioscience, 54, Issue 12, 1092-1100. Ana S. L. Rodrigues Search for other works by this author on: Oxford Academic Google Scholar

Rookmaaker, L.C. (1980). The distribution of the rhinoceros in eastern India, Bangladesh, China, and the Indochina region. *Zool. Anz*, 205, 253-268.

Rookmaaker, L.C. (1997). Records of the Sundarbans rhinoceros (*Rhinoceros sondaicus inermis*) in India and Bangladesh. *Pachyderm*, 24, 37-45.

Rookmaaker, L.C. (2006). Distribution and extinction of the rhinoceros in China: review of recent Chinese publications. *Pachyderm*, 40, 102-106.

Rookmaaker, L.C. (2006). The demise of the lesser Indian rhinoceros. Souvenir of Kaziranga Elephant Festival 2006, *Airawat*, 4, 27-28.

Rookmaaker, K. (2011). A review of black rhino systematics proposed in *Ungulate Taxonomy* by Groves and Grubb (2011) and its implications for rhino conservation. *Pachyderm*, 50.

Roth, T.L., Macrae, M.A., Brown, J.L., Kroll, J.L., Bellum, A.C., O'Brien, J.K. & Romo, J.S. (1998). The reproductive physiology of a living fossil – the Sumatran rhinoceros (*Dicerorhinus sumatrensis*). *Biology of Reproduction*, 58 (Suppl.1), 176.

Roth, T.L. (1999). Rhino reproductive physiology - what we know and what we need to know tomorrow for ensuring long-term stability of our captive breeding programs. In: Mehrdadfar, F. et al. Proceedings of the First Rhino Keepers' workshop 1999, sponsored by Disney's Animal Kingdom.

Sadjudin, H.R., Djaja, B & Lo, Y.K. (1981). Sensus Badak Jawa (*Rhinoceros sondaicus* Desmarest, 1822) di Semenjung Ujung Kulon - Maret 1981. IUCN/WWF Project 1960. Indonesia - Ujung Kulon Javan Rhinoceros. Fak. Biologi Univ. Nasional, Jakarta. Special Report 3.

Sadjudin, H.R. (1984). *Studi Perilaku dan Populasi Badak Jawa (Rhinoceros sondaicus Dem. 1822) di Ujung Kulon.* Jakarta: Fakultas Biologi Universitas Nasional.

Sadjudin, H.R. (1987). The Javan rhino (*Rhinoceros sondaicus* Desm.) census in Ujung Kulon National Park. *Rimba Indonesia*, 21, 16-26.

Sanders, R.W. (2012). Taxonomy of Lantana sect Lantana (Verbenaceae). *Journal of the Botanical Research Institute of Texas*, 6(2), 403-442.

Sandom, C.J., Terborgh, J. & Valkenburgh, B. Van. (2015). Collapse of the world's largest herbivores. *Sci. Adv*, 1, 1-12.

Santiapillai, C. & Suprahman, H. (1986). The Proposed Translocation of the Javan Rhinoceros (*Rhinoceros sondaicus*). *Biological Conservation*, 38, 11-19.

Santiapillai, C., Widodo, S. & Darmadja, B.P. (1989). Citation from Conservation of Rhinos in Indonesia. IUCN & PHPA, Bogor, Indonesia.

Santiapillai, C., Widodo, S. & Darmadja, B.P. (1990). Status of the Javan rhino in Ujung Kulon National Park. *Tigerpaper*, 17(2), 1-8.

Santiapillai, C., Giao, P.M. & Dung, V.V. (1993a). Conservation and management of Javan rhino (*Rhinoceros sondaicus annamiticus*) in Vietnam. *Tiger Paper,* 20, 7-15.

Santiapillai, C. & Suprahman, H. (1993b). Conservation and management of Javan rhino (*Rhinoceros sondaicus*) in Vietnam. Pp. 248-256 in proceedings of an international conference: rhinoceros biology and conservation (O. A. Ryder, Ed.). Zoological Society of San Diego, San Diego, California.

Santosa, Y, Rahmat, U.M., Prasetyo, L.B & Kartono, A. P. (2013). Javan Rhino (*Rhinoceros sondaicus* Desmarest 1822) Utilization Distribution and Habitat Selection in Ujung Kulon National Park, *JMHT*, Vol. XIX, (1), 31-38.

Saptoka, S., Aryal, A., Baral, S.R., Hayward, M.W. & Raubenheimer, D. (2014). Economic analysis of electric fencing for mitigating human-wildlife conflict in Nepal. *Journal Resource Ecology,* 5, 237-243. https://doi.org/10.5814/j.issn.1674-764x.2014.03.006

Save the Rhino International (2016c). Mozambique's role in the poaching crisis. Save the Rhino International, London. https://www.savetherhino.org/rhino_info/thorny_issues/mozambiques_role_in_the_poaching_crisis (Accessed 27 December 2017).

Sayer, J., Sunderland, T., Ghazoul, J., Pfund, J.L., Sheil, D., Meijaard, E., Venter, M., Boedhihartono, A.K., Day, M., Garcia, C., van Oosten. & Buck, L.E. (2013). *Proceedings of the National Academy of Sciences of the United States of America*, Vol.110, No.21, 8349-8356.

Schaffer, N.E., Agil, M. & Bosi, E. (2001). Utero-ovarian pathological complex of the Sumatran Rhinoceros (*Dicerorhinus sumatrensis*). In Abstracts of the International Elephant and Rhino Research Symposium, (eds. H.M. Schwammer, T.J. Foose, M. Fouraker and D. Olson), pp. 322. Vienna, Austria.

Schaller, G.B., Hu, J., Pan, W. & Zhu, J. (1985). *The giant pandas of Wolong.* Chicago, IL; University of Chicago Press.

Schaller, G.B., Dang, N. X., Thuy, L. D. & Son, V.T. (1990). Javan rhinoceros in Vietnam, *Oryx,* 24, 77-80.

Schenkel, R. & Schenkel-Hulliger, L. (1969a). Ecology and behaviour of the black rhinoceros (*Diceros bicornis* L.): a field study. Hamburg, Paul Parney.

Schenkel, R., Schenkel-Hulliger, L. & Ramono, W.S. (1978). Area management for the Javan rhinoceros (*Rhinoceros sondaicus Desm.*), a pilot study. *Malayan Nature Journal,* 31, 253-275.

Schenkel, R. & Schenkel-Hulliger, L. (1969a). The Javan Rhinoceros (*Rhinoceros sondaicus* Desmarest, 1822.) in Ujung Kulon Nature Reserve: its ecology and behaviour. Field Study 1967 and 1968. *Acta Tropica,* 26, 97-134.

Schenkel, R. & Schenkel-Hulliger, L. (1969b). The last remnants of the Javan rhinoceros in Ujung Kulon Nature reserve, Java. *Biological Conservation,* 2, 68-70.

Shijie, L., Qigao, J., & Tao, D. (2022). Body mass of the giant rhinos (Paraceratheriinae, Mammalia) and its tendency in evolution. *Historical Biology,* 1-12.

Schlitter, D. A. (2005). Wilson, D.E.; Reeder, D.M. (eds.). *Mammal Species of the World: A Taxonomic and Geographic Reference* (3rd ed.). Baltimore, Maryland, USA: Johns Hopkins University Press. p. 530.

Schneider, C., Hodges, K., Fischer, J. & Hammerschmidt, K. (2008). Acoustic niches of Siberut primates. *International Journal Primatology*, 29, 601-613.

Schwartz, M. W. & Martin, T. G. (2013.) Translocation of imperiled species under changing climates. *Annals of the New York Academy of Sciences,* 1286, 15-28.

Schweithelm, J. (1998). The Fire this Time, an Overview of Indonesia's Forest Fires in 1997/1998. Worldwide Fund for Nature.

Sectionov (2013). Control of Invasive Arenga Palm (*Arenga obtusifolia*) in Habitat Suitable for Javan Rhino (*Rhinoceros sondaicus*) in Ujung Kulon National Park. Presentation to the 2013 International Elephant and Rhino Conservation and Research Symposium.

Seidensticker, J. (1987). Bearing witness: Observations on the extinction of *Panthera tigris balica* and *Panthera tigris sondaica*. In: *Tigers of the World: The Biology, Biopolitics, Management, and Conservation of an Endangered Species, ed. R.L. Tilson & U.S. Seal,* 1-8. Park Ridge, NJ, USA: Noyes Publications.

Setiwan, R. & Yahya, A. (2002). Population and Distribution of Javan Rhinoceros (*Rhinoceros sondaicus* Desmarest, 1822), Based on the Calculation of Feces Collection and Footprint in Ujung Kulon National Park (eds.) Adhi Rachmat Hariyadi and Gert Polet, Cooperative project WWF Indonesia Project ID0091.07 and Ujung Kulon National Authority Directorate General of Forest Protection and Nature Conservancy, 1-38.

Setiawan, R., Gerber, B.D., Rahmat, U.M., Daryan, D., Firdaus, A.Y., Haryono. M., Khairani, K.O., Kurniawan, Y., Long, B., Lyet, A., Muhiban, M., Mahmud, R., Muhtarom, A., Purastuti, E., Ramono, W.S., Subrata, D. & Sunarto, S. (2017). Preventing Global Extinction of the Javan Rhino: Tsunami Risk and Future Conservation Direction. *Conservation Letters*, April 2017, 00(0), 1-9. Doi:10.1111/conl.12366

Shadwick, R.E., Russel, A.P. & Lauff, R.F. (1992). 'The Structure and Mechanical Designs of Rhinoceros'. Dermal Armour. *Philosophical Transactions of the Royal Society, London,* 337, 419-428.

Sharma, U.R. (2017). Cooperative management and revenue sharing in communities adjacent to Royal Chitwan National Park, Nepal. *Banko Janakari,* 11, 3-8.

Sheil, S. & Wunder, S. (2002). The value of tropical forests to local communities: complications, caveats, and caution. *Conservation Ecology,* 6, p.9.

Shrader, A. M. & Owen-Smith, N. (2002). The role of companionship in the dispersal of white rhinoceroses (*Ceratotherium simum*). *Behavioral Ecology and Sociobiology,* 52, 255-261.

Silk, J.B. (2007). The adaptive value of sociality in mammalian groups. *Philosophical Transactions of the Royal Society,* 362, 539-559. (doi.org/10.1098/rstb.2006.1994).

Skinner, J.D. & Mitchell, G. (2011). Family Giraffidae (Giraffe and Okapi), Pp. 788-805 in: *Handbook of the Mammals of the World.* Vol. 2. Hoofed mammals (D.E. Wilson and R.A. Mittermeier, Eds.). Lynx Edicions, Barcelona, Spain.

Smith, R.J., Muir, R.D.J., Walpole, M.J., Balmford, A. & Leader-Williams, N. (2003). Governance and loss of biodiversity. *Nature,* 426, 67-70.

Sodhi, N.S.., Koh, L.P, Brook, B.W. & Ng, P.K.L. (2004). Southeast Asian biodiversity: an impending disaster. *Trends Ecological Evolution,* 19, 654-660.

Sodhi, N.S. & Brook, B.W. (2006). Southeast Asian biodiversity in crisis. Cambridge University Press, Cambridge.

Sodhi, N.S., Posa, M.R.C., Lee, T.M., Bickford, D., Koh, L.P. & Brook, B.W. (2010).
The state and conservation of Southeast Asian biodiversity. *Biodiversity Conservation,* Doi: 10.1007/s10531-009-9607-5

Sodhi, N. S., Lee, T. M., Sekercioglu, C. H., Webb, E. L., Prawiradilaga, D. M., Lohman, D. J., Pierce, N. E., Diesmos, A. C., Rao, M. & Ehrlich, P.R. (2010). Local people value environmental services provided by forest parks. *Biodiversity Conservation,* 19, 1175-1188.

Sody, H.J.V. (1941). Das Javanische neushoorn, *Rhinoceros sondaicus* historish und biologisch. Archipel Drukkerij en 'T Boekhuis, Buitenzorg, vii+156pp.

Sody, H.J.V. (1959). Das Javanische Nashorn *Rhinoceros sondaicus* historish und biologisch. *Zeitschrift für Säugetierkunde,* 24, 109-240.

Spellmire, T.J. (1981). Bioacoustics of the black rhinoceros (*Diceros bicornis*): A preliminary report. Proc. ABS Regional Behaviour Conf. In Press.

Srivastava, V. (2015). Science Research Reporter, March 2015. http://xaam.org.science-reporter-2015-compilation (Accessed 25 October 2018).

Sriyanto, A., Priambudi, A., Haryono, M. & Hasan, A. (1995). A Current Status of the Javan Rhinoceros Population in Ujung Kulon National Park. Unpublished report presented at the 1995 Meeting of the IUCN/SSC Asian Rhino Specialist Group at Sandakan, Sabah, Malaysia.

Stankey, G.H. & Shindler, B. (2005). Formation of Socially Acceptibility Judgments and Their Implications for Management of Rare and Little-Known Species. *Conservation Biology,* (2006), 20, No. 1, 28-37.

Statistics Indonesia Banten Province (2019). Statistics of Banten Province. http://banten.bps.go.id/kegiatanLain/view/id/2 (Accessed 28 May 2019).

Steinmetz, R., Chutipong, W. & Seuaturien, N. (2006). Collaborating to Conserve Large Mammals in Southeast Asia. *Conservation Biology,* 20, 1391-1401.

Sterling, E.J., Hurley, M.M. & Minh, Le Duc. (2006). Vietnam: A Natural History. Yale University Press, New Haven and London.

Stevenson, M. F. & T. B. Poole. (1976). An ethogram of the common marmoset (*Calithrix jacchus jacchus*): General behavioural repertoire. *Animal Behaviour,* 24, 428-451.

Stoner, S., Verhij, P. & Jun Wu, M. (2017). Black Business: Illegal rhino horn trade dynamics in Nhi Khe, Vietnam from a criminal perspective case study. Wildlife Justice Commission. https:// wildlifejustice.org/wp-content/uploads/2017/09/Black-Business-FINALpdf.pdf.

Strange, M. (2012). A Photographic Guide to the Birds of Indonesia. Second Edition. Tuttle Publishing, Tokyo, Vermont, Singapore.

Sunquist, M.E. & Sunquist, F.C. (2009). Family Felidae. Pp. 54-169 in *Handbook of the Mammals of the World*. Vol 1. Carnivores (D.E. Wilson and R.A. Mittermeier, Eds.). Lynx Edicions, Barcelona, Spain.

Supriatin. (2000). Studi kemungkinan adanya pengaruh alelopati langkap (*Arenga obtusifolia* Blumme ex. Mart) terhadap pertumbuhan semai tumbuhan pakan badak Jawa (*Rhinoceros sondaicus* Desmarest, 1822) di Taman Nasional Ujung Kulon. PhD dissertation. Institut Pertanian Bogor, Bogor, Indonesia.

Sutherland, W. J. (1998). The importance of behavioural studies in conservation biology. *Animal Behaviour,* 56, 801-809.

Swaisgood, R.R, Lindburg, D.G, White, A., Zhang, H. & Zhou, X. (2004). Chemical communication in giant pandas: experimentation and application. In: Giant Pandas: Biology and Conservation (Ed. By D. Lindburg & K. Baragona), pp. 106-120. Berkeley, California: University of California Press.

Swenson, J.E., Sandegren, F., Soderberg, A., Bjarvall, A., Franzen, R. & Wabakken, P. (1997). Infanticide caused by hunting of male bears. *Nature,* 386, 450-451.

Talbot, L.M. (1960). A look at threatened species: a report on some animals of the Middle East and southern Asia which are threatened with extermination. Fauna Preservation Society, London, United Kingdom.

Talukdar, B. K. (2002). Tiger predation on rhino calves in Kaziranga National Park, Assam, India. *Tigerpaper,* 24 (4), 18-20.

Talukdar, B.K. (2018). Asian Rhino Specialist Group report. *Pachyderm*, 59, 27-30.

Taman Nasional Ujung Kulon (1996). Laporan Sensus Badak Jawa. Taman Nasional Ujung Kulon.

Taylor, C.D., Schultz, K.J. & Doebrich, J.L. (2009). *Geology and nonfuel mineral deposits of Africa and the Middle East.* U.S. Geological Survey, California.

Tembrock, G. (1963). Acoustic behaviour of mammals. In: Acoustic Behaviour of Animals. (Edit. R.G. Bushnell) Elsevier Publ. Co., Amsterdam, 751-785.

Thapa, K. (2010). Effectiveness of crop protection methods against wildlife damage: A case study of two villages in Bardia National Park, Nepal. *Crop Protection,* 29, 1297-1304.

Thapa, K., Nepal, S., Thapa, G., Bhatta, S.R. & Wikramanayake, E. (2013). Past, present, and future conservation of the greater one-horned rhinoceros (*Rhinoceros unicornis*) in Nepal, *Oryx,* 47, 345-351.

Theobald, D.M. (2000). Fragmentation by inholdings and exurban development. Pages 155-174 in R.L. Knight, F. W. Smith, S.W. Buskirk, W. H. Romme, and W.L. Baker. (Ed.) Forest fragmentation in the southern Rocky Mountains. University Press of Colorado, Boulder, Colorado, U.S.A.

Theobald, D.M., Spies, T., Kline, J., Maxwell, B., Hobbs, N.T. & Dale, V.H. (2005). Ecological Support for Rural Land-Use Planning. *Ecological Applications,* 15 (6), 1906-1914.

Tougard, C., Delefosse, T. Hanni, C. & Montgelard, C. (2001). Phylogenetic Relationships of the Five Extant Rhinoceros Species (Rhinocerotidae, Perissodactyla) Based on Mitochondrial Cytochrome *b* and 12S rRNA Genes. *Molecular Phylogenetics and Evolution*, Vol. 19. No. 1, 34-44.

TRAFFIC (2011). 'Wildlife Trade: What is It?' www.traffic.org/home/2011/5/24/lid-lifted-on-vietnamese-rhino-horn-trade.html (accessed 24 November 2014).

TRAFFIC (2016). TRAFFIC's engagement on African rhinoceros' conservation and global trade in rhinoceros' horn. TRAFFIC, Cambridge, United Kingdom. http://www.traffic.org/rhinos/ (Accessed December 2016).

Triguero-Mas, M., Olomi-Sola, M., Jha, N., Zorondo-Rodrigues, F. & Reyes-Garcia, V. (2010). Urban and rural perceptions of protected areas: a case study in Dandeli Wildlife Sanctuary, Western Ghats, India. *Environmental Conservation,* 36, 208-217.

Tuft, K. D., Crowther, M. S., Connell, K., Müller, S. & McArthur, C. (2011). Predation risk and competitive interactions affect foraging of an endangered refuge-dependent herbivore. *Animal Conservation,* 14, 447-457.

Tuttle, M.D. & Ryan, M.J. (1982). The role of syncronised calling, ambient light and ambient noise in anti-bat behaviour of a tree frog. *Behavioral Ecology and Sociobiology,* 11, 125-131.

Ullrich, W. (1964). Zur Biologie der panzernashorner in Assam. Zool. Gart. LPZ, Vol. 28, 225-250.

Ujung Kulon National Park (UKNP) (2012). *Report of the death of Javan rhinoceros, Banten, Indonesia.* Jalan Perintis Kemerdekaan, Banten, Indonesia, 1-10.

Ujung Kulon National Park (UKNP) (2014). *Report of the death of Javan rhinoceros, Banten, Indonesia.* Jalan Perintis Kemerdekaan, Banten, Indonesia, 1-15.

UNEP-WCMC & IUCN (2016). Protected planet report 2016. https://wdpa.s3.amazonaws.com/Protected_Planet_Reports/2445%20Global%20Protected%20Planet%202016_WEB.pdf. (Accessed 10 January 2020).

United Nations Food and Agriculture Organisation (2009). *Harvesting Agriculture's Multiple Benefits: Mitigation, Adaptation, Development and Food Security: Policy Brief* (FAO, Rome).

United Nations Office Drugs and Crime (2014). Wildlife crime worth 8 to 10 billion dollars annually, ranking it alongside human trafficking, arms and drug dealing in terms of profit. https://www.unode.org/unode/en/frontpage/2014/May/wildlife-crime-worth-8-10-billion-annually/.html

Vaglio, S., Minicozzi, P., Romoli, R., Boscaro, F., Pieracinni, G. & Moneti, G. (2016). Sternal gland scent-marking signals sex, age, rank and group identity in captive mandrills. *Chemical Senses,* 41, 177-184.

Van Gyseghem, R. (1984). Observations on the ecology and behaviour of the northern white rhinoceros (*Ceratotherium simum cottoni*). *Zeitsschrift fur Saügetierkunde,* 49, 348-358.

Van der Made, J. & Grube, R. (2010). "The rhinoceroses from Neumark-Nord and their nutrition". In Meller, Harald. *Elefantenreich-Eine Fossilwelt in Europa.* Halle/Saale. 382-394.

Van, Merm, R.H. (2008). Ecological and Social Aspects of Reintroducing Megafauna: A case study on the suitability of the Honje Mountains as a release site for the Javan Rhinoceros (*Rhinoceros sondaicus*). MSc thesis, Saxon Universities of Applied Sciences (NL) and Greenwich University (UK).

Van Strien, N.J. (1986). The Sumatran rhinoceros *Dicerorhinus sumatrensis* (Fisher, 1814) in the Gunung Leuser National Park, Sumatra, Indonesia: its distribution, ecology and conservation. Hamburg, Paul Parey.

Van Strien, N.J. & Sadjudin, H.R. (1995). Ujung Kulon National Park: Javan rhino, current status, protection, and conservation management. Report to Asian Rhino Specialist Group: 1-32.

Van Strien, N.J. (2005). Javan rhinoceros. Pp. 75-79. In: Fulconis R. *Save the Rhinos: EAZA Rhino Campaign 2005/6 Info Pack.* London, Save the Rhinos. 1-164.

Van Strien, N.J., Manullang, B., Sectionov, Isnan, W., Khan, M.K.M. & Sumardja, E. (2008). *Dicerorhinus sumatrensis*. In, The IUCN Red List of Threatened Species v. 2014.3.http://www.iucnredlist. org/ (Accessed 22 May 2015).

Van Strien, N.J. & Rookmaaker, L.C. (2010). The impact of the Krakatoa eruption in 1883 on the population of *Rhinoceros sondaicus* in Ujung Kulon, with details of rhino observations from 1857 to 1949. *Journal of Threatened Taxa*, January 2, 633-638.

Varada, S. & Alessa, D. (2014). Saving their skins: How animals protect from the sun. *Jama Dermatology,* 150, 989.

Velho, N., Karanth, K.K. & Laurance, W.F. (2012). Hunting: A serious and understudied threat in India, a globally significant conservation region. *Biological Conservation,* 148, 210-215.

Venables, W.N & Ripley, B.D. (2002). Modern Applied Statistics with S. Springer, New York.

Venter, P. & Hanekon, J.J. (2010). Automatic detection of African elephant (*Loxodonta africana*) infrasonic vocalisations from recordings. *Biosystems Engineering,* 1-9.

Verdaasdonk, M. (2018). Analyzing the drivers behind the distribution patterns of the southern white rhinoceros across the South African savanna landscape. Utrecht University, South African Wildlife College, MSc Thesis, 1-33.

Vigne, L. & Martin, E. (2008). 'Yemen's Attitudes towards Rhino Horn and Jambiyas', *Pachyderm,* 44, 45-53.

Von Martens, E. (1876). Die Preussiche Expedition nach Ost-Asien. Nach Amtlichen Quellen. Zoologischer Theil. Erster Band. Allgemeins und Wirbelthiere. Verlag der Koniglichen Geheimen Ober-Hofbuchdruckerie, Berlin, Germany.

Von Koenigswald, G. H. R. (1933). Beitrage zur Kenntnis der fossilen Saugetiere Javas. Wetenschappelijke Mededelingen Dienst van den Mijinbouw in Nederlandesch-indie 23:1-185.

Wiley, R.H. & Richards, D.G. (1978). Physical constraints on acoustic communication in the atmosphere: implications for the evolution of animal vocalisations. *Behavioural ecology and Sociobiology*, 3, 69-94.

Wake, D.B. & Vredenburg, V.T. (2008). Are we in the midst of the sixth mass extinction? A view from the world of amphibians. *Proceedings National Academy of Science United States of America*, 105, 11466-11473.

Wall, W.P. (1989). The phylogenetic history and adaptive radiation of the Amynodontidae. In D.R. Prothero and R.M. Schoch, eds., *The Evolution of Perissodactyl*, 341-55. New York: Oxford University Press.

Walpole, M.J. & Goodwin, H.J. (2001). Local attitudes towards conservation and tourism around Komodo National Park, Indonesia. *Environmental Conservation*, 2, 160-166.

Waser, P.M. & Brown, C.H. (1986). Habitat acoustics and primate communication. *American Journal Primatology*, 10, 135-154.

Wege, D.C., Long, A.J., Vinh, Ky, M., Van Dung, Vu. & Eames, J.C. (1999). Expanding the Protected Areas Network in Vietnam for the 21st Century: An Analysis of the Current System with Recommendations for Equitable Expansion. Birdlife international Vietnam Programme, Hanoi.

Western, D., Groom, R. & Worden, J. (2009). The impact of subdivision and sedentarization of pastoral lands on wildlife in an African savanna ecosystem. *Biological Conservation*, 142, 2538-2546.

Wikramanayake, E. *et al.* (eds.) (2002). *Terrestrial Ecoregions of the Indo-Pacific: A Conservation Assessment.* Washington, D.C.: Island Press.

Williamson, E.A., Maisels, F.G. & Groves, C.P. (2013). Family Hominidae (Great apes), Pp. 792-854 in: *Handbook of the Mammals of the World*. Vol. 3. Primates (Mittermeier, R.A., Rylands, A.B. & Wilson, D.E. Eds.). Lynx Edicions, Barcelona, Spain.

Wilson, D.E. & Mittermeier. R.A. eds. (2011). *Handbook of Mammals of the World. Vol. 2. Hoofed Mammals*, Lynx Edicions, Barcelona. Pp. 177-181.

Wilson, D.E. & Mittermeier. R.A. eds. (2009). *Handbook of Mammals of the World. Vol. 1. Carnivores*, Lynx Edicions, Barcelona. Pp. 646-647.

Wilson, D.E. & Reeder, D.M. (1993). *Mammal species of the world: a taxonomic and geographic reference,"* Smithsonian Institution Press, Washington, DC.

Wilson, D.E. & Reeder, D.M. (eds.) (2005). *Mammal species of the world: a taxonomic and geographic reference*, 3rd ed. Baltimore, MD: Johns Hopkins University Press.

Wilson, S.G., Hockings, G., Deretic, J.M. & Kark, S. (2020). More than just mud: The importance of wallows to Javan rhino ecology and behaviour. *Pachyderm,* Vol. 61, August/September 2020.

Wilson, S.G., Biggs, D. & Kark, S. (2021). Protecting an icon: Javan rhino frontline management and conservation. *Oryx*, Vol 56(1): 1-7, August/September 2021.

Wilson, S.G., Rookmaaker, K., Haryadi, A.R, Sectionov., I, Leslie., D.M, Long, B, Sunartos., S, Rahmat., M. & Mahmud., R. (2025). Chapter 6, Javan Rhinoceros *R. sondaicus* Desmarest, 1822, 135-151pp, in (Melliti, M, Talukdar, B. & Balfour (eds.,) (2025). Rhinos of the World, Springer Nature Switzerland AG, 423pp, https://doi.org/10.1007/978-3-031-67169.2

Whittaker, R.J., Willis, K.J. & Field, R. (2001). Scale and species richness: towards a general, hierarchical theory of species diversity. *Journal of Biogeography,* 28, 453-470.

Whittaker, R.J. & Heegaard, E. (2003). What is the observed relationship between species richness and productivity? *Ecology,* 84, 3384-3390.

Wood, J.D., McCowan, B., Langbauer Jr, W.R., Viljoen, J.J. & Hart, L.A. (2005). Classification of African elephant *Loxodonta africana* rumbles using acoustic parameters and cluster analysis. *Bioacoustics*, 15, 143-161.

Woodroffe, R., Thirgood, S. & Rabinowitz, A. (2005). The future coexistence: resolving human-wildlife conflicts in a changing world. *Conservation Biology Series Cambridge,* 9, 388.

Worden, J.S. (2007). Fragmentation and Settlement Patterns in Masaailand - Implications for Pastoral Mobility, Drought Vulnerability and Wildlife Conservation in an East African Savanna. Ecology. Colorado State University, Fort Collins, Colorado. p.295.

Worldometer (2019). Indonesian population statistics. http://www. worldometers.info/world-population/indonesia-population (Accessed 28 May 2019).

World Population Review (2019). http://worldpopulationreview.com/ countries/-population. (Accessed 28 May 2019).

World Wildlife Fund for Nature (2012). Javan rhino extinct in Vietnam. *Journal Newsletter of WWF Singapore,* Vol: 5.

WWF - IUCN (1982). *Mystery of Dead Javan Rhinos.* The Environmentalist, Vol. 2, No.3.

World Wildlife Fund for Nature (2016). Unsustainable and illegal wildlife trade. http://wwf.panda.org/about_our_earth/species/ problems/illegal_trade/ (Accessed 16 October 2018)

Yahya, A. (2002). *Studi Populasi Badal Jawa* (Rhinoceros sondaicus) *Melalui Kamera Penjebak Ifra Merah Di Taman Nasional Ujung Kulon.* Indonesia, WWF.

Yayasan Badak Indonesia (2010). Preparation Phase for Javan Rhino Study Conservation Area Establishment in Gunung Honje Area, Ujung Kulon National Park.

YMR, WWF & IPB (2002). *Laporan Akhir Studi Persaingan Ekologi Badak Jawa* (*Rhinoceros sondaicus*) *dan Banteng* (*Bos javanicus*) *di Taman Nasional Ujung Kulon.* (Final report on the study of ecological competition between Javan Rhino and Banteng in Ujung Kulon National Park). Bogor, Indonesia.

Zuraina, M. (1982). The West Mouth, Niah, in the prehistory of Southeast Asia. *Sarawak Museum Journal,* 31, 1-20.

Key Rhino Organisations (contact details)

International Rhino Foundation
General information and enquiries
Email: INFO@RHINOS.ORG
Website: https://rhinos.org

Yayasan Badak Indonesia–Rhino Foundation of Indonesia
Website: https://badak.or.id

World Wildlife Fund
Website: https://www.worldwildlife.org

World Wildlife Fund–Indonesia
Website: https://www.wwf.id

NGO Aaranyak
Email: info@aaranyak.org
Website: https://aaranyak.org

International Union of Conservation and Nature (IUCN)
IUCN SSC Asian Rhino Specialist Group
Website: https://iucn.org

International Union of Conservation and Nature (IUCN) Red List of Threatened Species
Website: https://iucnredlist.org

Australasian Society of Zookeeping
Website: https://aszk.org.au

American Association of Zoos & Aquariums
Website: https://aza.org

Rhino Resource Centre (RRC)–(provides references/images/rhino data)

Website: https://www.rhinoresourcecenter.com

Wildlife Asia

Website: https://wildlifeasia.org.au

Asian Rhino Project/Wildlife Asia

Email: info@wildlifeasia.org.au
        clare.campbell@wildlifeasia.org.au

Save the Rhino

https://www.savetherhino.org

Abwak–Association of British and Irish Wild Animal Keepers

Website: https://abwak.org

BIAZA–The British and Irish Association of Zoos and Aquaria

Website: https://biaza.org.uk

EAZA–European Association of Zoos and Aquaria

Website: www.eaza.net

Rhino Recovery Fund (created by the Wildlife Conservation Network)

Websites:
- https://rhinorecoveryfund.org
- https://wildnet.org

NGO Auriga Nusacantara (natural resource sustainability)

Website: http://auriga.or.id
Email: info@auriga.or.id

www.ingramcontent.com/pod-product-compliance
Lightning Source LLC
Chambersburg PA
CBHW052109030426
42335CB00025B/2907